WORKING

FOR THE PEOPLE

WORKING

FOR THE PEOPLE

PROMISE AND PERFORMANCE
IN PUBLIC SERVICE

By ROBERT MOSES

Foreword by Herbert Bayard Swope

 HARPER & BROTHERS NEW YORK

920
M911w

Library of Congress catalog card number: 55-8550

Contents

Foreword

by Herbert Bayard Swope

ROBERT MOSES, MASTER BUILDER, HAS DONE A LOT to New York in his brief span of years. Fortunately, he will do more, for he is driven on by a passion for service that stops at no limits, or state lines or politics.

Bob began as an Al Smith Republican (and that is an accolade of approval, for this writer thinks Al Smith represented one of the finest flowerings of American democracy). He is claimed as a Republican when that party is anxious to show it has character and capacity in its ranks. But he is without partisanship.

Bob Moses has made the pattern of give and take dominant in his life's attitude. But there has been far more give in his relations. He has never sought favor, although he appreciates it when it comes spontaneously from those whose judgment he values. He has never hesitated to punch, and punch straight, when he meets the phony or the pretentious. He has vision, and that is why he and his works will live.

Moses is a stern schoolmaster. He has impatience with mistakes and, occasionally, with those who differ with him. For example, he is harsh with me because I think tunnels are better than bridges in these days of pinpointing targets for bomb carriers. He has frequently made me feel the weight of his disagreement, although, in a wee, small voice, unlike Oliver Cromwell reproving his parliament, I dare to say he has not always convinced me.

Nor has he convinced himself about the value of the telephone. He is one of the most civilized men of our day, but he walks with Disraeli who said that comforts are too often called civilization. He really hates the device, which is strange, for his hearing is tops. It seems to be a personal peccadillo.

In the lifetime he has given to public service there are characteristics that stand out:

1. He has a patient step-by-step approach to his objective. He knows what should be done and why as well as how.

2. The broadening of concept and administrative responsibility, due to the various areas of effort overlapping one another, is to be found deep in his make-up. With him it has not been a mere collecting of different hats with different labels.

3. He does not fight merely for the sake of fighting, although he is not slow in swinging his mental fists. He dislikes and scorns soft soap and appeasement, but he is quick, under pressure of truth, to admit an error. There is no personal bitterness, no venom in the man. He thinks that is bad for mind and body, and ends nowhere.

Bob Moses is a man of strong ability and a deep sense of justice. He is direct, understanding, independent but appreciative. He gets things done; he knows how to trust people; he can delegate authority. He is one of the few worthy of John Galsworthy's prayer:

> Oh Lord of Courage grave;
> Oh Master of this night of Spring!
> Make firm in me a heart too brave
> To ask Thee anything.
> —"COURAGE"*

Bob Moses has convinced the public that he is their devoted servant, and they trust him wholly. Of how many can that be said? When the time comes along, years away, that he needs an epitaph, let that be said of this man who makes our dreams come true:

Citizen Moses—he worked only for the people!

* From *The Collected Poems of John Galsworthy*; copyright 1934 by Charles Scribner's Sons. Reprinted by permission of the publisher.

Preface

FROM TIME TO TIME I HAVE BEEN ASKED TO WRITE a book based on my experiences as a public official. Some publishers have suggested an autobiography, others a textbook which might be useful to those interested in the practical aspects of public work.

I have had to decline such invitations. As to an autobiography, even if I had the time, and could overcome the objections of my family and friends, such a work would involve official and personal relations which in many cases should not be exploited. To attempt a formal textbook of the usual kind would be contrary to my philosophy which is based on practice rather than theory.

Nevertheless, I have been persuaded, rather reluctantly, that an account of some of my past activities and experiences might throw light on certain obscure aspects of public administration, lead to a better understanding of the everyday problems of government and promote recognition of the yawning gaps between planning and accomplishment, millennial programs and realizable objectives, promise and performance.

Even this limited effort would have demanded more time than I could spare if I had attempted by myself to do the research and other work involved. I therefore agreed to an edited compilation by my friend Cleveland Rodgers, derived in the main from reports, speeches, letters and articles produced for specific occasions or to emphasize some currently debated phase of public administration and policy.

This little book makes no dogmatic pretensions and no claims to profundity. It is a factual account of certain developments in the field in which I have been engaged for many years, and of the hard lessons learned by experience. Perhaps it will bring some current problems into proper perspective so that the present and new generation may discover that there is indeed nothing new under the sun, that some progress has been made and that there is a sound basis for confidence in the future.

The book has one virtue at any rate. Under Mr. Rodgers' honest and competent hand it contains only original contemporary, not contrived, ex-post-facto stuff. It is not an amended, modified and corrected edition representing what I should like to have said and done, had I my life to live over again. Mr. Rodgers has not corrupted the text in the interest of diplomacy and friendship.

We face emergencies in this country other than those forced on us by the cold war and atom bombs. These are domestic emergencies arising from the new and expanded tasks of government. They can be met only by finding, training and encouraging the right kind of people to carry on public administrative work; but first we must have a better understanding of how government in a democracy functions and what must be done to shake off illusions and get down to realities. If this purpose is in any measure served by the record of what I have written, said or done, I shall be well satisfied.

Besides Cleveland Rodgers, the editor, I am indebted to Ordway Tead for help in putting material together; to my old friend and mentor, Herbert Bayard Swope, for his kindly and provocative foreword. Finally my thanks are due to the following publications for permission to use excerpts from articles by me previously appearing in their pages: *The New York Times Magazine* and *Book Review*, *Life* magazine, *St. Louis Post-Dispatch*, *Architectural Forum*, *New York Daily News*, *Elks* magazine, *Town and Country*, *Christian Advocate*, *Woman's Day*, General Motors prize-winning essay, and others.

R. M.

WORKING

FOR THE PEOPLE

1

Democracy's Problem Number One

ONE OF THE MOST URGENT PROBLEMS FACING THIS country and the free world is to find capable men and women willing to do the work democratic government is called upon to do. If we are to continue to progress, expanding the functions of government to meet increasing needs, and if we hope to maintain present standards, to say nothing of raising them, ways must be found to get the right people into public service and to keep them there.

This need is manifest at all levels of government. It applies to everyone on the public payrolls, from the highest elected officials to the lowest grade employees in civil service. Nominating and electing the right people for public office is a special problem. It is political and depends upon the intelligence of the electorate and the state of the public purse and pulse at election time.

Manning the vast machine which actually performs the various services entrusted to government is a more technical matter. To be sure, it involves politics of a kind, but helpful policies and principles can be adopted without referendums, revolutions or too much palaver. All that is needed is recognition of the tremendous increase in the demands being made on government, the complicated and technical nature of these demands and the obvious weaknesses in our methods of public administration. It is time for theories, misconceptions and misguided idealism to give way to common sense and realism.

The Growth of "Bureaucracy"

Many people are appalled by what they regard as the endless pro-liferation of so-called "bureaucracy." During the past quarter of a century public payrolls in this country have trebled and there is a widespread impression that the army of people in government serv-ice represents a conspiracy on the part of politicians to rob the tax-payers. There may be more people engaged in public work than are necessary, and politics may be blamed for some of the padding, but if we look closely at the budgets we find that the agencies these people serve were all created to provide some service for which there was a popular demand or to complete the perfection of man-kind.

Our usual method of remedying wrongs, or of bringing about re-forms, is to create new agencies. We have legislated too many agen-cies and there are needless duplications, but the motives were political only in the sense that legislators were carrying out what they regarded as the will of the people. That is the democratic way of getting things done. It is costly and inefficient, but not necessarily corrupt, and it is not irremediable. Our problem is to make democracy work despite its cumbersome governmental machinery.

There are vast spaces on the globe where nearly everyone works for the government; where private initiative, as we use the phrase, has dried up and opposition to the corporate public will is liquidated. Give me liberty, with all its connotations, pleasant and unpleasant, stimulating and irksome, rather than that death of the spirit which is bound to be visited on those who live under an exclusive and all-powerful government. I should rather work in the maddening and infuriating atmosphere of American politics, and accept the rules, risks and uncertain rewards of the game as we play it, than receive an ironclad commission from a dictator, coupled with the assurance that any interloper who got in my way would be strung to the nearest lamppost, exiled or *spurles versenkt*.

Life is competitive, and will continue to be so in these United States for a long time to come. I cannot conceive of politics, government, administration, physical progress and the coordination of public and private enterprise in any other terms.

Competition is itself a great discipline. An athlete cannot break training without running the risk of losing a game; competition keeps business and industry on their toes; the individual who aspires to any kind of success must discipline himself to assure achievement. Our progress as a nation depends upon such competition, and we must not deny to competitors the rewards that come from self-imposed discipline. This is recognized in most fields of activity. Yet, strange to say, it is not widely practiced in government.

How the Russians Manage

To man our public machines, government must compete with private interests, which offer definite rewards for special abilities and put premiums on ambition, initiative and energy. When it comes to administrators, government often has to beg for volunteers who are willing to make substantial sacrifices to enter public service. Getting good men to run for office or to take responsible commissions is becoming increasingly difficult because of smear fear.

The Russians have a more realistic approach. While the Communists have liquidated private initiative and enterprise, they recognize and reward the people who can serve their purposes. They use slave labor, but when it comes to technical administrators they seek the best men they can find. They do not let their fanatical ideology stand in the way. They have used engineers known by them to be anything but true believers to get their big jobs done. They may put half a dozen spies to watch over their experts to see that they do not commit sabotage, and they may be liquidated later, but they keep the experts on the job until it is finished.

We should not let our abhorrence of communism blind us to the fact that we are in competition with an aggressive, ruthless government that is exerting every effort to train scientists and technicians to carry out their objectives. The Soviet regime does not have to compete with private interests to man its government and it does not have to depend on volunteers. Public service is the only field open to young Russians of ability. In this country public service is often regarded as one of the least attractive of vocations.

SOME COMMON MISCONCEPTIONS

There are more misconceptions about public service than about almost any other career in American life. A friend once said to me, "Isn't it a fact that practically all career public jobs are drudgery of a dull and routine character?" I explained that this wasn't a fact at all. Some government jobs are humdrum, but thousands of others are stimulating, exciting, even dangerous and in a high sense rewarding.[1]

There is nothing dull about keeping impoverished families from breaking up, fighting to halt an epidemic of polio, damming streams and impounding water for reclamation, power, flood control, navigation and other purposes. There is nothing dull about locating, designing, financing and building housing developments which replace slums, or building great crossings like the George Washington and Triborough bridges and the rapid transit and vehicular tunnels and their arterial approaches and connections in New York City, making possible a civilization which more and more runs on rubber.

Another thing I hear is, "There's no opportunity for individual enterprise in the public service." This annoys me. I think of public servants like those who invented the Garand rifle; who developed the system for purifying uranium used in processing atomic energy; or who used biochemistry to produce a new vaccine against epidemic typhus, saving millions of lives.

The remark, "You can't get recognition and promotion in the public service," is also untrue. Hundreds of men and women have climbed from the bottom to the top of important and respected government agencies. I also hear statements which go to the other extreme, exaggerating the advantages of public service. Typical is the widespread belief, "Government employees have soft, lifetime jobs. They can't be fired."

I am not impressed by the hunger for that kind of security. Regardless of that, however, the fact is that public service employees can be disciplined and dropped. In one recent year alone thousands of Federal employees were discharged for misconduct, inefficiency and similar reasons.

Herbert H. Lehman, Thomas McWhinney, Clifford Jackson, Robert
Moses and Alfred E. Smith at the dedication of Heckscher Park, 1929

With Governor Roosevelt at Jones Beach
State Park, 1931.

Conferring with Alfred E. Smith before
the Constitutional Convention of 1938.

With Herbert Hoover and George E. Spargo at hearings on the
Reorganization of the Federal Government, 1948.

Mayor La Guardia, Alfred E. Smith, and Robert Moses at the
Belt Parkway opening.

Inspecting the ruins of Berlin
in 1947.

Celebrating the twentieth anniversary of Jones Beach with Governor
Dewey, 1949.

With Trygve Lie at Hofstra College.

Brooklyn Borough President Cashmore, Cardinal Spellman, Manhattan
Borough President Wagner, Robert Moses and Mayor William O'Dwyer
at the dedication of the Brooklyn Battery Tunnel, 1950.

nferring on parks with Governor Mey-
r of New Jersey at Jones Beach, 1955.

Mayor Impellitteri, Bronx Borough President
Lyons, Queens Borough President Lundy,
R. H. Gould and Robert Moses at Hunts
Point Sewage Disposal Plant, 1952.

orge V. McLaughlin, Robert Moses, Borough President Wagner
d William J. Tracy at the opening of the Airlines Terminal, 1952.

Governor Harriman, Rob-
ert Moses, Emil Prag
and Charles Poletti cu
ting the ribbon at the S
Lawrence Power Projec
1955.

Surveying Niagara Falls with Richard L. Hearn, Chairman of the
Hydro-Electric Power Commission
of Ontario.

Mary Martin, Lauritz Melchior
Robert Moses and Guy Lombardo
at Jones Beach, 1955.

With his granddaughter, Caroline
lins and James F. Evans at Fire I
State Park, 1955.

Politics Is a Dangerous Trade

There are three chief kinds of public service posts. The first is elective office. To get one you must, as a rule, make a career of politics. This can be a fine thing for the right man—and we need more high caliber men in office—but it is a dangerous trade. I would recommend it to the man who has an established income, a profession, business or talent he can fall back upon if he fails of re-election.

Next is appointive office. It can give great prestige and gratification, but it is also a risky business. These risks and uncertainties, it should be added, must be shared by the family of the official.

You may find yourself on the outside when your party, if you have one and if this association helped you in, gets beaten at the polls or your chief decides to pay a political debt with your job. There are, however, many appointive officers in exempt and normally unprotected positions whose prestige and usefulness are great enough to keep them in high positions irrespective of politics.

The third sort is the permanent, protected job in Federal, state or local government. This is a field with excellent opportunities, but it has some serious drawbacks and disadvantages. It is an enormous field. The Federal government employs about 2,300,000 persons, state governments about 650,000, county governments about 375,000 and municipalities some 934,000. And these figures do not include teachers or those in the military services. Most of the jobs are filled by competition, and promotions up close to the top are also competitive.

There are openings in the public service field for virtually every sort of talent and training known to man. The Federal government is the biggest employer of scientists in the world. State and local agencies employ thousands more. Everything from entomology to probing the mysteries of the cosmic ray is included. The number of legal positions on public payrolls open to women as well as men is colossal, and government uses vast numbers of economists, accountants, psychologists, welfare workers, athletic directors, writers, editors, librarians, musicians, artists, and other skills.

One of the country's most noted scientists, who had given up a high-paying industrial job to work for less money on a secret Navy project in Florida, once said to me: "I have the feeling that I'm doing something for my country. It means a lot more to me than money." This man derives satisfaction from the work itself and from the respect of his fellows, even without high pay, ribbons, titles and luxuries. There are other advantages in public service. Government employees, I can say from experience, are by and large honest, helpful, interesting people to work with. Working conditions are usually good, with short work weeks, long vacations with pay, sick leave and fair pensions.

As to salaries, no one will ever make a Hollywood salary in the public service. Nevertheless, starting salaries for college graduates who enter the Federal government are, in the main, as good as those offered by private industry. In the middle brackets Federal salaries are in some instances superior to those in private industry. And many public servants earn such salaries. New York City, for example, not long ago was seeking junior engineers, just out of college, at $3885 a year. Most governmental agencies give automatic salary increases and provide machinery for promotion. The public authorities in the fields of turnpikes, thruways, bridges, tunnels, electricity, port development, etc., which get their funds from the sale of revenue bonds to private investors, pay excellent salaries and are relatively free from politics and upsets of personnel.

RED TAPE AND OTHER HEADACHES

There is, of course, a darker side. The public employee is often hog-tied in red tape. The man who wants to move decisively in some situation frequently finds his hands bound by cumbersome regulations and customs and by timid superiors and subordinates. Public funds are involved, and there are intricate regulations to protect them from misuse. With changes of administration new policies may be adopted which the conscientious public servant may find difficult to swallow. Politics and influence are never absent.

I remember the battle I had to keep politicians from turning jobs at Jones Beach, Long Island, into political plums. I was able to stop this and other patronage raids, and political leaders have let me more or less alone for years. Sometimes, however, without a lot of public support it cannot be done, and the honorable public servant is made miserable.

These are a few of the headaches of public service. There are more. Public servants get used to being classified as "bureaucrats," "second-raters who couldn't make good in private industry," "feeders at the public trough." At times it is fashionable to magnify the shortcomings of public employees and to exaggerate the number of dishonest, disloyal and lazy ones. The average is at least as good as elsewhere.

Apparently some intelligent and discriminating leaders in private industry do not share this negative view about public employees. Many men in civil and military service have in a sense graduated, or perhaps I should say, migrated into high positions in private business, big firms and consulting practices. Having made good in public, they have gravitated naturally into private affairs. Many a big corporation is headed by a former public official. Public work has been the stepping stone for these men, but they are exceptions which support and emphasize my main point. There are plenty of jobs in government which call for the special abilities possessed by men who go from public to private positions because the rewards and satisfactions in private industry and business are greater.

THE PUBLIC ADMINISTRATOR'S HANDICAPS

One reason why an able public administrator may turn to a private position is because he has greater freedom in selecting men and directing the work for which he is responsible. An administrator, to be effective, must have a responsive, capable staff. He must have a degree of freedom in selecting those who are to carry out orders. He must be in a position to reward good work and to penalize sloth and inefficiency. He is apt to find his best men in his own organization, but he must have the authority to promote them to positions of increasing responsibility, and to see that they are adequately compensated. That is where our system is lamentably weak.

THE BRITISH CIVIL SERVICE

I have always had great admiration for the British civil service, and once wrote a book on the subject. My purpose was to stimulate interest in improving civil service and public administration in the United States. The British system was first introduced by Macaulay in India and later adopted in England, where university graduates were selected by competitive examinations, with tests varying with the positions, which meant dividing civil servants into classes.

I was impressed by the appeal to the best scholars in British universities and felt that the success of the system was owing to this fact. My criticism of the American civil service at the time was that while it was honest, based on open competition, and offered fair opportunities for promotion, it did little to attract young university graduates. I have long since altered my ideas as to the proper training for public service. One of our outstanding public officials was Alfred E. Smith, who was almost entirely lacking in formal education. Yet government on and below the national and international levels includes all kinds of service, from technical and professional work—where college and university degrees are prerequisites—to elected officials, where there are no fixed requirements. It includes executive, legislative and judicial offices, part-time as well as full-time service, line as well as staff work, administration as well as research.

There is no easy road to constructive service and success in any field of government. Personality, luck, and the indefinable qualities of leadership enter into it as well as education. Extraneous matters having little to do with qualifications or accomplishments are likely to be more prevalent and influential in public than in private affairs. We have drifted a long way from what the Founding Fathers called representative government—meaning putting in office outstanding leaders and trusting them—toward government by the lowest common denominator, which assumes that in a true democracy all people are the same size and equally endowed for the highest positions.

At the same time, we have made tremendous advances in all fields of activity where special knowledge and training are necessary. The armies, navies and air forces of tomorrow will be manned by technicians, and in every branch of government there is a demand for specialists and expert administrators and executives. Government is the biggest business there is, and the most diversified. It is time we ceased to theorize and became realistic in facing the task of running it.

The Weaknesses of our Civil Service

Our civil service has greatly improved in recent years, but it still has some of the weaknesses attributable to its original concepts and others to the tremendous expansion that has taken place in the past few years. The original civil service was an ideal conception. Its purpose was to protect public servants from the scandalous abuses of the political patronage system. We could not begin to have decent public service until we gave government employees protection from the rapacious political jobsters.

In addition to offering this kind of protection, competitive examinations opened the door to anyone who aspired to a government position. Once installed the public servant was assured of tenure, promotions, a pension and other benefits. Government was ahead of industry in providing such security to employees, and the country, as well as the public servants, benefited.

Unfortunately, as the system has evolved, and the economy of the country has expanded, unforeseen weaknesses have developed. Civil service, devised to protect the government employee, has become a serious handicap to him or her. Government has not been able to meet the competition of industry and business in the matter of salaries, and, despite promotions, civil service rules have become something like a conspiracy to penalize ability and ambition and to hamper efficiency.

The competent public servant who deserves promotion may take examinations and move up a few grades, but he soon finds himself in a blind alley, or trailing far behind men in similar work outside of government. His worth may be recognized by his superior, but the latter can do nothing about his case. He cannot pick out one man from a group in the same grade and promote him.

The lack of flexibility in the system, of discretionary authority on the part of administrators, and the futile attempt, through standardized examination tests, to spell out the qualifications which fit an individual for advancement, are deadening influences which rob employees of ambition and leave them stranded in routine jobs, while frustrated administrators try desperately to find the help they need to carry on the important work of government.

We must become realistic about this situation. The problem is serious in New York City and in New York State. It is worse in Washington, and every subdivision of government in the country faces the same kind of problem. In New York City we have an annual expense budget of over $1.5 billion. Another half billion of capital expenditures must be administered, along with Federal and state funds which go into highways, housing and other projects. This is big business. Decisions as to how these funds are to be administered, the details of the daily progress of public work, call for the best brains.

We talk about the need for efficiency and economy in government, but we do not go to the roots of the problem. We do not get efficiency and economy by slashing budgets. We can get it by getting good administrators, giving them competent help, and holding them responsible for results.

THE CRY FOR VISION

Government has spread rapidly into fields hitherto preempted by private enterprise, and whether we like it or not, this movement can at best be slowed down but not stopped. It has therefore become more and more obvious that a democracy which still leans to private enterprise can survive only through the most ingenious and fruitful cooperation between business and government. The notion that there are fixed and unchangeable areas in which public and private officials function independently is now entertained only by the most unteachable mossbacks and doctrinaires, and has been abandoned by all pragmatists.

Our primary difficulty is not one of debating the relative values, merits and demerits of private as against public enterprise, but of accepting the realities and finding the people for both government and business who are able and willing to cooperate and to meet the challenge of a new day. The chances of finding the right people as leaders in business are excellent, largely because both talent and incentives are present. The likelihood of attracting them to government is not nearly so promising, partly because competent people have shied away from the risks of public service, partly because of the absence of incentives comparable to those in business, and partly because government has in recent years been given a bad name by those who confuse the misdeeds and efficiencies of a few with the essentially sound character of the great majority of public employees.

MORE TECHNICIANS ARE NEEDED

For both public and private engineering we must have an assured supply of well trained young men. The universities are not supplying enough of them. To enable the universities to meet this demand, corporations, and particularly those which have some logical relation to engineering, should contribute much more liberally, especially to endowments, laboratories, chairs and scholarships. This can be done out of their earnings under the Federal 5 per cent exemption rule. Better faculties, salaries and facilities, less academic red tape and faster promotion of capable people will help the profession by attracting to it the most ambitious youth of the country. Americans are a technical-minded people. The natural urge of youth is toward scientific work. All that is necessary is to encourage this trend.

The engineer, perhaps because of his unnecessarily narrow technical training, is often whipsawed between the skilled trades and the bosses. The mechanic with his trade union to fend for him does well. He often makes more than the graduate engineer. The boss usually has nerve and savvy rather than education. I get a little weary of the type of union leader who thinks a job begins and ends with digging, mixing concrete, putting up steel, bricklaying and electric wiring.

I once asked one of these leaders whether those of us who think up, sell, finance, design and operate big improvements, contribute anything as compared to the union men. His reply was: "If you didn't do it, someone else would." Similarly, the old theme, in its various costumes and settings, of the boss who was smart enough to refuse an education, who hires educated men and can get 'em by the dozen, palls when you have heard it a hundred times. The funny thing is that this type of boss always sends his son to college.

We need more good engineers and technicians in government, and they must have broad culture and discrimination. I am not an exponent of digging and construction just for the devil of it. The first rule is to preserve, the second to restore, the third—only the third—is to build. I apply these rules to land and seascape and to genuine inherited treasures: not to slums. Here the wrecker is the indispensable ally of the planning engineer. Engineering is action, and when all is said and done action is the great aim and purpose of mankind.

Government not only keeps order: it paves the way for private risk and profit. The maker, the agent, the purchaser, the supplier and the repair man in the saga of the automobile are all dependent upon the engineers, contractors and workmen who plan, build and maintain the roads; upon the executives and legislators who furnish the ways and means, and finally upon the forgotten man who pays the bills. This pattern of public and private works is the same in almost every field.

There is no speculative building without streets, parks, and utilities; no permanent art without public or semi-public museums; no shipping without publicly dredged channels and public docks; no railroad without publicly acquired rights-of-way; no flying field without usually exorbitant government subsidy; no river crossings without public bridges and tunnels; no adequate supply of pure water, or disposal of waste; no traffic control, protection against crime or fire, and no preservation of health, treatment of sickness, care of dependents of one kind or another without public works which increase in complexity and cost with the growth and concentration of populations and with ever rising demands and standards of an emancipated people.

Being a government employee is of itself no longer a distinction in a country in which an ever mounting percentage of all the working population is in this category. Men work in sewers, in slaughterhouses and at open graves. They voluntarily enlist in armies in times of peace. They risk contagion in hospitals and laboratories. They fly, crawl over steel girders, climb steeples, swing on the trapeze, and go down to the sea in ships and diving suits. Public service is a fascinating mixture or compound of all these dangerous occupations.

What is needed by way of equipment for such service is strong nerves, backbone, ability to argue a case by the written and spoken word, the instinct for combat, the hide of a rhinoceros, and a willingness to work like a dog for an occasional rain-washed bone. A bit of evangelism is also a prerequisite. It is no more possible to comprehend what attracts people into high public office and keeps them there than to understand the quirk that makes a man a sand hog, a jet plane pilot, or a trapeze artist. It all adds up to the conclusion that we Americans are still an essentially simple, romantic and adventurous people, not nearly as much interested in the dollar as some foreigners suppose.

What we need is to get rid of some of our romantic notions about government; to clear up misconceptions as to how government actually operates, and to apply in the field of public service some of the creative realism that has enabled us to forge ahead in other ways.

2

Politics, Parties
and People

A MAJOR OBJECTIVE OF EVERY DECENT CITIZEN who has any stake in the community, by birth, inheritance or other interest; of anyone who has pride in his or her city, its reputation, its functioning and its advancement, and who has children for whom he wants to guarantee a better life, must be to establish and maintain a government which will afford a framework for good living and successful private enterprise.

Anyone, man or woman, of whatever station, who needlessly smears his city, state or nation; who exaggerates its faults, lacks and hindrances; who slanders the vast decent majority by magnifying the misdeeds of a relatively few bad eggs, is a poor citizen.

When only a fraction of enrolled voters turn up in an important primary, when too few register and even fewer vote, when the vote falls off sharply after the top choice has been made, and constitutional amendments are practically ignored, how can we be proud of the exercise of the franchise which is our fundamental right and duty? Elections are expensive largely because the parties have to put on a big show to get people to the polls—which does not mean much, because you can lead a voter to the polls but you can't make him think.

If anything remotely approaching the sustained interest and critical judgment of our baseball fans—meaning a large part of the entire population—were applied to elections, what an improvement there would be in government! If the voters followed politics as they do the Yankees and Dodgers, the Indians and Giants, there would be players and contests like those we see in a World Series. Able direction, good sportsmanship, team work, no stalling, no sustained wild pitching, no Caseys at the Bat.

If Dr. Kinsey could be persuaded to take a vacation from sex, he might do some really useful research on the Political Habits of the Adult American Voter. Those voters who follow the party blindly irrespective of its candidates, who are moved mainly by extraneous social, religious and racial prejudices, who vote against instead of for candidates, must be charged with blame for "balanced" tickets, a poor roster of choices and driving away competent people from public office. The bosses try to give the public what it wants.

POLITICS IS A SERIOUS BUSINESS

Former Postmaster General James A. Farley made this shrewd remark in a speech in New York City: "We must not shrug off our responsibility by washing our hands of politics as a dirty business. Politics is not a dirty business unless we allow it to become so. It is rather a most serious business which has need of the most highminded and the most generous hearted among us."

We have no right to criticize candidates offered to us to choose among if we have made no effort to influence the party choices, if we avoid party service, if we do not help persuade the right people to run, and if we do not vote in primaries; but simply wait for election day to roll around. It is the independent party man to whom we must look for courage in primary contests, because today primary contests are a joke, and every obstacle is thrown in the way of independent candidates who must create overnight their own machinery to oppose that of the leaders. Contrary to the general impression, however, political leaders ordinarily do not attempt to force their choices on the ballot. They want to find out what the voters are thinking about pro and con. The average leader is not thirsting for defeat and martyrdom. He wants to win.[2]

The regular party workers, the party officials from captains and district leaders on up, are as important as the candidates. If we don't care who operates the party machinery, we have no business complaining that it isn't run well. Incidentally, patronage which, however mitigated, conditioned and controlled, is an inescapable feature of politics, is in the hands of these leaders. If its distribution astonishes, pains or appalls us, we shouldn't complain if we haven't done our part in the selection of the leaders.

If the voters' standards are low or nonexistent, if they want backslappers, baby kissers, sweet singers in local quartets, or exclusively members of their own church, racial origin, school or club, there is no use assuming that the leaders will attempt to rise much above the rank and file. If the voter doesn't want leadership and competence, he won't get them.

In spite of the fact that national and state issues have in theory little place in grass roots, sidewalk and domestic administrations, the established political parties in the nation and state do function in municipal government. Theoretically we should have non-partisan government of municipalities. In some small communities this has worked. It is, however, dangerous to generalize. The larger the municipal unit the more difficult it is to exclude national and state parties, which at bottom depend on local organization.

WHY PARTIES ARE NEEDED

Whether or not we like all manifestations of politics, there can be no national or state government in a democracy without parties. Therefore, parties should be respected and good citizens should not regard them as gadgets which are dusted off and put into motion every two or four years. They are something more than obscure conspiracies against good government which for unaccountable reasons we have to tolerate.

In national and state affairs we need strong parties with genuine principles and objectives, based upon natural lines of cleavage. We are fortunately a two-party country. Occasionally a third or fourth party bobs up but it does not last long. I cannot conceive how our democracy, or for that matter any other, could continue to flourish in a multi-party system.

What Splinter Parties Mean

In France, for many reasons inherent, no doubt, in French history and character, government is based upon proportional representation, which deliberately encourages splinter parties in order to prevent any one party from becoming strong and to discourage men on horseback. As a result it has been impossible to achieve national unity. The kind of man who can be elected President is one who in the course of many years in the Chamber of Deputies has made no enemies. He in turn must pick premiers who can hold together a dozen or more splinter parties for a short time. In some respects, the French President suggests the male in certain branches of the insect world. When he has produced a Premier his function is about over.

French ministries are formed and reshuffled like cards in the hands of an expert dealer, and men in one cabinet turn up in another in different posts in a manner bewildering to most Americans. There can be no leadership, no continuity, no responsibility, no loyalty and no public respect under such a system, and if the French continue to cling to it they will go down as other gifted nations have before them.

These are people of culture of whom it may be said that they could not compete in the modern world because, in spite of their great resources, they were unable to compose their internal differences and make small sacrifices for the common good. The nearest thing to a nihilist is a French peasant. He is against all government, particularly national government, and of course opposed to all taxes. He avoids politics and parties. His idea of local administration is a bureau of vital statistics. We are, of course, hopeful that France will succeed in breaking away from some of her old political habits.

Proportional Representation

Proportional representation is the architect of communism and disorder. Its twin objectives are to enfranchise minorities as such and to kill big parties. The encouragement of splinter groups, by giving them representation based on the total votes they cast in large areas, destroys neighborhood voting by those who know the candidate best;

encourages the formation of professional, trade and other pressure groups, and the candidacy of demagogues, crackpots and otherwise irresponsible people; ruins party responsibility and therefore orderly government; and plays straight into the hands of the Communists and other radical extremists who first infiltrate government and then by obstruction destroy it.

Our occupation officers who helped write proportional representation into the new German constitution after World War II did that country and us a great disservice. In New York City, proportional representation was an abject failure and was enthusiastically repealed. Merely as a piece of voting mechanism, it is a most complex balloting and counting device, conducive to trickery, expense, confusion and delay.

It is claimed by enthusiasts that proportional representation is especially useful in keeping national and state parties and party leaders out of what is essentially nonpartisan housekeeping. Actually, the professional politician has an essential and often honorable part to play in the municipal picture. His role should not be underestimated. It is a mistake to assume that the show can go on nicely without him. He is the one who anticipates fires and puts them out, quiets feuds, reconciles claims and ambitions, and distributes the favors as evenly as possible. He may comb off something in the process, but not always or even often. Usually he wants the best government consistent with his running it.

The Role of the Independent Voter

Our major parties do not always function on logical principles. For a long time the Republican party was the party of strong central government and the Democratic party that of states' rights and municipal home rule. Their roles have in many respects been reversed, especially since the advent of the New Deal. Similarly the Republican Party was the abolitionist party, and the Democratic Party that of Southern white domination. Here again the roles to some extent have been reversed, due in part to the great city Democratic machines. As to fundamental principles, however, the Republican Party is still the party of conservatives, whether they be progressive or ultra-progressive; and the Democratic Party, with some exceptions, that of the so-called liberal element. This is a natural, logical line of cleavage.

Those who join one party or the other need not vote for all its candidates or endorse all its policies. One can be a party worker without being either reactionary or radical. There is no reason to be revolutionary, for bigotry or for bitter partisanship. We ought to have a sense of humor about these things. There is no reason to despise the other man's party any more than there is a reason to despise the other man's fraternal organization, or his college, or his taste in houses or clothes.

The average American is a middle-of-the-road man. He tends to one side or the other but is neither far to the right nor very far to the left, and it is the independent voter, whether affiliated with a party or not, who makes the final decisions. This is true even under the British parliamentary system, because if some of the members of the House of Commons did not change their minds between big elections there would be no votes of loss of confidence, and no ministries would go out of office until the full term ran out.

One does not have to make a profession or a full-time business of party membership. This is one field in which the part-time worker is welcome and useful. As a public official I have no place in ordinary party work, but I am an enrolled party member and have never hesitated to express myself on the larger issues. Even those of us who have been in the more or less permanent service realize how important it is that the parties which furnish us with those who make policies, and whom we advise and assist, shall be truly representative of the best in democracy.

LOCAL POLITICAL FORCES

There seem to me to be six great forces in municipal government. The first force consists of the bosses. The second is the elective officers whose success or failure depends largely on the bosses and on their own native strength and endurance. The third is the high appointive officers who in turn depend on the elective officers, on their own fortitude and on the usefulness and loyalty of the permanent staff, usually protected by civil service, who constitute the fourth class. Fifth, comes the press, and last, but not least, the public.

Some years ago I read a book, *You're the Boss*, by the late Edward J. Flynn, long the successful Democratic leader of The Bronx in New York City. There is too much cant and solemnity in most of our textbooks on government, and only an occasional wink of the right eye and a good dig in the ribs saves us from sour smugness. I was thankful for the touches of pure Irish blarney which here and there enliven the pages of Mr. Flynn's apologia for political bosses.

Some smart bosses do pick men for the top jobs in government who have the savvy, the modesty and the common sense to leave the real work to competent assistants, usually in the civil service. Mr. Flynn was right in saying that Boss Murphy of Tammany Hall supported Alfred E. Smith through thick and thin, ran the interference against the opposition and shenanigans of other practical politicians, and thereby helped Smith to demonstrate that a boy from the Bowery could be a first-rate Governor.

Mr. Flynn was refreshingly frank in discussing the "boss" system, the rules and gimmicks of practical politics and the distribution of patronage. However, the volume contains hardly a reference to the purposes and objects of government. Apparently what government has to do, that is, the problems it has to deal with from day to day, are of minor interest to the best of bosses. Not the job to be done, but who is to hold it, is the important thing. Therefore the qualifications of the incumbent are secondary, if, indeed, they are considered at all.

The operation of the boss principle often produces ludicrous results. I remember a conversation with Governor Smith at the time I was working with him on the reorganization of the state government. The immediate problem was the introduction and explanation of legislation. There was strong Republican opposition but there were a few independent Republicans who were ready to introduce the bills. It was essential that in the sponsorship of each bill there be a Republican in one house and a Democrat in the other. The difficulty was to find Democrats in the Assembly who could do the job. This discussion led to an insistence on the part of the Governor that some promising young Democrats who could be really useful to him be: picked from New York City. Mr. Murphy readily agreed, and by way of explaining how some candidates were selected, he told the story of a man by the name of Makachek.

It seems that a number of Bohemians had moved into a previously German district and it appeared desirable to nominate some one of Bohemian extraction. He took Makachek from a list because he could pronounce and remember his name. He said he kept thinking of "make a check." Otherwise he knew nothing about the man. For all I know Makachek may have turned out to be an admirable legislator, but, if so, it was an accident. Ordinarily, selections for elective and high appointive office are on racial, geographical and religious lines, and on the "make a check" basis. Our genius for political compromise in such matters is, however, always dressed up as a matter of high principle arising out of what is called the democratic process.

Other Important Factors

After the bosses and elective and appointive officers comes the permanent governmental staff. Civil service has done much to protect it, but the process of shielding this group and offering it security and pensions, bureaucracy, lethargy, clock-watching, lack of enterprise, and fear of showing one's head above the crowd, has done much to undermine efficiency. Radical unionism and veterans' preference have further reduced efficiency and will militate more and more against the promotion of the best talent. There should, of course, be some veterans' preference in initial appointments, but it should not be an absolute preference and should not extend for half a century to promotion, thus slamming the door in the faces of able young men unless they in turn become veterans by participating in a third world war.

There are, to be sure, structural standards in municipal government as well as in engineering and building. A compact government, with a recognizable head clothed with both power and responsibility, with a few elected officers chosen at general elections separate from those at which the top Federal and state executives are voted on, with a small number of compact, consolidated departments, with a legislative body of limited membership—these standards are tried and true. A small municipality with little more than housekeeping functions may in some instances be operated by a nonpartisan council and city manager, but a big city, town or county needs an elected personality at its head. Complete elimination of political parties on the assumption that they should function only on state and national levels is impossible.

Crusades to improve municipal government in these United States have had more banners than swords, and have been characterized more by fleeting noble impulses than by stubborn persistence. We are at last waking up to the fact that the gadgets advocated and touted for so many years will not cure the more deepseated troubles of municipalities. By gadgets I mean efficiency schemes like model charters, city managers, home rule, legislative reapportionment—to give the big cities fairer representation in the influential state governments—frequent popular referendums on everything debatable, performance budgets and other similar mechanical devices. There are still doctrinaires who believe in salvation by legislation alone. Legislation of itself wins no victories. It is simply the vehicle on which stamina can ride. A stumble bum can do nothing with a fine bicycle in a six-day race.

As to the press, good local government is more and more dependent upon it for correct information and support, but competent local officials who do not have a flare for publicity and showmanship, and who aim at action and accomplishment rather than melodrama, find themselves almost shut out of the news. Much of the press puts too much emphasis on controversy and is happiest if it can egg on a fight or trap the unwary into some controversial utterance. In addition, editors, especially New York editors, as distinguished from reporters, rarely have a first-hand acquaintance with municipal government problems, and frequently do not even know the geography of their city. It would be a good thing if the best reporters were permitted to rotate as editors when municipal affairs are under discussion.

Finally, we get to the public, which in most municipalities, especially in big cities, is preoccupied with other matters and gets its governmental information only from the press, radio and television, and from infrequent and casual contacts with public officers. What is more serious is the tendency, particularly in cities with a mixed population of varying origins and associations, to confuse all kinds of extraneous issues with matters of local self-government.

The man who votes for an elective official because he is clever at reviving ancient racial, religious, sectional, professional or other grudges, or votes against him because he refuses to inject such issues into his campaign or administration, is the fellow who makes first-rate local self-government impossible. He plays into the hands of minorities and pressure groups, and has no right to expect even as good government as he gets today. Public service, like water, cannot rise much above its own level, and the people can, in the long run, expect of its public servants no higher standards than those of the average voter. This, however, constitutes no reason why we should have the rule of the lowest common denominator.

It is becoming obvious that we face a showdown between our free enterprise, capitalistic democracy and out-and-out autocratic communism. In this struggle we pit honest information against political propaganda and downright misrepresentation. Illogical party alignments, the manifest deficiencies of our public service, the stupidities of our more reactionary and less teachable tycoons of money and industry, and the contentiousness, loafing and poor leadership of much of our organized labor are severe handicaps.

We are dealing with ruthless radicals who have no capitalists, no labor unions, no honest ballots and no home rule to worry about, and to whom individual liberties are eyewash. Absolute government has enormous advantages in such a struggle. Democracy is bound to be relatively inefficient because the happiness of countless individuals, rather than the triumph of the state, is its purpose. We cannot afford to be as careless, wasteful and happy-go-lucky as we are today, relying on our scientists, our head start in atomic invention and our great natural resources to keep us at the head of the procession. It is a challenge but, given leadership and public education, I am convinced that we have the stuff to meet it.

3

The Personal Equation

EVER SINCE GILBERT AND SULLIVAN MUSICALLY promulgated the patter that any ambitious young fellow, by polishing up the handle of the big front door, can become the ruler of the Queen's Navy, other less gifted authors have used fine phrases about the nobility of public service and the cardinal virtues which will enable the ambitious to bob to the top like a cork, with happy references to Horatio Alger and advice à la Dale Carnegie.

In politics, as in other fields, the personal equation cannot be disregarded. While government, as distinguished from politics, can be exciting, much of it is humdrum business, largely in the hands of gagged or inarticulate permanent experts who are dependent on high officials to tell their story. Personality certainly counts here, but it has its limitations.

A young scion of a leading American family once came to Governor Smith for advice on running for Congress as a Democrat in a Republican stronghold. The Governor asked:

"What makes you think you could buck the machine in that rotten borough?"

"Well, Governor," the young man replied, "I suppose I shouldn't say it, but the family thinks I could win on my charm."

This reply, which floored the Governor and gave him one of his best after-dinner stories, was not as preposterous as it may seem. If that incomparable genius of politics Jimmy Walker did not go places on personality, what propelled him?

24

Governor Smith and Jimmy Walker were fountains of humor and balls of fire compared to other executives of their day. The difference between them was that Smith's talents were used to reduce to homely fare and popularize great and complicated issues, while Walker's were largely sleight of hand to make the issues disappear and to dramatize the magician.[3]

Walker was Democratic leader of the state Senate in 1923, when the Democrats had a majority of one. One of my tasks, as an assistant to Governor Smith, was to keep Senator Walker informed on the Governor's program. Given a few whispered words outlining an argument, Walker could make a complete, fluent speech. When all else failed, he fell back on his wit for a gibe or a catchy phrase to overcome a serious opponent.

On the eve of the extraordinary session of the Legislature in 1924, called by Governor Smith to fight for Heckscher State Park on Long Island, Walker had not shown up. He was discovered at the Ten Eyck Hotel barbershop on Monday morning, at the hour when the Legislature convened. He had no preparation for his part as majority leader, but was unabashed and full of wit and sangfroid.

Five minutes before the morning session, Jim arrived at his office in the capitol, viewed the mountain of mail on his desk with mock alarm, asked his secretary, Eddie Stanton, if there were any checks in the letters and, being told that there were not, swept the entire accumulation off to the floor and asked me, as the head of the state park system, to tell him quickly what was brewing!

The Decline of Oratory

Perhaps it is a sign of my age that most oratory has lost its charm for me. Where, indeed, are the Ruperts of debate? The growling, rumbling voice of one surviving Old Man Eloquent still echoed around the English-speaking world in 1955, but there is no successor to Sir Winston, and it looks as if his mantle were going straight to the Costume Museum. We like to believe that there is no accounting for the former British Prime Minister's extraordinarily buoyant and resilient personality, his restless and varied activities and his divine talent, save on the basis of his half English and half American inheritance. Certainly, he did not pick up these talents as a backward student at Sandhurst. He developed them by omnivorous reading, painful, old-fashioned elocution in front of a mirror, and endless practice as a journalist, correspondent and debater.

Churchill swallowed biography, memorized the purplest passages of English prose and verse, cultivated a biting and incisive style, as well as the honeyed tongue of men and angels, and added élan and bravura all his own. He explored, soldiered and reported throughout the length and breadth of the British Empire. He roamed from Land's End to John O'Groat's, from Dan to Beersheba, from Kashmir to the Deccan. He was thus magnificently prepared to rally his people with unforgettable oratory in their darkest and finest hour.

In my youth I admired the magnificent bellows of William Jennings Bryan, and the fact that there was nothing much above the Adam's apple did not detract from the expansive organ tones in which he prayerfully adjured labor not to let capital press the crown of thorns upon its brow, and proclaimed that the great basic American virtues were the exclusive province of the hardy pioneers who braved the wilderness that the desert might blossom like the rose and the voices of the little children mingle with the voices of the birds.

I can remember the succession of great Irish orators with their flowing periods, throbbing vocal chords and Milesian metaphors. When he studied elocution at St. James' Parish, Governor Smith learned to imitate them. He could do the whole series of Burke Cockran's orations on the several professions. There was, for example, the talk on the statesman, repeated over and over, and appliquéd and embroidered with shamrocks, wolfhounds and lovely little Irish harps. According to the Governor, it ran something like this:

"Is the politician happy? Far from it. When the sceptre of power finally drops from his nerveless fingers, he is condemned to an isolation the more unbearable because of the adulation to which he has become accustomed."

In the old days, folklore has it that there were great toastmasters, men of wit, of resource, of subtlety, of comedy and humor. These were men of the stripe of Joseph H. Choate, Simeon Ford, Job Hedges, Bishop Potter, Mr. Murphy, of Mark Cross. They could keep speakers in order, stimulate them, slap them down if they got tiresome, and run off a dinner in jigtime. They functioned before the days when men who own dinner jackets will put up with anything which will keep them away from home.

Oldsters still chuckle over the dinner at which Simeon Ford, who ran the Grand Union Hotel opposite the Grand Central Station, introduced Joseph H. Choate with many sly references to previous Josephs—among them he of the coat of many colors and the one Mrs. Potiphar took such a yen to. Choate rose to the occasion: "I am not," he said, "the Joseph of the coat of many colors, nor yet the Joseph who was tempted by Potiphar's wife, but had I been so tempted and had I succumbed, I know at whose hotel we would have registered."

Governor Smith had the shrewdness, the feel for an audience, the gaiety, and the guff that passes for logic in politics. At the end of the hard-fought campaign in which Smith finally defeated Judge Nathan Miller, he triumphantly marched up State Street in Albany to the Mansion through a continuous ovation I have never seen equaled for sincerity and emotion. Judge Miller had made an address at Troy, a reasoned, judicial, fair, but narrow, unsympathetic, cold-blooded budgetary analysis, unredeemed by anecdote, humor or happy metaphor. In it he claimed he had saved, I believe, $40 million, which Smith would have poured down the drain. This of course was bookkeeping with a thin "waste not want not" appeal.

Governor Smith started working on an earthshaking, devastating reply on the previous Saturday morning, but one thing or another intervened. There was mail; lots of friendly visitors; church; radio; and wine. Saturday disappeared; Sunday flew by; and the big speech was neglected until we started for Troy at seven on Monday evening. I asked the Governor what he expected to say. He replied that everything was jake.

At eight the Governor approached the lectern. There was radio, or "raddio" as he impishly preferred to call it, but that did him no good because he was away from the mike half the time with mimicry, crouching, comprehensive gestures and other appeals which brought him right down into the audience. After many flattering references to the concentrated native intelligence, judgment, patriotism, fairness, etc., of the people of Troy, Cohoes and surrounding towns, the Governor drew from his pocket an account of Judge Miller's speech, quoted the $40 million saving, referred sympathetically to the lateness of the hour and the importance of sparing the audience tiresome and confusing details and said, "I can sum it all up for you in one sentence: If Governor Miller saved forty million bucks, where is it and who's got it?"

There was a shocked silence, and soon you could see that the people in front were repeating the question to each other and were ready to go after Judge Miller in a big way. I told the Governor afterward that it was a magnificent sockeroo in a heavyweight bout, but just a trifle below the belt. But it worked. It was short and to the point, and it represented something different from the oratory we listen to these days.

Apt humor is always a sharp weapon against Ciceronian orations. Jimmie Walker in a dozen ways was the peer of them all when it came to impromptu, sophisticated wisecracks. He was no paragon to hold up to youth. He was the product of a crazy age, impish, urbane, polished, sardonic. He was at his best when he was dependent solely on his wits, when he was unprepared, unrehearsed and seriousness was purely coincidental.

At the one-hundredth anniversary of the Erie Canal the Port Authority put on a big lunch to celebrate the union of New York City and the Great Lakes. Frothing rivers flowed. Filet mignons were piled up like flapjacks. Oratory flowed, too. The guest speaker was a charming old gentleman from Buffalo, a grandson of the De-Witt Clinton who built the big ditch, resting peacefully after an honorable local career, unknown to fame and vastly astonished to find himself so honored. He determined to do the occasion full justice and read quietly, historically and monotonously for forty-five minutes. This was after lunch!

He was followed by counsel for the Port Authority, an estimable lawyer who claimed to have invented the Authority idea and also the extraordinary legalistic device known as and/or, with the 45-degree line in between. This gentleman, with the precedent before him, also spoke forty-five minutes!

As the audience began to filter out, deterred only by curiosity as to how the Mayor would get himself out of this situation, Beau James lifted himself lightly to his feet, pointed to the clock and said: "I see before me the busiest and most powerful leaders of the world of industry. They must get back to their desks. Neither wind, nor snow, nor rain, nor gloom of night, nor Jimmie Walker shall keep them from their appointed rounds. Gentlemen, this meeting is adjourned for one hundred years." It is an art which few possess.

When Governor Smith asked my opinion of Walker as a candidate for Mayor of New York, I told him that aside from other objections, none of them personal, the Governor could not support him because he was incapable of sustained effort. I did not think he would last through one term, much less almost two. In the end it was irresponsibility that got him and forced his resignation under fire, thus paving the way for reform in New York City.

OTHER MAYORS I HAVE KNOWN

I am not old enough to have known the hard-bitten, tough, sententious Judge Gaynor, who leaned on Epictetus for his inspiration and epigrams. When John Purroy Mitchel, a gallant young reformer, fresh from college, reached City Hall, it was—though he did not then realize it—the twilight of efficiency engineering, expertizing and municipal research, and the dawn of disillusionment about salvation by governmental gadgets. The age of "scientific management" in government, with its fancy lingo, was drawing to a close.

It was a period of disillusionment for me, for I worked for a time with the Mitchel administration, and the Bureau of Municipal Research. I know of nothing actually accomplished by the sterile Mitchel administration excepting Edward M. Bassett's launching of the zoning system. The zoning boat was loaded down with all kinds of junk; it had reciprocating engines instead of turbines; it made little speed, but it floated and went places. Almost all the rest of the Mitchel proposals were pipe dreams. It was an honest outfit

committed to saving rubber bands, using both ends of the pencil
and similar efficiency devices, and to the impossible promise of making vast physical improvements without spending more money.

"Red Mike" Hylan was a dull, plodding, decent political hack,
picked because he was the most pliable, respectable material that
could win without effort. He swelled, instead of growing, in City Hall,
and his pathetic two terms ended when Governor Smith could take
no more of his clowning.

Judge John P. O'Brien, who succeeded Walker for a brief period,
was a kindly, respectable, bumbling family and church man, distinguished for turgid opinions and unimpeachable personal integrity.
In the course of a single year of futility and wurra wurra, he gave
Tammany a quiet, dignified funeral and Fiorella H. La Guardia,
interpreter, consular employee, who studied law while he worked,
full of reform and Mediterranean fire, leaped into City Hall and
set it to shuddering, heaving and quivering for twelve eventful years.

La Guardia was an extraordinarily picturesque and photogenic
character, and he made an irresistible appeal to all who admire stout
hearts, keen, honest minds and salient personalities. There was, too,
another side to his nature which was not lost upon the public—
his enormous loyalty to his family and his abiding affection for all
children. He had his faults. Like the City of New York, he was a
bundle of contradictions. He was the first reformer to succeed himself. He was a many-sided man, torn by conflicting emotions. He was
uncertain as to whether to be a national, an international or a local
character; whether to be a legislator whose every act is privileged, or
an executive who must be responsible tomorrow for everything he
does today; whether to be a conservative or a radical; an artist or a
tough boss, a broad-minded cosmopolitan or an uncompromising reformer. Yet he was the best Mayor in New York's history.[4]

I have had a responsible part in New York City's administration
since 1934, when La Guardia first appointed me Commissioner of
Parks. I did not agree with him at all times, but we worked well together. In the mayoralty campaign of 1945, when William O'Dwyer
was the Democratic candidate, I supported Newbold Morris. Nevertheless, Mayor O'Dwyer asked me to continue in office and supported

the programs I proposed. I favored O'Dwyer's re-election. When he resigned, shortly after his re-election, I supported Vincent Impellitteri, who was elected. Under him, our city improvement program was further advanced. I took no direct part in the campaign of 1953. Following his election, Mayor Robert F. Wagner requested me to continue in office.

I do not know why anyone in his right senses wants to be Mayor of New York. It is the best way of inviting stomach ulcers, gout and beri beri, swamping the family, hastening early baldness and denying that sufficient unto the day is the evil thereof. But Mayor Wagner has the training to do the chores, suffer the slings and arrows, and tackle the real problems and glories of what is aptly described as the second biggest political post in the nation. He was brought up by an affectionate, humorous, tolerant and highminded father, who rose from obscurity to become a highly respected statesman and humanitarian.

Young Bob went to the best college we have—by far the best, and it gave him much. He studied some more, began at the bottom of the government ladder and rose, rung by rung, to the chief magistracy. In his first year in that office he earned widespread goodwill. Millions want him to succeed.

I like many things about Bob Wagner. What I like best, however, is that he cares deeply and sincerely about New York and is willing to work unstintingly and singlemindedly to make it better. These are his great fundamental virtues, and to those of us who are privileged to work with him, he can look for technical aid, for honest, if sometimes disconcerting, advice, and for the unswerving loyalty to which every executive who gives genuine leadership is entitled.

Some Governors I Have Known

The great trouble with most of the Governors of New York has been that they have been diverted from local administrative matters by the irresistible lure of the distant shining dome of the Capitol at Washington.

John A. Dix was a cipher, and William Sulzer, who was removed from office, was a befuddled imitation of Henry Clay. Alfred E.

Smith was, in my opinion, the greatest Governor of our time. He was a great executive because he had a warm heart, vision, shrewdness in picking men, and the generous impulse of all great administrators to build up his associates, trust and reward them.

Nathan F. Miller was one of the toughest as well as the deepest, narrowest and most cold-blooded state executive I have known. He had the uncompromising and inflexible honesty, financial vision and range of sympathies of a bank auditor, the habits of mind and social approach of an appeal judge of the McKinley era, enormous industry and courage and complete indifference to fame, personal popularity and promotion. His conception of the state was that of Alexander Hamilton and John Adams. He almost ruined the Republican Party by his unwillingness to meet the rising demand for progress and change. Governor Miller, however, held no grudge against the public for turning against him and his policies, which shows what sterling stuff he was made of.

Although I opposed him politically and differ with Herbert H. Lehman on many matters, I have great respect for him and think he was an able Governor. I have had my differences also with Thomas E. Dewey, but supported him and worked closely with him over many years, and I am now working harmoniously with Governor Averell Harriman for many years an enthusiastic and generous supporter of the State Park system.

THE ARISTOCRAT IN POLITICS

Shortly before he died, Ogden L. Mills published a book entitled *The Seventeen Million*, and I was asked to review it for *The Yale Review*. No one, with the possible exception of Herbert Hoover, had so clear a title to speak for the 17 million anti-New Dealers as Ogden Mills and at the time no one, not even excepting Mr. Hoover, faced an audience so packed and papered against the speaker.

Born at Newport when it was most fashionable, brought up among the "Hudson bracketed" estates of Dutchess County, all his life one of the ablest living Republicans, Ogden Mills tried in vain to escape the connotations of his name and background. Earlier in the century it was no handicap to be frankly a gentleman of wealth in politics. In 1937, but for a glaring exception, the camel could walk through the needle's eye more easily than the conscious native aristocrat out of Harvard by Groton could be elected to high public office.

Here was the greatest of all American political puzzles, for not a Dutchess County apple's throw from the Mills estate at Staatsburg is Hyde Park, where another boy of old New York lineage, wealth and what is commonly regarded as snobbish upbringing, spent much of his youth. What, then, shut the gate of political preferment to Ogden Mills and opened it wide to Franklin Roosevelt? It is one of those political freaks which show that we are not yet grown up in politics.

Mr. Mills was at his best in attacking the New Deal by analogy with other tyrannies, and in particular in emphasizing the lessons of Communism and Fascism. He was not so strong in his reference to the industrial revolution and its effects on individual freedom and private initiative. Another weakness was his almost pathological fear of public spending. This can be one of the most dangerous of all phobias, and there are occasions when the miser in high public office can be as dangerous as the drunken sailor.

In reading his book, I could not get it out of my mind that Ogden Mills was one of the Republican high command in New York State in the decade from 1918 to 1928 when the Republican Party was busy building up Governor Smith by opposing every constructive plan he offered that cost money. The depression was good for practicable conservatives and Ogden Mills profited by it almost more than any other conservative I know.

I do not know why more men of this type do not enter public service. It has been suggested that titles or decorations not forbidden by the Constitution would make our public life more glamorous. Even Socialists have been seduced by knighthoods, the Order of the Bath, the Legion of Honor, and titles like Pasha and The Honorable. Mark Twain shrewdly observed that we publicly scoff at titles but privately hanker after and even buy them. He said that the human race must be stripped to be a real democracy and that the introduction of even a rag on tiger skin or a cow-tail would make a badge of distinction, and end in monarchy. Mark Twain was wrong.

These ribbons would become so numerous and prevalent that they would mean no more than a Davy Crockett cap or a Deputy Sheriff's badge.

THE PRESIDENTS OF MY TIME

Although as a Yale man I had great admiration for William Howard Taft, my first presidential vote was for Theodore Roosevelt. I still think T. R. was far ahead of his time in many things, his interest in conservation, for example. I do not know why I failed to appreciate Woodrow Wilson while he was alive. I thought he was just another professor. At the risk of sacrilege, it may be suggested that for a comparatively long time after his martyrdom, another Evangelist, the greatest of them all, made little impression on his contemporaries.

With Wilson I would link Franklin D. Roosevelt and Wendell Willkie as three of the great American evangelists. A century or two from now, when the current concerns and acerbities of our time are forgotten, our descendants will perhaps know the true significance in world history of men like these. In the meantime, let us assume that the road of international brotherhood is long and broken, and that on the journey there are honorable places both for the evangelists and for the step-by-step conservatives. The important thing is to see that we are all headed in the same direction.

I was serving as Secretary of State when Governor Smith ran for the Presidency, and I took no part in that campaign. As a Republican I had plenty of reservations regarding some of Smith's supporters, but I voted for him, and was appalled by some of the scandalous attacks made on Smith. The effects on him of his defeat were tragic.

Herbert Hoover is our foremost engineer, and is recognized everywhere as a great administrator. It is a triumph of democracy that after years of misrepresentation, detraction and caricature, this distinguished American at last came into his own with the recognition of his prodigious efforts for public service at home and abroad.

Our foremost political realist is, of course, Bernard M. Baruch, who has earned the right to speak his mind freely, and is the wisest of philosophers as well as a great humanist and generous philanthropist. Another durable personality with whom I have had many political differences is James A. Farley, one of the most respected figures in American public life.

AN INDEPENDENT REPUBLICAN'S VOTE

As an independent Republican, I was asked by the editors of *Life* magazine to comment on the candidates in the 1952 Presidential campaign. I had never seen Governor Stevenson, nor had I met General Eisenhower. All I knew about the candidates was what I saw in the pictures, heard on the radio, read in the press and gathered by talk and osmosis.[5]

That the two nominating conventions should have ended so well was something of a triumph of our curious election system. Somehow the system works. Our republican form of government was not invented in Russia, nor have the Communists been able to produce the chain reactions which in our political atomic explosions follow the release of the imprisoned sunlight we call democracy.

The Democrats moved toward the center from the left, the Republicans from the right. Economic royalists and New Dealers were equally disappointed. Both candidates were first-class men. One knew more about foreign and the other more about domestic affairs. Adlai Stevenson is one of the literate political figures of our time and a welcome departure from spellbinders and demagogues. He is a phrasemaker, but a phrasemaker with a conscience.

Unfortunately, Stevenson does not always distinguish between verbal facility and wisecracking. Ordinarily our electorate is not keen on sly and clever raillery. These are dangerous practices. If the argument were reduced to metaphors, it seemed to me that the average voter was likely to say that General Eisenhower might not be so quick on the trigger but knew more about guns than Governor Stevenson, and hit the target oftener.

General Eisenhower was both straightforward and diplomatic. As to previous records, if relatively long and heavy responsibility was to be the measure, the advantage was with Dwight Eisenhower. Stevenson's docket showed only inconspicuous service in a number of relatively minor positions, excepting three years of noteworthy but inconclusive service as Governor of Illinois.

The difference between the General and the Governor, as I

saw it, was one of growth. The former represented a fruit or vegetable which had ripened slowly on the vine and the latter one picked a little too green and forced artificially to quick maturity.

Leaving aside the two platforms, which were neither revealing nor very different and required interpretaton to give them meaning, the two candidates promised much the same things. We therefore had to look elsewhere for the basis of an honest choice. I was for General Eisenhower primarily because he not only promised but was bound to give us a new administration at Washington in place of one which was stale, tired, discredited at home and abroad, incompetent and powerless to restore confidence and meet the challenges of a new day. General Eisenhower had no alternative, no conceivable motive for doing otherwise, no reason not to clean house, no pulls, attractions, influences, loyalties or obligations tying him to high officials in the government whose public usefulness was manifestly at an end.

I had no illusion that all the new faces introduced by the General, if elected, would be transfigured by a passion for service and that all his decisions on appointments would be untouched by political considerations. But the faces would be new ones and many would be those of people of genuine ability long excluded from the hope of high position and opportunity.

No doubt Stevenson would in a limited sense have been his own man. He would not be led around by the nose. He would not condone all that had gone before. He would have some new advisers and doubtless a better cabinet, but the machine would still be there and the fixers and influence peddlers on the sidelines in Washington would draw a breath of relief, then settle down to the same old influencing and fixing. What our house of government needed was a new set of architects, engineers and builders, not just a change of janitors.

There are those who said it was silly to ask for a change for the sake of change. But that is exactly what millions wanted, including independents and many Democrats as well as Republicans. These millions were mortally afraid that a Stevenson victory, no matter how fine a man Stevenson might be potentially, would mean en-

trenchment of demagogy and autocracy and the end of periodic
healthy competition for the right to govern. If it turns out that the
Republicans have been in long enough, Adlai Stevenson will still be
young and available. I believe there was a force at work which defies
ordinary arithmetic and the laws of political gravity. It is the innate,
sure, canny instinct of the American voter for the real underlying
issue. In the last campaign the necessity of a complete change of
government was the issue.

We may accept the dictum that the less government we have the
better off we are, and still concede that the minimum of official
planning, financing, and administration demanded in the atomic age
is something different from the laissez-faire theory of the nineteenth
century. Since we are bound to have powerful officials, or at least
officials with heavy responsibilities, they ought to be good ones, and
their lives might well be made a little tamer, a trifle more respected
and rewarded, and somewhat less rocky and hazardous. I suspect that
good officials will be made rather than educated, but whatever the
process there seems nothing wild or revolutionary in the vision of a
limited, highly competent, democratic government in a land still
dedicated to individual freedom and private initiative.

We cannot eliminate the personal equation from politics, but we
can strengthen the machinery. My mind runs a good deal in the
direction of building up a really fine permanent secretariat, one step
or grade below the cabinet officers. It could not only develop ideas
but keep the governmental machine running with or in spite of
political changes involving personalities and all manner of extraneous matters.

4

Theory and Practice in Politics

IN THE COURSE OF ASSOCIATION WITH MANY ABLE and interesting personalities in public administration, I am about ready to accept the conclusion reached by Plato and Aristotle two thousand years ago and aptly expressed by Alexander Pope when he said:

> For forms of government let fools contest;
> Whate'er is best administer'd is best.

Men make government just as they make business, but government is not simply public business. There should, no doubt, be much more business in government, but the idea that any successful tycoon will make a good public executive is an exploded American superstition. There are elements which enter into high public office, elective or appointive, which have no parallel in private business, and the bland assumption that a certain type of corporate organization under an imposing and impressive board of directors, answerable to big stockholders, must necessarily work in government is moonshine. The analogy between stockholders of a business corporation and the great rank and file of voters at the polls will not stand close scrutiny.

A good form of democratic government, with executive, legislative and judicial powers reasonably separated, and executive functions, power and responsibility concentrated in one man, will enable that man, if he really has any substance, to succeed better than if he were constantly adjusting and fighting checks and balances in a ramshackle organization rigged to prevent action. On the other hand, no form of government will make a strong executive out of a weak one, or automatically elevate third-string people to the first rank; and it has been proven again and again that strong people with good objectives and public support can accomplish astonishing results in the face of extraordinary difficulties. In spite of Communist mouthings, robot government has not worked anywhere yet. The human equation is still predominant. People were not made for the government, and any system which does not respect their natural rights will in the end bite the dust.

THE FALLACY OF EXPERTIZING

I have had considerable personal experience with the improvement of forms of government. As I said in a letter to the then Comptroller of New York City in 1951, this experience taught me to be wary of salvation by new organization charts and efficiency installations, and extremely suspicious of extravagant claims of net dollar savings in government. Men, not charts and measures, make good government. The ideal thing, of course, is to have first-class men operating first-class machines, but first-class men can operate any machine and third-rate people can not make the best and most modern gadgets work. Budget, efficiency and planning surveys usually avoid the big immediate problems in favor of small economies, or propose long-range revolutionary plans not realizable in our lifetime.

Government is not just another business with the profit motive left out—a business which, once divorced from politics, can readily be improved by itinerant experts armed with the lingo of efficiency. Capitalism, whose practices government is asked to imitate, has not always been internally healthy and without sin, and it has even been whispered among the unregenerate that great corporations have their own diseases, paralleling those of government, including politics, deadheads, nepotism, illusions of grandeur and hardening of the arteries. Spasms of reform and efficiency get us nowhere. Wise reformers do not give too many cathartics. We need firm objectives. These are orderly growth, wider horizons, decent standards. Toward their realization we require steady, reliable sources of income.

I am for genuine economy, for cutting out waste, for the smallest practical number of competent, decently paid and well treated employees and for savings which do not cut services; but I ask the experts to concentrate on the big problems of financing and refrain from making mountains out of molehills, or trying to reestablish the economic and civic standards of the nineteenth century. There is undoubtedly waste in government, and it should be mercilessly exposed and rooted out, but not at the expense of morale and service.

THE RISING COST OF LOCAL GOVERNMENT

We must keep a sense of proportion about expenditures and taxes. We must remember that it is the Federal government which siphons off most of our incomes. While the big cities and the states in which they are located battle endlessly over pennies, the Federal revenuers run off with the dollars. If our national and global statesmen could find means of cutting down on defense and spending abroad to buy friends and raise the general level of subsistence, there would be plenty left for good local government.

I do not trust uplifters, reformers, taxpayers' groups, and commercial organizations, researchers and pundits who may say that by hiring efficiency experts and appointing business managers who despise politics and love double-entry bookkeeping we can reduce the actual net cost of administration in growing, ambitious municipalities inhabited by people who want better services and insist on competing with progressive communities elsewhere. Certainly, we should not countenance waste, improvidence, slipshod work, laziness or superfluous help, not to speak of crookedness and other reprehensible shenanigans; but let's look at the record, as Governor Smith used to say.

Most reform administrations, following revolutions that toss out the local political machines, go on the rocks because the eager-beaver amateurs who come in are committed to both expensive improvements and budget slashing. They promise the millennium for nothing, and end up with no improvements and no savings. Then the politicians who are more sensible and less offensively pious come trooping back, their standards, if we are lucky, somewhat raised by years of penury and exile.

Similarly, unit cost accounting is standard in business. When it is translated into a so-called performance budget, and applied to scientifically unmeasurable services of local government, it becomes just another way of piling up paper work for analysis by increasing hordes of statisticians and examiners. The mysterious words "performance budget" have become part of the cliché vocabulary of most lecturers on government, municipal experts, civic and trade secretaries and press pundits. As a result, most candidates for office embrace the phrase enthusiastically, just as they adopt other slogans which sound good before election and need not be embarrassing later on. When all the gadgets have been tried, the simple fact remains that it is men, not ingenious schemes and mechanical devices which make municipal government good, bad or indifferent.

Pundits also try to persuade us that business and government have their absolutely separate fields, recognized by all smart people, that business is by far the larger field, that government preempts parts of it at the price of free enterprise, and that the dollar put into business is a wise investment but the one spent on government is usually wasted or stolen. It is just foolish to say a dollar spent on producing cars is laudable but one put into the roads on which the cars must run is boondoggling and waste.

Equally foolish is the assertion that there are separate, clearly distinguishable boxes marked respectively Federal, state and municipal administration, that every public function belongs logically in one or the other, that there is no overlap, that the abnormal growth of the Federal field spells tragedy, that the state field too becomes swollen and dropsical and that the city field is overrun by selfish groups and wild spenders.

There is no fixed line between business and government. There are many twilight zones between them. There are no separate boxes which contain our three types of government. The only intelligent approach is the pragmatic one. Granted sound objectives, the agency best equipped to do the work is the right one, and in many instances there must be partnership of business and government and of Federal, state and municipal governments. Oversimplification, dogmatic assertions and rigid formulas are the worst possible approaches to the satisfaction of wants in a growing and thriving democracy.

WHY GOVERNMENT IS DIFFERENT

The after-dinner speaker at the local merchants' association or
Rotary Club who declares for more business in government and less
government in business will no doubt get a big hand from the
assembled brethren, but with the delivery of this chestnut he has
probably exhausted both his ideas and his vocabulary. Business
methods should of course be made to prevail in the ordinary routine
clerical and housekeeping areas of government. The economies which
good management dictates apply to public just as much as to private
offices. There is no reason or excuse for waste because it is paid for
by appropriation of taxpayers' money. As we go up the scale, however, we find that the basic functions and practices of business
and government are fundamentally diverse and not easily reconciled.[6]

Government is indeed our biggest business and is, for better or
worse, getting bigger all the time. It invades more and more of the
territory hitherto preempted by private enterprise. Under Fascism
and Communism government absorbs and runs everything. Under
Socialism its aims and activities and the limits of nationalization are
ill-defined, fluctuating and uncertain. In democracies, the territories
occupied by business, on the one hand, and public administration, on
the other, vary enormously. There is, in between, a no-man's-land or
twilight zone of quasi-public activity where churches and charities,
authorities, limited dividend companies, cooperatives, mutual institutions, museums with ex-officio trustees and many other agencies
operate. The tendency of the times is to encourage the government
and twilight zones to expand, and to force the business zone to contract.

If we look at the fundamental laws, we see that our three separate
and equal constitutional branches of Federal and state governments
—executive, legislative and judicial—have no analogy in private business. This separation of powers is a political concept which, on the
whole, seems to suit our temperament and has lasted longer and
brought greater blessings than any other democratic expedient.
We aim primarily at checks and balances, not at efficiency and
economy. We do not ordinarily elect our Presidents or Governors

because they are the best businessmen to be found, nor our judges because they are the most learned members of the bar, nor our representatives because we want the best brains of the community to whom we are ready to entrust decisions between elections.

The governorship and mayoralty of cities are not unlike the presidency when it comes to qualifications. Business skill and executive ability may be factors, but ordinarily not prime ones, and extraneous considerations are even more numerous, weirder and weightier than in national affairs.

Some Harmless Illusions

A Mayor, particularly of a big polyglot city, must be close to all sorts of people, many of whom are more interested in his views on the North of Ireland, Israel, Liberia, Socialism in England, Franco Spain and Peron Argentina than they are in his knowledge of finance, the budget, public improvements, education and transportation. The notion of reformers and business groups that every big city really yearns for a carefully selected, appointive city manager, as distinguished from an elected Mayor, is one of those harmless illusions by which we seek to explain the failures of local government and extol the triumphs of American business.

Only a fool or fanatic would insist that in the choice of political executives the extraneous considerations we have mentioned, if intelligently applied, are inherently bad. All elective and high appointive offices—Federal, state or municipal—all judges and magistrates, all legislators cannot be of the same type, origin, residence and persuasion. All Supreme Court judges cannot be selected from New England or the Middle West. We have, however, gone to absurd and dangerous extremes in applying to politics arbitrary rules and practices of sectional, trade, professional, economic, racial, religious, sex and social apportionment, and have produced as a result undemocratic travesties on the great ultimate objective that the best shall serve the state.

If a job which has, for reasons long since obscured or forgotten, once been held by a Roman Catholic, Protestant or Jew, a veteran, a Negro, a woman, a man of German or Irish descent, a resident of a particularly sensitive district, the word goes out that it "belongs" to the element or place in question, that no outsider may be considered, and that any move to change this custom will alienate thousands, create schisms, rifts and riots, and put the leader who loses the plum, together with all his captains, in the political doghouse for life. No successful big business could be run on such a basis, but that is what happens regularly in politics.

As to legislative offices, democratic government has its enormous virtues, however unbusinesslike it may be. Without the matching of wits, the airing of views, convictions and prejudices, the shifts and compromises, and the ensuing curiously assorted understandings and friendships which come out of congressional, state and municipal legislative sessions, the inherent conflicts between city and country, creed and religion, labor and capital, class and class would flare into civil war and half the nation would be in constant turmoil. That is a problem business need not worry about.

POLITICAL PULL AND PATRONAGE

Appointive and administrative as distinguished from elective officials, function under a rigid, inflexible, expanding civil service system. The higher positions are usually filled by promotion from the lower ones. Exceptionally able people can be brought from outside only in the face of great difficulties, and skipping grades is almost impossible. It takes so much ingenuity, persistence and courage to outwit the bureaucrats who administer the laws and rules of public service that few executives are willing to try it even if their sole purpose is to attract into a department or promote persons who can effectively administer the more and more complex and responsible activities which government has assumed.

There is, to be sure, plenty of patronage, pull and family pressure in big corporations. Directors and trustees are often chosen for reasons no better and sometimes much worse than those which guide the voter at the polls. Business executives have been known to take care of their friends and relatives and even to pave the way for promotion to the top positions by interim appointments whose only purpose is to smooth the progress of those destined for the top.

This, however, is not the standard practice. It is particularly dangerous in competitive fields. It is the exception and not the rule. Nevertheless, any honest observer or historian of American big business must admit that there is plenty of personal politics in business, though it is not as prevalent and not nearly as hard to root out as it is to introduce business methods into government.

The growth of government at the expense of business is not all chargeable to the tendency of the times, to the ambition of politicians or to the machinations of radical Socialists. Private trade has contributed its share to alienate public opinion. The price of bad conduct in business is absorption by the worst monopoly of all, the monopoly of government. The penalty of bad government is more of it.

Businessmen lead a comparatively sheltered life. They have their arguments with labor and with bureaucracy. They may be attacked by raucous demagogues as economic royalists, predatory interests and princes of privilege, but they are relatively immune from the lively, profitable and easily capitalized issue of Communism—which in public life has become a convenient instrument of smear, slander and vicious innuendo to drive from influence and office many fine, basically patriotic people of open, inquiring mind. Business is lucky not to be plagued with our irresponsible native Fascists who, almost equally with the Communists, poison our public life today and drown the voices of reason and decency.

What Officials Must Face

I am not sure that over the years wagging tongues have not hurt public servants more than the other groups, but the tradition of slandering those in office is old if not honored. In the seventeenth and eighteenth centuries, Pope, Swift and many others added spice to coffee-house gossip and journalism by open attack and innuendo aimed at those in the government. The Junius Letters in our early American days were on the same level, and we have some contemporary ghoulish columnists, commentators and biographers who strike at the dead in their tombs.

The answer of the public man, I suppose, is to imitate the efficient prehistoric animals who saved themselves by thickening their hides, growing weapons of defense and attack and putting on protective coloring. For the permanent government employee—as distinguished from the elective officials—who need to seek publicity, protective coloring is probably the best device because it makes the wearer obscure, indistinguishable and almost invisible.

We have a good right to boast of our inventive genius, Yankee ingenuity and know-how in business and industry. We have, unfortunately, not encouraged these attributes in government. When it comes to inventive boldness, fertility in ideas, originality, drive, interest in the unusual, the original, the novel, public employees have hard sledding among the icefloes of politics. The average American official, except in occasional radical administrations and among legislative minorities, shudders at the thought of ridicule, and a hint of caricature terrifies him.

INCENTIVES AND REWARDS

Another great difference between business and government has to do with incentives and rewards. Business, even under a punitive tax system, can do much more to compensate the higher, the technical and in many cases the rank and file employees than public service. Business guarantees somewhat less security, but more and more the tendency is to provide continuity and pensions in private enterprise. Executives in business get more and they can keep more. By stock and other devices they can be given a share in the business. The income of many of them, therefore, comes under the more favorable capital gains tax.

Our public service may be overstaffed but it is certainly underpaid, and other incentives are lacking. It is a dubious honor to be identified with public service at a time when it is popular to make fun of government employment, to crack jokes about feeding at the public trough, and to identify the overwhelming majority of decent hardworking people in government employment with a few thugs and malefactors who link up crime with high officialdom.

It is unnecessary again to stress the depressing effects of veterans' preference, state apportionment in the case of Federal service, local residence requirements and the other devices by which government hamstrings itself in recruiting personnel. "Cost plus" defense work, with plenty of overtime at enormously swollen wages, has put a further crimp in the happiness of public employees on fixed low salaries. It has no doubt also embarrassed ordinary private business not lucky enough to have defense contracts, but such private establishments are in many instances able to meet the competition. Government cannot.

Public officers who are not protected by law from summary removal serve at tremendous risk to themselves and their families in the most dangerous, exciting and interesting trade in the world. The gratitude of the board of directors of a company and of its executives and security holders is more dependable than that of the general public, whose memory is short and whose attention is easily diverted.

Yet public service has its rewards for those who retain their enthusiasm, thicken their hides, accept its handicaps, and count their modest blessings. Among these blessings are the privilege of working in the most fascinating laboratories in the country where things are done on a grand scale, planning and executing for people rather than money, and demonstrating that the democratic system, with all its checks and balances, is the best yet devised by man.

We need not argue just where the line should be drawn between public and private enterprise. It changes from time to time and place to place, but there is a line, and if it is pushed too far to one or the other side, or wiped out, nothing but trouble results. We can, to be sure, have too little as well as too much government enterprise. There are many things private capital cannot do, but the worst thing that can happen to a nation is to nationalize all services and activities, and thereby to assume that the equal distribution of poverty means wealth for everyone.

Those who make a sharp distinction between public works, which they label as waste, and private enterprise, which alone in their philosophy is constructive, are just about as wrong as radicals who denounce free enterprise as fascism and monopoly, and demand that government plan and run everything. The sensible man knows that there must be balance. He takes a pragmatic view of the roles of public and private responsibility. Nothing belongs absolutely to either government or business. It is all a question of which in the long run works best in a particular place and context. We should not expand public enterprise beyond our capacity to govern, nor permit private business to function or expand at the expense of the welfare of the average citizen.

5

Some Planning
Limitations

PRAGMATISM IS TO PLANNING WHAT RELATIVITY IS to physics. Man is in the grip of new forces which he has recently discovered, but is as yet unable to control. What we need is free trade, not necessarily in goods but in brains. The worst barriers are those of prejudice. The best imports and exports are ideas, even if they are at variance.

The most absurd of all notions is that physical planning is something invented in recent times by bright minds newly escaped from the thralldom of systematic architecture, engineering and public administration. It has been painted in recent years as a new discovery like fission and antibiotics; as though there was never previously any forethought, preparation, prudence and program in the layout, construction and growth of cities until the new science sprang full grown from the brows of renegade architects, engineers seeking outlets into a new world, assorted professionals eager for power, and reformers bent on smashing the present sorry scheme of things and molding it nearer to the heart's desire.

Planning is as old as man, and just about as chequered and unpredictable. Excavations and researches have proved beyond question that there were well-planned cities in Peru long before the Christian era. In his *Introduction to Town Planning*, Julian Julian quotes from Livy's *History of Rome* to show the difficulties, mistakes and successes of the Romans in planning. According to Livy, "they built rather with a view to future numbers than for the population which they then had." The population trends of Rome were, however, hard to figure out, just as they are in modern cities.

Our problems are further complicated by the shifting of populations, not only from country to town and back again to suburban areas, but in New York City, for example, where we have enormous shifts in people from borough to borough, and from one part of a borough to another, creating new demands on government for all manner of facilities.

Quoting from Suetonius, Julian Julian points out that Nero was a famous Roman planner who "being offended, as it were, with the ill-favoured fashion of the old houses, as also with the narrow, crooked and winding streets, he set the city of Rome on fire." The author adds:

Tacitus does not appear quite so confident that it was Nero's anxiety to carry out a town-planning scheme which led to the burning of Rome, but his lengthy account gives many interesting details as to the crowded buildings, the narrow streets of the old city, the more orderly arrangements for protection against fire, and for promoting the public health in the new city.

OTHER ANCIENT CITY PROBLEMS

Nero's planning regulations provided, among other things,

. . . that the buildings themselves should be raised to a certain height without beams, and arched with stone from the quarries of Gabia or Alba, that stone being proof against fire; that over the water springs, which had been improperly intercepted by private individuals, overseers should be placed to provide for their flowing in greater abundance, and in a greater number of places for the supply of the public; that every housekeeper should have in his yard means for extinguishing fires; neither should there be party walls, but every house should be enclosed by its own walls.

Continuing on the subject of Ancient Town Planning, Julian says:

In 478 B.C., after Athens had been twice burnt by the Persians within two years, Themistocles recognized that the city should have a new and regular plan, that it was desirable to have a new capital by the sea, and that a strong navy was needed, but as, on religious and other grounds, it was difficult to transfer or transform the capital, he decided to found the port town of Piraeus.

Dr. Curtius' history of Greece contrasts the older Athens and the new city by the sea:

While Athens, hastily rebuilt amidst her ruins, as necessity demanded, was disorderly, devoid of plan, and full of narrow and crooked lanes, the Piraeus, on the other hand, was a modern city, with large open spaces, roomy cloistered halls, broad and rectangular streets, . . .

Julian also devotes considerable space to the planners who sprang up after the London fire of 1666.

Within a few days of the fire three plans for rebuilding the city were submitted to the King . . . [and] for nearly two centuries there was an English statute which required four acres of land to be attached to each cottage, except those built in large towns. This, however, was found to so seriously restrict the building of cottages that the law was repealed in the reign of George III.

This is precisely the kind of thing which happens today. Real estate developers and big owners find standards too high, and by influence, pressure and the judicious use of lawyers, get them reduced or virtually eliminated. We think our traffic problems are a new thing without precedent, and we offer solutions which appear to us to represent modern genius. Both problem and cure are as old as the hills. For example, the Roman police edicts forcing heavy traffic to move at night and preventing daytime parking. *The Daily Life in Ancient Rome*, by Jerome Carcopino, shows that this was attempted in the most drastic fashion nearly twenty centuries ago.

The New Planning Jargon

Practitioners of the new planning science have invented a jargon of their own. This terminology is not only unnecessary but has become ludicrous and offensive to the average citizen. We get sick of hearing about "satellite cities," "freeways," "environs," "regions," etc. We become even more weary of elaborate statistical studies which have no foundation in common sense. I remember one pamphlet full of mathematical formulas which sought to estimate the future population of a community by breeding blue flies in a bottle on some fantastic theory that the conditions governing the multiplication of the flies were similar to those controlling the multiplication of human beings!

Here is another example, taken from the New York *Herald Tribune*, with the author's name omitted:

———, of Washington, city planning economist, has recently completed a study of Aurora, Ill., applying a new dimension to usual city planning methods. This new technique combines a thorough analysis of the economic, social and political structure of an area as it stands today with the actual physical environment and growth potentials. These closely related factors are projected forward in time, then rebalanced to give direction to plans for expansion and to stimulate this growth. The fundamental idea behind this kind of planning is that the central core of commerce and industry and the surrounding area which has an economic stake in this core should be planned to be as self-sustaining and competitive as possible within the larger economic structure of the nation as a whole. To gain this objective, it is necessary to enlist the aid and co-operation of all the civic, political and municipal authorities within a specified area so that the development program can move forward as a unified effort.

Note that there is no mention of the planning that depends on intimate knowledge of a community and affection for it, and that no distinction is drawn between the visiting diagnostician and the resident family doctor. All we have is the glib itinerant expert who knows everything and is at home everywhere. The extremists tell us that big cities are dated, urbanism is dead, regionalism is the thing, and green belts, dispersion, decentralization and satellite towns of just 60,000 inhabitants are the answers to population growth.

The fact is that men have always made physical plans, that they have usually been inadequate because of selfishness and indifference, that today we are more and more conscious of our responsibilities to the future, that in our brief journey we look ahead as far as we can, and that most of us recognize and accept the need of restraints in the form of comprehensive city maps, zoning, capital programs and budgets, and of a definite framework within which private enterprise can expand and flourish.

OTHER PLANNING LIMITATIONS

It is hard to say how far ahead we can look in government work where specific programs of construction and government services involve large expenditures. The principles of democratic government are supposed by some people to be immutable. On another theory, our Constitution, while based on principles, is so flexible that it will meet the needs of any age. Yet we accept with little question the most dogmatic assertions as to the limits of the police power in sustaining planning and zoning laws.

I am convinced that many of the limitations on planning imposed upon us by elderly gentlemen who fought and bled for the original statutes no longer exist in fact, that much more drastic and comprehensive regulations may be constitutionally adopted governing buildings, as well as setbacks, heights and their appearance.

How can we plan for the future of cities and suburbs and, in many cases, of the open country, unless we know much better than we do now what are the legal limits of zoning and planning? Some years ago I raised the question whether, in the subdivision of property, a municipality can insist upon the dedication of space for playgrounds as well as the layout of adequate streets. I was told that this would be unconstitutional. I do not believe it. It makes no sense to me, and is one of those legalistic fetishes imposed by technical authorities who do not want to take a chance on being wrong in the courts and who hate to take back any of the pontifical rules which they themselves have laid down before.

There are, of course, many other factors which set limits to long-range planning. Who can foretell the future of the automobile or the airplane? A popular sport is to poke fun at all those who laid out our cities years ago. The gridiron plan of Manhattan Island, adopted in 1811, has been a special object of ridicule. But were these early planning commissioners so short-sighted? They made their plan before the days of the railroad, the internal combustion engine, elevators and skyscrapers.

The planner who professes to be able to see clearly a hundred or more years ahead is an egoist or a visionary who cannot safely be trusted with immediate decisions in public office. On the other hand, the public official who looks ahead only ten years is a fool. Somewhere between these two extremists must be found the answer to the limits of planning, at least physical planning. My own feeling is that by and large the official who can confidently look ahead fifty years in these days is a pretty smart fellow, and even he takes a chance of being proven ridiculous or tragically wrong in some of his prophecies.

CURRENT PLANNING LITERATURE

In the artificial, limited form in which the word "planning" is used today by so-called experts, it means, I suppose, laying out new towns, subdivision of unincorporated land and rebuilding and zoning heavily populated, established communities. The practitioners of the art of planning, dreamers, sociologists, geographers, architects, engineers, landscapers, builders, realtors, writers and what-not are eager beavers, and in their burrowing turn out many piles of somewhat less than aureate earth.[7]

From Plato and Aristotle, from More to Frank Lloyd Wright, there has been a growing and fascinating literature bearing on new cities springing out of the wilderness. Canberra, New Delhi, the Levittowns, the aluminum and oil towns of Venezuela and Canada, the United Nations headquarters in New York tell the story.

Here planners have a free field and little but the stubbornness of nature and the shortage of funds to hinder them, slow them down and dampen their noble rage. One of the lessons we may learn from their doings is that you can make a company town almost over night, but not a city with personality, character, flavor and a soul. The making of a real polyglot city as distinguished from a robot factory takes time, leadership, the hands, brains and imagination of many men, and designs not ordinarily found on the drafting boards of engineers and businessmen.

As to the second category of planning—minute subdivision of estates and farms into single or multifamily housing and retail or other business—the available literature is unsatisfactory. It is too technical, too statistical, too academic, too biased, or too biographical to give an accurate picture of the rapidly growing and largely uncontrolled suburbs which represent the overflow of big cities.

We ought, among other things, to have more literature about real estate advertisements in the daily press, which show in picturesque and often misleading superlatives and hyperbole that should be subjected to heavy discount and depreciation, what the rank and file of so-called developers are really up to. These are the people who make the villages and cities of tomorrow. Their layout men, architects, engineers, material, production, advertising and financial staffs are the down-to-earth planners of the communities we must live in, near or with.

A few honest, fearless, informed critical books on the doings of these exploiters would be more valuable than all the ballyhoo inflicted on us by the academic planners, ultra-modern designers of conspicuous and completely untypical projects, the cynosures of big business and the ingenious creators of modest little machines for living at $60,000 to $100,000 apiece.

Finally we come to the most difficult and important phase of planning—the rebuilding of established cities. The literature of city planning of this kind is monumental, but far from satisfying because it is too often written by those who lack the combination of qualities and experiences to justify printing and to command respect and attention.

In planning we must decide between revolution and common sense—between the subsidized lamas in their remote mountain temples and those who must work in the marketplace. It is a mistake to underestimate the revolutionaries. They do not reach the masses directly but through subsurface activities. They teach the teachers. They reach people in high places, who in turn influence the press, universities, societies learned and otherwise, radio networks, the stage, the screen, even churches. They make the TNT for those who throw the bombs. They have their own lingo, cabalistic writings, and secret passwords. People in this group have to an astounding extent captured public attention, invaded the universities, preempted space in the press and on the air, and while their support is neither solid, substantial, nor lasting, it is a force to be reckoned with.

Somehow or other the itch of planners to take the big cities apart and reconstruct them is stronger than the itch to reorganize smaller communities. Perhaps it is because these planners cannot find an

audience and a living in the great open spaces. Those who would
drastically decentralize a metropolis, break it up into satellite towns,
rebuild it in its entirety, make sheer logic prevail in the relocation
of trade, residence, art and recreation, may continue to paint pictures and deliver homilies for long-haired listeners. New York and
other large cities are too tough for them and they had better keep out
of the rough and tumble of the marketplace.[8]

Federal vs. Local Planning

The ivory-tower planners tell us that nothing short of a complete
revolution in present conceptions of land ownership and control will
permit the decentralization of population which is essential to decent
living. They would rebuild metropolitan areas on satellite village and
greenbelt theories. They advocate all-wise and all-powerful planning
boards, superior to the executive, legislative and judicial branches of
the government. They will have no piecemeal improvements and no
limited objectives. They are not afraid to expand the fields and
functions of civil service beyond our capacity to govern. They will
have no truck with what they call half-baked public works programs.
The cost is of no consequence. If we cannot have a revolution, they
say, let's not have anything.

I am a believer in limited objectives, and step-by-step progress
toward goals which are not too far ahead, and which can be realized
in this generation without breaking the bank. Like Cardinal Newman, "I do not ask to see the distant scene, one step enough for me."
Above all, the conservative middle roader fears Federal domination
of local affairs, be it in business or in government. He fears nationwide planning by distant bureaucrats who stifle local initiative either
by design, by routine paperwork or by sheer stupidity.

During the New Deal planning era there appeared a book by two
Federal works officials entitled *New City Patterns*. The authors were
sold on the idea that the country should be run from Washington,
where all the answers were known, where the tall thinking was done,
and the big medicine was brewed. Federal planning control must,
they said, extend into municipalities because all levels of government
are concerned with metropolitan areas and must cooperate on "new
city patterns."

This outwardly impressive volume quickly went into a familiar song and dance: Cities have failed; we cannot modify present patterns and must therefore have entirely new ones. The narrow tax base of local governments can be adjusted only by the higher levels of government. The metropolitan area is the only logical local planning unit since planning problems cut across local political boundaries and since local governments are ill-equipped to cope with their home problems.

The best kind of metropolitan planning commission, they suggested, would consist of eleven members, two Federal members, including an economist and planner, two state members, including an administrative analyst and a highway engineer, three central city members, including a municipal public works engineer, an expert in municipal administration and an architect, and four county and suburban members, to wit: a landscape architect, a sociologist, an attorney and a realtor.

They proposed a metropolitan master plan to regulate local uses, a long-range capital improvement program scheduling projects over a period of thirty to fifty years, and an immediate five-year program. They would see to it that local, metropolitan and Federal planning agencies establish friendly collaboration based upon "interdependence and mutual assistance," make the local officials "realize that they are participating in and are important to planning processes," make "a goodly number of the local citizens metropolitan-minded" and, of course, establish and cultivate "proper contacts with newspaper reporters and feature writers." In order to be sure that the press does not go astray "the reporter's copy should be checked by a member of the planning staff to assure a fair and correct statement of the facts!"

Here and there throughout the volume were statements grotesquely out of line with facts and conditions. For example, it was stated categorically that local recreation space should consist of four acres of parks and playgrounds for each eight hundred people, a conclusion completely at variance with all experience, and calculated to bankrupt any large city. Similarly it was proposed that maximum housing densities in New York and other large cities should be fifty to sixty families per acre net, and thirty-one to thirty-seven families gross where land values are high, and twenty to thirty families net and twelve to eighteen families gross per acre in intermediate areas. Obviously no large city could exist and function on this basis.

The authors ignore the fact that every room must have light and air, and that the vertical pattern, provided that land coverage is not too great, is the only one which makes sense in such areas. The authors' answer to this was naive. They said that the trouble is that "private developers are forced to maintain an economic relationship between the total rentable floor space in their buildings and the cost of the site." This relationship they regarded as intolerable.

There are, to be sure, differences to reconcile, plans to coordinate and rigid, arbitrary geographical and political lines to cross in the solution of metropolitan problems, but Federal control is no solution. It is hard, no doubt, to work with many local agencies and laws, but it is the way of democratic government, and our progress based upon reasonable compromise has been impressive. Democracy is a thing which comes out of the soil and the sidewalks, not a ukase or directive issuing from Washington or the Kremlin. It may also be conceded that there are legitimate fields of Federal as well as state influence in local regional matters, but they are limited and do not mean regimentation of our daily lives by distant bureaucrats.

The realistic middle roader has to work with the authority, the money, the help, the instruments, the time and the opportunities he can get. He is held responsible for failure, and gets little recognition of success. He has to fight in a highly competitive field against others, some of them just as sincere as he is, for the limited resources which are available. He has to reconcile and coordinate his program with that of private enterprise, in the face of the curious notion entertained by a large section of the press and an astonishing number of otherwise intelligent people that these two interests are wholly different, mutually exclusive and quite irreconcilable.

Ever since Hiroshima and Nagasaki, the advocates of urban decentralization have embraced the new major premise of early, inevitable and inescapable atomic destruction of all concentrated industry and society. Before we abandon our present civilization with its manifest imperfections and return to the caves and huts of our ancestors, I suggest that we exhaust the tenets of faith and religion, the arts of diplomacy, the sanctions of law and economics, the dictates of common sense and the fundamental decency of the average man.

Most of us must accept with enthusiasm, resignation or regret, as the case may be, the inheritance of the past, and in our planning aim to modify, adapt and improvise rather than raze, dynamite and revolutionize. I hate compromise more than most public officials, but I realize that it is at once the curse and the glory of the democratic process. He who wrestles to some purpose with the physical problems of an old and stubborn city or mushroom suburb deserves, in my poor opinion, somewhat more credit than the builder of a Canberra.

No public body or private patron has as yet endowed me with the power and money to do one of those de novo, blank-slate jobs which seem to fall so invitingly into the lap of genius. When Kubla Khan decrees a stately pleasure dome, Frank Lloyd Wright or Le Corbusier is sent for. I get into the picture when there is a remote, disputed barrier beach, an abandoned salt meadow, or a rundown, ragged, misused shorefront to be reclaimed, a narrow parkway right-of-way to be torn foot by foot from reluctant, embattled and avaricious estate owners and subdividers, or a forlorn gashouse and slum to be carved out with an axe or scalpel.

Those of us who lean a little to the right ask only that the revolutionists prove the worth and durability of their ideas and products before they demand universal acceptance. What could be fairer than that?

6

Common Sense
Planning

ALTHOUGH PLANNING IS AS OLD AS CIVILIZATION, many factors contributed toward making this a country of comparatively unregulated growth. Large acreage, new frontiers, relatively few people, hatred of regimentation, the spirit of freedom and private enterprise, opposition to the expansion of government, apparently bottomless natural resources, and a dozen other conditions and characteristics have made us what we are.

As the country filled up, the geographical frontiers disappeared, natural resources began to be exhausted, less room was available at the top for private enterprise, and more people realized that they were in compartments, grooves, and groups from which they could not easily rise. Unfavorable conditions developed which private enterprise did not seem to be able to correct. Then men began to look more toward government for assistance and to waive, at least temporarily, their inherited dislike and fear of official regulation. Naturally there was no lack of political thinkers and leaders to meet this demand and to exploit it to the full.

I like to believe that I am a forward-looking conservative, that is, a person who recognizes the law of change, wants to keep abreast of the times and to anticipate the future to the extent that it can be visualized, but who wants to hold on to what is good and what has proven its worth before jumping to something new just because it is new. I do not believe in cure-alls, nor in the possibility of accomplishing anything really worth while in human progress without immense and sustained effort over a considerable period of time.

OFFICIAL PLANNING AGENCIES

As to government, I do not fear expansion just because it is expansion. I fear it because I foresee that we may expand government beyond our capacity to govern. I am not horrified when I hear that government has branched out into something new. I want to look over the new enterprise to see whether it is necessary, to find out where private business fell down or was otherwise inadequate, discover whether regulation rather than control would solve the problem, see what kind of people the government can find to substitute for those who functioned privately before or to fill the gap if there is one. I see no reason to get hysterical because government expands or tries something new, but by the same token I do not propose to be bulldozed by partisans, enthusiasts, crackpots and fanatics into accepting as new gospel things tried hundreds of times in the past under slightly different guises and found lacking.

Planning in government, as I have said, is merely a new name for a very old thing. A budget is a plan; a cabinet, a council, a legislature, a board of estimate, a committee on finance or ways and means, or any other legislative committee, a constitutional convention—all these are planning bodies, straining their eyes into the future, seeing through a glass darkly, some with unclouded retinas, some with a jaundice of ignorance or bias, some applying a microscope when they ought to use a telescope, some looking for mirages and rainbows and imagining that they see them close at hand, some forming extraordinary impressionistic pictures which mean little or nothing to anyone else.

The problems of city planning bodies, such as we have in New York, do not lie in the character of their membership. They lie in the inevitable complications arising from their relations with other branches of the government, including the elected officers who have, or believe they have, a direct mandate from the people, and other administrative municipal agencies which are jealous of their prerogatives and insist that they shall not be lost sight of.

State, as distinguished from municipal, planning bodies have not made much progress and, in my opinion, will not make much. The state is too large a unit to be controlled by a planning board. Such boards usually run afoul, if not of the Governor, at least of the members of his cabinet, the budget director, fiscal officers, legislative bodies and other boards and agencies who are doing definite pieces of planning work even though they are not labeled as such.

These state planning boards have a strong tendency to degenerate into a combination of library, ivory-tower debating society, planetarium, and watercolor club. So long as appropriations hold out, any research staff will turn out reports, make pretty pictures, discuss what other people are actually doing, claim credit for accomplishments toward which they have contributed little, and generally go through the governmental Swedish exercises and St. Vitus dances necessary to show that the bureau is alive and kicking. The greatest activity, of course, is apparent at just about the time the annual budget is being made.

In the physical sense there are no insoluble urban problems, once we get into the mood to be serious, honest, cooperative and unselfish about them. We can rid ourselves of slums, untangle traffic except at infrequent peak loads, provide all the modern works and services that are good for us, stimulate trade, commerce and business, welcome and encourage the arts, provide wholesome recreation and generally establish the framework for happy and productive living.

In the higher sense of order and good citizenship, however, we have a long way to go. We have not learned how to control a small but virulent and vicious minority of assorted troublemakers and lawbreakers of all ages. Partly because of generous but confused thinking and partly because of shock, we have handled them in a gingerly fashion. We have let them run loose and endanger the entire fabric of our lives. We shall have to come to grips with them because 3 per cent of the people who have no regard for law, no respect for anyone else and no notion of good citizenship and patriotism, cannot be allowed to overrun the other 97 per cent who understand liberty and realize that its enjoyment involves obligations to others.

As to the great majority of essentially fine people of many strains, we have learned to live together in democratic fashion. We all stand for the same thing, but we do not know just what it is. The creative central theme of our symphony is not yet clear and triumphant. That requires not only harmony but the baton of leadership. And how do we acquire leadership? Not by pinning braid, epaulets or stars, bars and chevrons on likely people, or by tapping the first passerby and giving him a hat marked captain or conductor. We need more respect for talent, for ideas, brains, nerve—for the uncommon man. Herbert Hoover said it well on the occasion of his eightieth birthday:

Among the delusions offered us by fuzzy-minded people is that imaginary creature, the Common Man. It is dinned into us that this is the Century of the Common Man. . . . The greatest strides of human progress have come from uncommon men and women. You have perhaps heard of George Washington, Abraham Lincoln, or Thomas Edison. They were humble in origin, but that was not their greatness. The humor of it is that when we get sick we want an uncommon doctor. When we go to war, we yearn for an uncommon general or admiral. When we choose the President of a University, we want an uncommon educator.

The imperative need of this nation at all times is the leadership of the Uncommon Men or Women. We need men and women who cannot be intimidated, who are not concerned with applause meters, nor those who sell tomorrow for cheers today.

Such leaders are not to be made like queen bees. They must rise by their own merits. America recognizes no frozen social stratifications which prevent this free rise of every individual. They rise by merit from our shops and farms. They rise from the thirty-five million boys and girls in our schools and colleges. That they have the determination to rise is the glorious promise of leadership among free men.

It is notable how the thinking of two men of widely different origin, career and political affiliation runs parallel. In the School of Business and Public Administration of the College of the City of New York, appropriately named after him, Bernard M. Baruch, another great elder statesman, said:

Government is only an instrument for regulating society. A limited democracy—the political form we live under—is bound to have its faults since none of us who make up this democracy is perfect. But this democracy has given each of us the opportunity to better his own condition by his own striving—and more than that no government can give us. . . . We, in this country, have succeeded because we have made Americanization synonymous with expanded opportunity. We have sought our goal of equality for all not by pulling everyone down to the same level, as has happened elsewhere, but by giving everyone the opportunity to rise.

When all is said and done, realistic, practical planning is merely common sense applied to limited objectives. Planners are born rather than made. The qualities which make a good planner were well established in the days of the leading executives of the Old Testament. The Greek philosophers recognized, isolated and described them. The Romans built an empire on them. No greater planning body ever existed than the convention which wrote our own Federal Constitution. In addition to common sense, a knowledge of history, good vision, first-hand experience in government affairs, tenacity, courage and an ability to write and speak trenchant English are requisites.

The Varied Aspects of Communities

In the field of physical planning of municipalities, a most important requisite is local knowledge. The planner must have his roots down deep in the community; he must realize that the results of experience can be applied only sparingly at home.

There is no one, convenient, predigested textbook plan for cities or states; no royal road to good government; no one plane of the Great Carpenter to cut down inequalities and even out opportunities. Each community has its own peculiar problems; the conservation and reclamation of its natural attractions, and the maintenance of its unique flavor and character are at least as important as its modernization, standardization and streamlining. What can be done in one place is anathema, poison, or a subject for ridicule in another. There is no single formula, recipe or prescription for municipal progress. Civic virtue wears a different shape and form in every community. She is as various and changeable as the lady in the Tin Pan Alley parody:

> She was bread in old Kentucky,
> She was apples in Orleans.
> She was pretzels in Milwaukee,
> And in Boston she was beans.

Some years ago I was invited to address the Boston Society of Civil Engineers and the Northeastern Section of the American Society of Civil Engineers. I was supposed to comment on a contest for a plan and program for metropolitan Boston. My suggestion was that if Greater Boston wanted a sane program it should not rely too much on the exotic Bauhaus influence of the Harvard School of Architecture. It should put its faith in New England common sense, and in the Celtic imagination and humor which the good Lord gave Bostonians to leaven the lump. I recommended a bill of fare as homely, as substantial, as nourishing and as economical as the bean and the cod.

It is easier to devise, adopt and carry through a plan of municipal reform and physical construction in a comparatively large city like Cincinnati, where there is a conservative population of roughly the same origin, habits, outlook on life, and high average of intelligence and civic sense, than in an enormous metropolis like Chicago with its wide and deep cleavages, its apparent indifference to high standards in government, and its sprawling ugliness, miserable housing and lack of inspiring leadership.

I do not have the gift of prophecy, but I predict that before long Lincoln-hearted men will arise in Chicago—the "City of the Big Shoulders," as Sandburg called it—who will galvanize its immense Midwestern energy and touch its latent pride; men and women who will point out that Michigan Avenue and the Lake Front are no more than a show window to distract attention from the ugliness and misery of the stockyards and the slums which lie back of them. No technical planners full of the pompous jargon of their trade can perform this miracle. It must have local inspiration, and even this will be vain without the help of plain, ordinary citizens fed up with what they see around them, who set their jaws and decide to do something about it.

SOME OLD AND NEW CITIES

In Miami we find our oldest and newest American civilization. My old friend Carl Graham Fisher, restless Hoosier promoter and authentic American genius, went there to find new frontiers, and made Miami's first plan. Bike, auto and balloon mechanic and racer, the internal combustion engine with its ramifications made him wealthy. He acquired an automobile race track and then looked for new fields in the sand bars and mangrove swamps of Florida. His Miami career is a fantastic story of transformation by power saw and dredge, by hoist and bascule, and by wholesale planting of palm and hibiscus.

It is a record of boom, bust and boom again. How, in such a hectic sweat and hurry, with a crew as various and curiously assorted as those of a California or Alaska mining village, could one expect much planning in the public interest? How, indeed, could anyone have anticipated that so many of the frantic boasts and circus superlatives of the pioneers would, after a fashion, be realized? The curious fact is not that so little, but that so much, was accomplished. The builders of Miami had imagination, ambition and elbow grease—perhaps a little too much of all three.

These pioneers, like many others along our newly discovered seaboard, did not know where to draw the line between a winter resort and a year-round city of homes; between an oriental bazaar, where shrewd merchants charge all the traffic will bear, and a solid business center built upon reputation, fairness and responsibility; between a catch-penny mechanical Coney Island run by barkers and concessionaires for absentee owners, and a garden community of homes, stores and orderly beaches operated by and for substantial citizens and respectable visitors seeking sunshine, warmth and comfort, and requiring little artificial stimulation to make them happy. That is Miami's planning problem, and no outsider, no carpetbagger, no foreign expert in blueprints and efficiency, no philosopher on a distant campus, can solve it.

Los Angeles, another city in the warm winter belt, is swamped by the influx of retired people from northerly farms and colder climates, kleig-lighted and magnetized by the fantastic, make-believe movie colony—vast, uniform, regimented, monotonous. It is a city which like New York and many another careless American municipality allowed its greatest natural heritage, the ocean front, to be exploited and fouled, and finally awakened to find that vast sums are needed to reclaim this heritage. Even with country, state and Federal help the problem of financing is not simple. It is no longer a matter of drawing pretty pictures of fine public beaches, approached by broad landscaped parkways. It is a problem of compromise and ways and means, of concentration on what is realizable in their time that faces officials more accustomed to gorgeous, colossal movie effects than to planning realities.

New Orleans is extraordinarily favored by nature and under heavy obligations to its early planners with respect to highways and transportation. Established as a seaport at a strategic bend in the Mississippi, New Orleans is more or less surrounded by water. Lake Pontchartrain cuts it off from the north, and on the south the Delta country sharply limits its growth. The main avenues of access are from the east and west. There is relatively little through traffic. Trade and transportation are attracted to New Orleans because it is one of the greatest ports in the country, and because of its unusual historical and natural advantages. The main arterial problem, therefore, resolves itself into getting into and out of the heart of the city from the east and west, and of expansion to the south, rather than getting straight through the city.

Another important factor is the radial system of broad streets and canals, spreading out from the Vieux Carré, laid out with great intelligence by early city planners. The canals and ditches which drain the city and provide for navigation have afforded and continue to offer splendid opportunities for conversion into broad avenues and highways for rail and highway transportation. As a result of these conditions, it is possible to devise a modern arterial program which requires the acquisition of few and relatively inexpensive rights-of-way.

The grand manner of French architects and planners and the necessity for an endless fight against rising water here happily conspired to produce a roadway pattern of extraordinary usefulness to future generations. The rights-of-way for countless vehicles, which could not have been anticipated in days long before the internal combustion engine was thought of, are ready-made for car, bus and truck as well as train. I doubt whether, throughout the continental United States, there is another modern urban highway program for which so little allowance must be made for acquisition of rights-of-way, disturbance of industry, commerce and business, demolition of homes and moving of people. The most important factor lies in the close relation of the vehicular to the railroad problem. Solution of the highway traffic problem is almost wholly dependent on the adoption of a program of railroad grade crossing elimination and terminal improvement.

PRACTICAL PLANNING QUESTIONS

There are certain elementary questions which may be asked of citizens and responsible officials interested in improving conditions in American cities. The answers to these questions will provide an intelligent, practical approach to the planning or replanning of such communities.[9]

If your town or city is alive and growing, ask if civic plans of the last ten to twenty years have made any sense; whether political leaders and elected officers have followed them; and what such plans, as distinguished from the unconnected efforts of individuals, have produced. If growth has been haphazard, figure out whether your luck will hold and how long any business, public or private, can live on momentum and chance.

How far has central dry rot in the oldest parts of town developed into a spreading cancer which threatens your taxes and integrity? Can you afford to leave it and let people and industry move out into the suburbs, or will you cut it out and rebuild at the heart of your community?

What can be done to keep young married couples in town? How can you stop the *drang zum land* which gives them sun, shade, play space, but makes the breadwinner a commuter dependent upon railroads or enormously expensive and usually unsatisfactory additions to municipal rapid transit? Has it occurred to you that in the long run it is cheaper to rebuild and rehabilitate central areas than to provide transportation for real estate promoters who tout the virtues of outlying vacant land?

Have you ever thought of better city schools and other services as the answer to suburban competition? Parks, parkways, playgrounds and tree-lined boulevards constitute the difference between a livable city and an inhuman factory of stone, concrete, brick and steel. Each week, man works 40 hours or so out of 168. Residence and recreation are therefore, if anything, as important as the workshop and its accessories. This is a fact which planners stress, but businessmen and officials generally ignore.

Have you done anything about new traffic arteries, for mixed as well as pleasure vehicles, running through and really tapping your city, relieving side-street congestion and lessening the parking problem? Have you done anything about parking, bearing in mind that this is almost always a midtown problem affecting only about 5 per cent of your total area, but is blown up into exaggerated proportions because of the annoyance it causes? Have you thought of making midtown business pay for surface, subsurface and garage facilities, of adopting zoning regulations which will compel new building according to new standards and prevent the fellow who lives on increased congestion from ruining the town for future citizens just so that he can exploit the last square inch of his lot?

Have you studied the successes and failures of plants which have moved out of town and often away from their logical labor market, to find out whether you can offer the inducements in town which the suburbs appear, often superficially, to offer?

Have you counted honestly your cultural and clinical advantages, bearing in mind that these exist for most people only in cities, and that without them your town does not have much to boast of?

Have you made it easy by good roads and other devices for the city man, who often lives in an apartment, to own a small place by the water or in the woods in the nearby country for weekends and vacations?

Have you figured out the power of the city dollar, whether invested or raised by taxation, to carry out a program of city capital improve-

ments by a combination of public and private enterprise and cooperation?

Have you studied by decibels or otherwise the tempo of your
town? Have you tested its magnetism in attracting those who love
competition and the "big time," its hospitality to outside talent, its
rewards and incentives, its attractions to casual visitors as well as
prospective residents, business and trade?

Have you figured out how large your town can afford to be in the
light of the demands upon your elected and appointed officials, your
business heads and the church, school and social leaders upon whom
you are dependent for your moral health? Many of our American
towns are too big for their civic boots. They are too much for the
people who are trying to run them. You must have big people for
big tasks. Grow, expand, reach out, but don't get elephantiasis.

SMALL-TOWN PLANNING

It is high time that the average American small city and village—
towns we call them in the vernacular—decided what it wants to look
like, what it should do to accommodate traffic, meet municipal needs,
restrain those who care nothing for neighbors or the community, and
get rid of what is cheap, ugly and a poor imitation of bigger places.
There is no need to go foreign, colossal, metropolitan, arty, ultra-
modern or Hollywood. The more local and natural the results, the
better, but we cannot expect a new native American culture in every
town, springing from the soil, without ancestors anywhere.[10]

Every municipality should have a definite, sane and realizable program of public improvements, logically related to private enterprise,
employment and residence, that is, a public physical program
integrated with a private economic one. The municipal plan should
not be theoretical, academic and revolutionary. It should not be the
iridescent dream of visionaries, nor the impatient pronouncement of
youthful reformers. Neither should the program be whittled down to
mere inescapable repairs by bankers and real estate owners who are
chronically opposed to every nickel of public expenditure which
affects the current tax rate and the debt limit. Between these two
extremes there is a happy medium where solid, sensible, middle-of-the-

road citizens can stand on common ground. As the Bible says: "Prove all things; hold fast that which is good." Intelligent, conservative citizens should not be influenced in their decision on such matters either by alarmists or by reactionaries.

Every municipality should have an independent and respected planning commission and an adequate zoning system which will prevent irresponsible and haphazard building, stabilize values and insure orderly growth. Every city should, through its leading citizens, its press and its officials, review its charter and determine to what extent it is obsolete and needs revision and modernization so as to provide a more efficient structure and functioning of the government. It should always be remembered, however, that a charter is merely the framework of government, and that it takes human talent to make it function.

Generally speaking the most intelligent approach to these problems is by example rather than by standardized, textbook teaching. In other words, the intelligent thing for local officials, interested citizens, civic and fraternal organizations and newspapers to do is to study what has actually been accomplished in other cities of comparable size, location and background. If so-called experts, engineers and planners are employed, they should be people who have not merely written on the subject and advocated this or that change, but who have a record of successful accomplishment, whose advice has been taken in the past and has proved to be good.

Those responsible for public improvements should not begin by assuming that all the talent in the world can be found at home and that no other community or individual has anything to contribute. There is nothing like an open mind on such subjects, and a determination to find out what has worked elsewhere and why. But it does not follow that what fits one community will be equally successful in another. Plans must be adapted to each particular municipality, after making allowances for its peculiarities as well as its needs.

We are living in a period of rapid change. Those towns which have developed first-rate leadership in business, banking, trade and civic organizations as well as in government, which have an alert and independent press, whose leaders have become accustomed to cooperate toward common ends and to sink petty differences for the common good, are those which will not only survive but grow and flourish.

Those which have no plan or program, no enterprise and local pride, no vision and leadership, no common ground on which politics, government, business, church, civic and welfare interests can meet, resolve differences and agree on objectives, will go back, decline, shrink and live largely in the past.

Enormous numbers of people have become accustomed in recent years to moving about from one place to another. They are no longer anchored for life in one spot. For better or worse, they have developed a mobility which they never had before. They are likely to move in future not only to find better jobs but also to obtain better living conditions in progressive communities which have anticipated such demands and have taken steps to meet them.

7

The Heart
of the Metropolis

IN WRITING ABOUT NEW YORK CITY, I OFFER NO apology. She needs none. The metropolis where I have worked for so many years is larger and in many respects more complex than other communities, but basically their problems are similar and I proceed from the particular to the general. This is true, also, of her people. In other words, we are much like the rest of America.

New York City has always been a magnet drawing ambitious people from the entire country and the world at large. The roster of unusual talent in our business, industry, the professions—in fact in every walk of life—shows an extraordinary number of natives from other parts of the United States and elsewhere. The survival of the city as a national center depends on the continuance of this process.[11]

Yet New Yorkers are charged with being insular, foreign and boastful. The first is true, the second false, and the third misleading. We are by geography and definition insular. We are not foreign in any but the statistical sense. We may lack humility, but no great city can be humble if it has any self-confidence. Visitors, if their minds are open, will discover in New York evidences of inward grace, demonstrations of the faith and hope from which our actions spring, and signs of the truth which is in us. And they will recognize here the same kinds of people they meet and live with at home.

The fascinating pageant of New York's history has been recorded by more competent pens than mine. Like England,

Time and the ocean and some fostering star
In high cabal have made us what we are.

To the three factors which made England we may add the successive
waves of immigrants swept upon our hospitable shores, bringing
talents and skills more valuable than the gold and silver, the ivory,
apes and peacocks of the biblical navy of Tarshish.

The logic of New York's founding is as cogent now as on that day
in 1609 when the mist of antiquity lifted and the *Half Moon*, leaving
the Bay, ascended the Hudson. After three centuries, our city flag
still flies the orange, white and blue of the Netherlands, an inheritance which has become more precious with time. In the cold light of
reappraisal of Europe since World War II the Dutch emerge as the
most fair-minded, civilized and admirable people at the crossroads,
a people who in spite of hell and high water never lost their sterling
character. May we keep the faith as well.

It is not, however, our task to keep our inheritance intact and
gilded as if it were an ancient treasure in a modern museum. We
must be impressed, not obsessed, by the past. Ours must be a living
faith, always meeting the challenge of the day. New York's place
on this continent and on the globe is more secure than it ever was
in the past, and its future is boundless, if the big city can continue to
produce the leadership which the times demand, an intelligent and
discriminating following and the legitimate pride which arises from
the conviction that its inhabitants are citizens of no mean city.

SOME MISCONCEPTIONS AND ANOMALIES

Unfortunately there are still people in other areas who regard New
York City not as part of the United States, but as a sort of excrescence
fastened to our eastern shore and peopled by the less venturesome
waves of foreigners who failed to go west to the genuine American
frontier. We have had a bad press in the hinterland, and New York
has the dubious distinction of leading the nation in exaggerating
and dramatizing its deficiencies.

A brief visit to Brazil once gave me a perspective on the amazing
effrontery of our less representative North Americans who criticize

government and business ethics in foreign countries, forgetting the blatant headlines and lurid expressions in print and over the air which describe all the unpleasant features of our own domestic lives, and play down or ignore the achievements and decencies which we expect others to recognize and appraise at their true values.

New York and other American municipalities have made the most extraordinary and inexplicable efforts to foul their own nests. We are lucky indeed that discriminating people in other countries see us in truer perspectives. Some of our antics are incomprehensible to others. It is well to attack scandal and crime, but at least equal attention should be given to the many signs of health and idealism in our municipalities.

SOME HIGHLIGHTS FOR VISITORS

It is futile to attempt to list or classify the mixed motives that draw people to New York, or to repeat worn clichés about the diverse racial origins of our people and the melting pot in which they are fused into that fictional character, the typical New Yorker. We have genial, itinerant columnists who pursue the city's sights and sounds and record the doings of local celebrities, characters and cards for the enlightenment of natives and readers of syndicated features.

We have roving raconteurs who catalog our bouquets from Gowanus Creek in South Brooklyn, where Gowanus No. 4 is distilled naturally, to the ship chandleries of our river fronts, fragrant with tar and oakum. We boast of gossiping gourmets who can tickle palates with specialités de la maison and guide visitors on an epicurean tour through Dinty Moore's corn beef and cabbage and livers and lights, Shavey Lee's sharks' fins, Gage & Tollner's bouillabaisse (Fridays only), the nourishing Coney Island Knish, the Rockaway dog—all beef, a yard wide and stuccoed with mustard—and that Gallic orphan known in the Roaring Forties as "Creep Suzette."

We have eloquent barkers and lecturers on sightseeing buses and yachts who can point out the precise bench in Central Park where our elder statesman, Bernard M. Baruch does all his thinking; the exact spot where Steve Brodie hit the East River in his famous bridge jump; the room in Bellevue charity ward where Stephen Foster died penniless; the ancestral homes of Annie Rooney and Mamie O'Rourke; and the Bowery hall where Irving Berlin was a singing waiter.

They salute the old-law tenement (actually long since demolished) where Al Smith was born, Fulton Fish Market, where he earned the degree of F.F.M., his home on Oliver Street, and close by St. James' Church, where he was a choir boy; the Mariners' Temple and the old Spanish-Portuguese Cemetery—monuments to the three faiths which shared the nickels and dimes left over when we finished paying for the Smith Memorial in the public housing project that bears his name.

Visitors' guides may wave airily at the wampum works of the Rockaway Indians and point out the remaining jazz joints in Harlem where vaunted descendants of the black and unknown bards of long ago sob spirituals, croon the blues, hammer out the dated rhythm of "Flat Foot Floogie and the Floy Floy," and release the tortured cacophonies of bebop. And they will identify the Greenwich Village saloon where Masefield, the British Poet Laureate, flushed mugs, cleaned cuspidors, dreamed of Ships, Cargoes and Spanish Waters and contemplated The Everlasting Mercy. Our museum guides, in three hours, can show visitors the arts and crafts of three thousand years, and the flora, fauna, feathers, furs and fins of all species which have enlivened biology since this revolving globe cooled sufficiently to support it.

Some Other Aspects of the City

My purpose is not to overpower readers with adjectives, but to deal with realities. We also have earnest reformers, planners and social workers who ceaselessly complain that too many of our midtown shrines of luxury and pride are flanked by the tenement clotheslines which shamelessly flaunt the short and simple flannels of the poor. It is innate humor, rather than any grimness, reticence or sophistication, which prevents New Yorkers from becoming sloppy and sentimental about their city.

A glance at a map of the greater city will show how relatively small, if not insignificant, is the Great White Way. The core of the city holds many of its greatest attractions. Without it there would be no motivating force, no concentrated high values and therefore no major revenues. But it is a mistake to assume that everything of consequence in New York is within three miles of Grand Central. What is news on the Rialto is gibberish along the Belt Parkway where, far from the frenetic hot spots of midtown, hundreds of thousands of our less advertised citizens keep the even, if not noiseless, tenor of their way.

Here are a few examples of progress in the field of municipal construction which some visitors may overlook: They should note the emerging new neighborhood patterns along the East and Harlem rivers in Manhattan—parks, parkways, housing, the United Nations headquarters, on what was until recently a shambles, reviving adjacent real estate values; the rebuilding of Astoria, across the river; the Triborough Bridge system; the Brooklyn Civic Center; Flushing Meadow Park and its burgeoning environment, with the corridors beyond it extending through Kissena and Cunningham parks to Alley Pond in Queens Borough.

Those interested in the new city that is emerging should note the vast reclamation areas in Queens, Brooklyn and Staten Island, the West Side and Henry Hudson renovations with their widespread repercussions and influences; the gradual reduction of slums in every borough; the salvaging of all of Jamaica Bay and its frontage; the great Soundview, Ferry Point, Whitestone, Rockaway and Clearview park projects; the many constructive achievements of the Port of New York Authority; the reconstruction of our museums; new schools and hospitals and health centers; the many modern city buildings housing courts, libraries and countless other services.

We would not expect visitors to appreciate our prodigious sewage disposal systems, the pure Delaware upland water supply flowing down by gravity. Our own citizens do not fully appreciate these things or what they represent in the way of hard work on the part of little-known people in the public service. What business, industry, trade and the arts and professions have done within this framework of municipal improvements is most impressive of all.

Local critics who refer mournfully to the exodus of industry from the city talk nonsense. They never see the new plants in the southeast

Bronx, trucking in Williamsburgh, and the amazing waterborne commerce of Newtown Creek and the Gowanus Canal. We have had something of a waterfront mess, but it is being cleared up and I doubt if other ambitious ports will draw away our shipping.

We are rebuilding New York, not dispersing and abandoning it. The city spreads into the suburbs, to be sure, and that, within bounds, is what should happen. The process, however, needs no speeding up. It requires no compulsion. It demands no metropolitan supergovernment by ambitious regional planners.

WE ARE REALLY METROPOLITAN

Those of us who have had a hand in these accomplishments are accused by captious and irresponsible mudslingers of failure to work together on a truly metropolitan basis. Committees and commissions are appointed or self-appointed to save us from insularity, narrowness and selfishness. What are the facts?

As an example of voluntary metropolitan cooperation the Port of New York Authority and the Triborough Bridge and Tunnel Authority have laid the groundwork for a vast extension of river crossings intricately meshed with the Federal, state and municipal highway pattern of the entire Atlantic seaboard. Looking up the Hudson from The Cloisters at Fort Tryon Park one may see Fort Washington and Riverside parks, the Henry Hudson Parkway and Bridge, Inwood, Spuyten Duyvil and Riverdale on one side and the New Jersey Palisades and Palisades Parkway on the other, accessible to New York as well as New Jersey, and preserved for all time by a happy combination of private philanthrophy, bi-state and municipal action.

Motorists reach Jones Beach over city and state parkways, over lakes and through parks on waterworks property in Nassau County dedicated to the state by the city, and over meadow and town lands given to all the people by townships of Long Island which existed before there was a state or a nation. Those responsible for these facilities made possible the vast suburban growth on Long Island and built up new values in the face of terrific initial opposition. In this as in other matters we try to steer a middle course between modesty and megalomania, abasement and boasting, placidity and restlessness, the crawl of the caterpillar and the speed of the salamander. Occasionally, due to a falling barometer, carelessness or cussedness, we veer or tack to one side or the other, but we soon get back on the course.

THE NEED FOR LEADERSHIP

New Yorkers, while not regionally governed, are metropolitan-minded. The city and state bark at each other, but they get along. We do not coerce people into leaving or force dispersion and de-centralization. Suburbs, too, have their problems. We do not believe big cities are dated. At any rate, New York is not. Speaking for the builders, our objective is modest: We aim to rebuild New York, saving what is still durable, what is salvageable, and what is genuinely histori-cal, and substituting progress for obsolescence. This is our big prob-lem.

New York, unfortunately, is woefully short of recognized, respected, natural leaders, leaders who are not just on the make but in some measure dedicated to the future of the community. The demand is for leaders who will do not merely their best but the best of the men they would like to be; leaders who are not intimidated by pollcats, who do not depend upon applause meters and sell tomorrow for the cheers of today; men who are gallant enough to do the right thing and leave the final decision to time and the ultimate good judgment of decent people.

New York is too big for village intimacies, small-town fellowship and cracker-barrel town meetings; I am aware of the tempo, the stratification and the anonymity of city life and the difficulties involved in bridging the gaps which separate the many groups, callings and lo-calities of which we are composed, in finding common purposes and in discovering those whom we are prepared to select, respect and follow.

Democracy, as we have been practicing it of late, is a kind of bed of Procrustes, in which all those who are too big are enthusiastically and vigorously cut down and only perfunctory efforts are made to stretch the short ones. The idea is to make all of us the same size. The notion that by such devices we can in the long run compete with our ruthless competitors, Communist and Fascist, who look for and encourage talent and leadership to promote their false ideologies, is absurd.

There is more private generosity in New York than civic spirit. Witness the widespread support of churches, hospitals, charities, welfare and education. There is philanthropy on a huge scale. But the breadwinners, large and small, are bombarded by appeals for myriads of good causes downtown, uptown, in the suburbs, in the slums, appeals in the press, through the mails, over the air. Every approach, charm, shock, lure and persuasion known to fund raising and public relations experts and to advertising salesmen trained in selling cigarettes, detergents, gadgets and nostrums are brought to bear on them. When the targets of these appeals get through selecting the claims they can afford to recognize—over and above fixed obligations and inescapable personal needs—and have tossed out the rest, there is little interest, time, energy and money left for the broader demands of citizenship. We ask the tired businessman to be serious, alert and noble when all he wants is to be relaxed and comfortable.

Among our most doleful domestic critics are representative big bankers and businessmen who solemnly warn that we shall go bust if we do not stop spending. Certainly we must balance our budgets, but economics, however essential, will not keep the total from increasing, because our needs and desires eat up the savings. We must pay taxes, tolls and rentals if we expect more and better services for a growing and ceaselessly demanding population, and if we continue to insist that the good things of life must be fairly distributed. We must work harder, loaf less and stop bellyaching about fear and want.

It is mortifying for New York City officials to have to go to Albany for state aid that is rightfully ours, but it should be even more humiliating to refuse to meet local needs locally and to have distasteful measures, which we ought to swallow without compulsion, ruthlessly rammed down our throats. There will always be disputes between acreage and people, between the big city and the widespread hinterland, between the rural and the urban point of view. We are, however, interdependent here in the Empire State and we should make a virtue of getting along. It is not possible completely to split sovereignty, and home rule, like states' rights, is a relative business.

There is no easy formula for the production of genuine leaders. There must be a popular demand for them based in part at least on impatience with compromising racial, religious and political exploitation, glassy-eyed banking, selfish labor leadership, and a press often more interested in controversy than in real issues.

You may search and philosophize until you are fuzzy over the decay of cities. You may weigh all the known factors. When you are finished you will conclude that the sun set on the isles of Greece, that Rome declined and fell, that Nineveh and Tyre were leveled to dust, that Carthage was destroyed and Venice became a museum because there were no longer men of light and leadership to overcome widespread selfishness, indifference, factionalism and cowardice.

THE LACK OF CIVIC PRIDE

Next to the dearth of leadership in New York, our greatest handicaps are lack of legitimate pride in our accomplishments, lurid advertising of our deficiencies and difficulties, snide criticism, malicious wisecracking, gossip, controversy for its own sake and sheer ignorance of our own town. I am tired of overnight experts, with a traveling radius of two miles from Times Square, who are barely able to find the television studio where they have the effrontery to lecture on the needs of Canarsie, Mott Haven, Richmond Hill, Inwood and Mariners Harbor; of civic secretaries who throw knives from safe places in the shelter of the wings at human targets out in front on the stage, and of prominent people who lend their names to every cause which sounds grand and impressive, but do not know what they are endorsing or attacking. We tolerate and laugh at sayings and doings for which the authors would be labeled as traitors and tarred, feathered and ridden out of town on rails in places where citizens are proud of their heritage and jealous of their reputation.

What is all this chatter of civic secretaries, muckraking commentators and sour critics about our planlessness, the curses of urbanism, municipal decay and rot, the hopeless burden of our problems, the ineffectiveness of our officials, the dog-eat-dog competition of businessmen, the doom toward which we move relentlessly? Why do decent thinking citizens permit this wailing to go on?

Admitting that we have troubles and fall short of perfection, we have done and are doing things here in New York, public, quasi-public and private, on a bigger and better scale than they are done anywhere else in this country or in any other. We have in large measure what the Communists lack and lie about. Our achievements have been phenomenal. It is acknowledged by those not blinded by prejudice. It is the envy of foreign representatives of totalitarianism who come here to scoff and rarely remain to pray.

The trouble is that none of these critics has any idea of what he wants. We must always remember that it is concentration of population which makes possible large department stores and fine shops, financial, management, trade and shipping centers, modern hospitals and clinics, the theater, the opera, the fine arts, the magnets of culture and letters, famous hotels, restaurants and cabarets, continuous athletic and sporting events, conventions and dozens of other human activities which require mass attendance. Without a core of scarce, vertically built, high-value land there is not enough to tax for the operation of city government. This is our dilemma—to keep the urban core active, magnetic and profitable, but not to let it choke us to death with mounting peak loads of traffic and people.

8

The Spreading City

THE URBAN TREND, WHETHER WE LIKE IT OR NOT, is undeniable. The shift from country to town is steady. There is little wavering in the graph but, like all statistics, these require both definition and honest interpretation.

The country is, of course, the area marked in green on the maps, whether wide open or thinly populated. The town—that is another matter. The town is not only the city in the legal sense but the large village as well, whether incorporated or not, the township in some areas, the metropolis in others. In measuring the trend toward the more compact, populous places, we must remember that as people move into cities many in the same cities move into the outskirts, the suburbs and the satellite towns.

Besides those who move from place to place because of their work, an astonishing number of people have homes in town and in the country. They divide their time about equally between an apartment in town and a house, camp or shack of some kind elsewhere. We have millions of city people of all income brackets who spend every weekend in the country and others who have made a habit of regular visits to national and state parks.

The city man is a weekend salt-water fisherman by instinct. He requires something unpaved, unencumbered, and monotonous to keep him sane. Perhaps it is an admission against interest to say that there are many of us who simply cannot take the city the week around.

Our parkways, turnpikes, expressways, thruways and other roads, which are being multiplied and improved to keep pace with the output of cars and the demands of the traveling public, will increase enormously the pressure on our highway system and promote mutual attraction and gradual unification of the country and the town.[12]

Meanwhile, the healthy, natural movement of young couples with growing families to houses and apartments at moderate prices in outlying areas of the city and in the suburbs has been accelerated. No compulsion, no artificial stimulus is needed to drive people out of town.

PREJUDICE AND POPULATION SHIFTS

Increasing leisure, longer paid vacations, larger pensions, earlier retirement, older people with the itch for travel and with unsatisfied curiosity about distant places break down more and more the artificial differences between the city man and the country man. The big question is whether the traveler seeks to broaden his horizons or to confirm his prejudices.

We should not pay too much attention to the dweller in the shadow of the "El" who would rather be a lamppost in Chicago than the whole Painted Desert. Or to the confirmed Gothamite who boasts that the city is the finest summer resort and that, as Mr. Dooley remarked: "Ivrything that's worth havin' goes to th' city; the counthry takes what's left." And by the same token, keep in mind that Thoreau spent only a relatively short time continuously in his crude shack at Walden Pond. There is no sense in assuming irreconcilable conflict between city and country people. We are not neatly divided between hayseeds and slickers. Acres have claims as well as concentrations of people, but there are no provable superior virtues attaching to the country or city when moral, spiritual, mental, or even health and hygienic factors are under consideration.

Cities were in many cases originally created for protection. This is about the only logic of urban growth which is no longer significant. All the other reasons for the establishment of growing cities are as influential today as they were when the pioneers founded them on the seaboard, the river, the valley, the hill, the rail center, the crossroads, the focal point of a farming, mining, fishing, manufacturing or other center, or the source of plentiful labor.

Academic planners and those who cannot stand urban competition or tolerate a certain amount of noise, tension, hurry, and the anonymity of urban life, advocate decentralization of cities and dispersion of population. But their prejudices will not materially influence the logic of the situation. There are good reasons why most cities persist. Those which decline do so because they no longer serve a function in the larger economy of the nation.[13]

SOME ADVANTAGES OF CONCENTRATION

It is not to be forgotten that civilization is an outgrowth and attribute of cities. Farms produce food; oceans support commerce; the suburbs are dormitories; the mines teem with energy and the forests with the solitude which promotes thought—but civilization flourishes only in concentrated urban communities. You need not live in a city, but you must be nearby or visit now and then if you expect to be recognized as a civilized man. A city need not be large but a village is not a city. To quote the lines of Vachel Lindsay:

> Let not your town be large, remembering
> That little Athens was the muses' home,
> That Oxford is the heart of London still,
> That Florence gave the Renaissance to Rome.
> —"ON THE BUILDING OF SPRINGFIELD"*

The American is restless and imitative. He likes contrast, change and assembly-line stuff. I believe it was Henry Mencken who described him sourly as an Elk in a Ford. Well, ours may not be a great civilization as measured by philosophers. It is no Cinque-Cento Italian Renaissance when it comes to aristocracy of the arts, but it has its points. This is the one nation on earth in which the average man can also be the well-rounded man with two residences, one in town and the other in the country. You do not have to be a millionaire here to own a flivver and a country bungalow.[14]

A proper reading of history shows that the permanence of cities is

* From *General William Booth Enters Into Heaven*; copyright 1916 by The Macmillan Company. Reprinted by permission of the publisher.

more significant than their decay. War and the acts of God have from time to time outraged them, but those which were established at navigable waters, at important crossroads and centers, strategic places of one kind or another, persist.

A one-industry town may dry up with its only attraction, but this is the exception not the rule. For every Auburn which fades as its bold peasantry declines, there is a Birmingham which still flourishes. Ol' Man River—Mississippi, Danube or Columbia—keeps on rolling along and most of the cities he has spawned on his banks still flourish. A city cannot live on Tyrian purple, or the sale of graven images of Diana, or on depleted mines, honkytonks or rundown aristocracy; but London, Stalingrad, Amsterdam rise from rubble because they were and continue to be the logical and traditional places for concentration and because they continue to have the men, the enterprise and the pride to keep up with or ahead of the times.[15]

The trouble with the prophets of doom of cities is that they do not think like the people who live in them. Lewis Mumford, Frank Lloyd Wright and their followers who damn urbanization because they cannot stand the gaff of city life no doubt honestly believe that all city people hate their existence. They do not realize that Brooklynites adore Brooklyn, idolize the Dodgers because they symbolize it, and cheer themselves hoarse at the mention of its name. Can Mumford and the aesthetes, and Frank Lloyd Wright and the back-to-the-land boys be right and three million Brooklynites be wrong? The community may survive a long time because there are, as Webster said of his old alma mater, those who love it, and because there are also those who cannot get away.

A town, like a British remittance man in Canada, can be supported by distant relatives. Some of our old villages are helped by natives who have gone to big cities and made good. We have towns that, like Colonial Williamsburg, have become museums and monuments which stir memories but have no grip on ambitious boys and girls. There are, to be sure, not many such communities in our new country. Those that exist should keep up standards but should not try to compete with rushing, raucous, new places. It is better to live on charm than to be an imitation Babylon.

Only the city can afford the arts in their broadest and most developed sense, because, it takes population to keep art centers alive and flourishing. The same reasoning applies to great medical centers which require the most nearly complete clinical facilities, to management headquarters of banking and big business, and to many mercantile establishments which have to be close together.

The nearby country as well as the suburb is meaningless without the city. Los Angeles supports a veritable paradise of truck farmers and orchards almost at its borders, and New York is the big market for the potatoes, ducks and shellfish of Long Island. Proximity of city and country, warm shorefront and glacial heights, ranch and bungalow, is what makes California such a strong rival of the Atlantic and Gulf seaboards and the Middle West. Our entire economy is depedent on urban, suburban and rural integration.

Obviously, city life is not doomed, although some particular town may be static, advancing or going back. In studying any particular community, there is no quick, smooth categorical answer to the never-ending challenges of growth and change. Intelligent citizens should study the main forces at work, the pulls and pressures. Much depends on the traditions of the town, on its special interests, on types of leadership and the strength of advocates of conservative improvement as against radical and revolutionary uprooting.[16]

DIVERSITY IN METROPOLITAN AREAS

It is a great mistake to assume that the overbuilt and deliberately overcrowded midtown section of every big city is the city, and that nothing else in it counts. Parts of big towns are like suburbs and even country. The significant and often prevailing and controlling outskirts, peripheries and relatively quiet residential places where respectable people keep the noiseless tenor of their way—places which make no pretense of being "stems," Broadway crossroads, "hot spots," "loops" and what not, and with no special bids to visitors—are more characteristic of the city, more redolent of its quality and flavor than the places ballyhooed by barkers and touted by advertisers. The barkers always show off the city slums, the Harlems, Bowery, Basin streets, Chinatowns, Little Italy, the former ghettoes, and so on, and picture them as a fixed, unchangeable, inevitable feature of city life. But it simply is not so.

In our cities the shallows murmur, but the deeps are dumb. There are more churchgoers than cabaret hounds, but they make less noise. The jazz joints, with their raucous snare drums and trumpets, are more obtrusive but much less important than the long-drawn aisles and fretted vaults where, as the poet said, the pealing anthem swells the note of praise.

The spreading suburbs also have their logic, not only as dormitories for commuters and garden spots for their wives and children, but also as places from which, by rail and road, the manifold attractions of the city can easily be reached without the distractions and handicaps of city life.

It is sad to see venal, weak or complacent local officials, indifferent to recent history, permitting the subdividers, real estate developers and their co-conspirators and victims to repeat the same tricks in the suburbs which made the slums of the cities a few generations ago— small lots, narrow streets, with parks, schools, and utilities of all kinds waiting for future assessments on unsuspecting purchasers. Higher standards must come from the average citizen. Water cannot rise above its own level.

The suburbs, too, often are leaderless. I worry more about the suburbs than about the cities. In the cities we are at least aware of and are trying to undo the errors of the past. In the suburbs these felonies are being compounded and perpetuated.

SOME SUBURBAN PROBLEMS

I do not believe that the metropolis is obsolete. The city is still the center of gravity of modern civilization. Parts of it of course are antiquated, especially slums and rundown, depressed areas which are the results of the past selfishness of capital, the weakness of government and the indifference of the citizenry. We have at least been educated above this level to some understanding of the difficulties, costs and sacrifices which must be made to remedy conditions which under better leadership would never have occurred.

Our big cities must be rebuilt, not abandoned. While this is being done the suburbs will continue to grow amazingly, and open country previously considered beyond commuting distance will become suburban. But let us not fool ourselves about the spreading city. There are just as many problems involved in rapid, uncontrolled, suburban growth as in the rebuilding of substandard midtown urban sections.

As we reflect on suburban growth we begin to recognize that this is not an unmixed blessing. I am not at all sure that the problems of the suburbs are not more serious and less understood than those of the city. I have never yet seen one of these big plans for suburban "developments" start out with a proper diagnosis of future problems.

The Levittown community on Long Island is an example. Here the builders took a number of farms, open land, and built some 17,000 houses to accommodate 75,000 people. When you live in the heart of the city you have facilities which, while they may not be just to your liking, do provide schools, streets, sewers, water, electric and gas utilities and some established forms of transportation. When you go out in the open country, however, all these problems gradually rear their ugly heads to plague you. I have seen them develop. You decide that putting in cesspools is safe to start with, but soon you are taking water out of the same ground to drink, no doubt at a different level, and then a water supply problem arises. Nobody pays much attention to drainage, and all of a sudden you have to do something about storm sewers.

Somebody is going to get the bills for that. Some one will be assessed. Bills also have got to be paid for sewage plants. Cesspools and well water for 75,000 people do not mix for any length of time. Transportation and schools must be provided. There is no use going through the roster of necessities. They descend upon the community as a whole after the developer, the fellow who has moved these people or industries to virgin territory has departed and closed his account books.

"Rus in urbe"

Only a pretentious scribbler would glory in the boast that Augustus Caesar found Rome built of brick and left it built of marble. Our watchword should be that we found our city a wilderness of stone and steel, crowded and inaccessible, and that we opened it to light and air, planted it with the green of parks and the laughter of playgrounds, and carved out wide spokes and rims for parkways and expressways to make the city and country one.

I dismiss as unworthy of serious consideration the gloomy prophets who label cities as obsolete because of the possibility of atomic bombing. If the hydrogen bombs actually fall, we shall all be finished. Meanwhile, apprehension and premature terror can paralyze us before anything really happens. These are just the objectives the Communists aim at in their cold, psychological warfare.

It is the ambition of every official responsible for the rebuilding and improvement of cities to increase the open spaces, reduce the coverage of land, salvage, restore and preserve natural resources; in fact, to approximate the old Roman idea of *rus in urbe*, the country in the city.

The city, rebuilt, modernized and humanized, will always be the great magnet which draws from the hinterland the eager, the young, the curious, the ambitious, the talented. These, from the dawn of history, have gravitated to big places where the incentives are most dramatic, where competition is strongest and rewards great. Ours is an emerging new people of many stocks and talents in a land of extraordinary variety. Country and city, we are knitted together.[17]

Our suburbs will in time somehow attain bouquet, flavor, character and personality. The residents, mostly young couples with small children, will form friendships. Acquaintances will cross the parkways and highways which separate one development from another. Marriages will cement the Montagus and Capulets of these scattered communities. Thus eventually they will produce leaders with vision and pride and by some mysterious alchemy develop a sense of unity.

9

Some of New York City's Problems

BECAUSE OF HER SIZE, SHAPE, POLITICAL SETUP and other unusual features, New York City has some problems which may be unique, but to some extent all large communities have difficulties of the same general nature. Solutions of these difficulties are not to be found in politics. Yet politics is a factor.

During the mayoralty campaign of 1953 the New York *Daily News* requested me to write a series of articles emphasizing the city's problems and desirable objectives as distinguished from the personalities of the candidates. While much progress has been made, these problems have not been solved and since many of the objectives have not been attained, I believe they should be restated.[18]

At the outset I recorded my firm conviction that New York's salvation is not coming from outside. Shortly before the election, the Kefauver Committee, with its television stunts, had guaranteed the millennium. The Senators sounded like the late Elijah Dowie, who came here years ago from Zion City to save us and left denouncing our people as "stinkpots."

The late Mayor Gaynor, a shrewd, crotchety and somewhat cynical old judge, but quite a philosopher, scouted the idea that the Mayor is the moral mentor of the city, and boldly asserted that the main objective of his administration was to maintain "outward order and decency." I commend this morsel of wisdom to pious investigators who track Original Sin from the White and Appalachian Mountains to

the Big City on the assumption that our parkways are roads to
Damascus lined with penitents eager to see the light. There have
been Magdalens in other places than New York. After all, it was in
New England that Hester won her A.

We have deep-seated internal troubles but these will not be cured
by television stunts, muckraking and political evangelism. The net
result of the Kefauver hearings was that the notion became prevalent
in political circles that by television you can sell almost any candidate
to the city as if he were a cake of soap. Even if this is so, I doubt
whether you can clean the city that way.

REALISM VS. EXPERTS AND CHARTS

I have less and less interest in forms of government, law, charter
and code changes with which ambitious politicians entertain the
voters in the weeks before election, but there is one important change
in the New York City Charter which should be made right away.
That has to do with the powers of the Mayor and other members of
the Board of Estimate, which is the main governing body of the city.
The Mayor should have four votes, instead of three; the President of
the City Council should have three votes, as at present, and the
Borough Presidents of Brooklyn, Manhattan, Queens and The Bronx
two each, and Richmond one vote. (Manhattan and Brooklyn now
have two votes each, Queens, The Bronx and Richmond, one.) That
would leave the total sixteen, as at present, but redistribute power.
The City Comptroller, who now has three votes, should be an auditor,
like the State Comptroller. He should have no administrative functions, and should not be on the Board of Estimate.

I have long since lost faith in municipal experts who prattle about
a grand master plan of the city, experts who cry for a program or
"performance budget"; and I do not believe in an imported, super-
duper city manager or assistant mayor who knows neither our people
nor our geography. Because a city manager is good for Wauwatosa,
Wisconsin (population 33,324) or a performance budget for Sauk
Creek, Minnesota, or a garage under a park in San Francisco does
not prove they will work in New York. To be sure we can learn from
others, but let's at least study the thing carefully and adapt it to our
own conditions.

I do not believe in economies at the expense of service and have never been persuaded that the people of the city will knowingly embrace any such thinking, no matter how cleverly presented. I do not believe that our capital budgets can be cut at all. Similarly, I believe that even if all practical minor improvements in current administration are met, the expense budget is bound to rise. Candidates who promise an actual net reduction in the expense budget are taking the voter for a ride because it cannot be done if at the same time they guarantee improvements in essential services.

Cities did not create postwar inflation and the fifty-cent dollar, yet how can they be explained away? Similarly, the candidate who promises to be loyal to his political friends and appointments and also to put better men in key positions cannot possibly make good.

Progress in Housing and Slum Clearance

Metropolitan New York has made more progress in providing good new housing than any other large city in the country. This is a long way from saying that enough has been done. We need more public housing for the lower income groups; more middle-income housing for those who cannot pay full rents; much more slum clearance, preferably with the help of private capital; public housing to take care of displaced persons; and more rehabilitation of individual houses in areas which are not yet slums but are on their way downward.

The steady movement of new families into outlying neighborhoods and suburbs will continue without artificial stimulus and will suffer no interruption, but the overbuilt central core, with its great attractions, will still be the objective both of those who like city life and those who cannot get away from it. Here is one of those problems which do not yield to statistics dimly illuminated by asterisks and footnotes. We have reached a state of stable equilibrium in our older residential areas. A closer view shows how it happens—the well-to-do stay, the relatively well-to-do move, the poor from Puerto Rico and the South come in.

At the first sign of a recession and unemployment, there will be trouble. Meanwhile, indifferent Federal authorities call it a local sidewalk phenomenon, and at election time, local candidates, eager for office and throwing wild haymakers at each other, duck this subject because it is dangerous and makes no votes. Let us have an end of evasion. An honest forthright approach is the first step toward a solution.

It is no criticism of the Spanish-speaking people in Puerto Rico to say that when 70,000 of them arrive in New York annually by plane, and over 50,000 remain, almost all poor and often unacquainted with our customs and language, not only shelter but many other problems are forced upon the city. Fifty thousand people are over 10,000 families. Decent new dwellings for them cost at least $10,000 apiece. That's $100 million a year, without counting the cost of schools, hospitals and other services. These people will make good citizens. They can be absorbed. They can add much to our life, but not at the present rate of arrival unless we make adequate and humane preparation for them. Economy drives, budget- and tax-slashing will not do the trick.

How can the Federal government honestly deny some responsibility for these people? It should contribute liberally; and the state, too, should help. This matter must be argued patiently, forcefully and intelligently with state and, above all, Federal officials. It should not be allowed to degenerate into name-calling for political advantage in local campaigns.

The public is not gulled by slogans to show whose heart beats loudest for the poor. No candidate who promises help by denunciation is going to get us anywhere. Nor is one who claims that his political connections are such that a word from him at the right capitol will bring instant cooperation. This is a matter on which the people of the state and country are divided, not so much on political as on ideological grounds, with the rural and inland groups showing little regard for concentrated urban populations. Only executive leadership can enlighten and persuade dissidents in the state Legislature and in Congress.

The big insurance companies and savings banks are timid about further ventures into equity as distinguished from mortgage participation in large-scale, controlled rental housing. They have been frightened by restrictive legislation and forced into court to obtain rent increases to which they were clearly entitled by agreements with the city. It is much simpler to loan to other landlords, invest in something less troublesome and controversial, or simply put government bonds on their shelves.

Closely related to housing is building inspection. One of our greatest difficulties lies in the fact that if all of the minute regulations in the Multiple Dwellings Law and applicable statutes were enforced, landlords could not possibly lift the violations. Immediate, uncompromising, ruthless and literal enforcement of every section of New York's meticulous Multiple Dwellings and related laws would dispossess hundreds of thousands and make them public charges. In many cases tenants would have to be put out while costly major repairs were made. In the process, rents would be decontrolled, and when the tenants attempted to come back, they would have to pay amounts beyond their means.

Banks and other mortgage holders cannot easily be persuaded to make new large uneconomical loans for repairs. Legislation to exempt such repairs from taxation would help, but the requirement of anti-discrimination pledges is a serious deterrent, not because landlords seek to discriminate but because they fear to lose control of the selection of tenants. It is one of the strange paradoxes of life that if you try to speed up a salutary evolutionary process, such as the brotherhood of man, you slow it down.

By far the most promising method of stimulating repairs lies in liberalizing Federal Housing Administration guarantees. But until we have more new housing in and near town, more vacancies in ancient rookeries, lower prices, larger government subsidies and guarantees, more help from the big banks which have in recent years abandoned decaying and changing neighborhoods, we shall have to concentrate in our inspections on vital safety and health requirements.

Obstacles to Providing Adequate Schools

A new organization chart has been adopted by the Board of Education which provides for several top assistants to the superintendent, covering the fields of teaching, planning, construction and repair, finance, etc. This reorganization was logical, but does not of itself solve anything. There are not enough teachers in most areas. Salary schedules must be revised upward. The attractions of teaching must be increased commensurably with new and unprecedented burdens. Good education is not cheap, nor is it the place for ruthless, hard-boiled slashing under the guise of economy.

School construction still lags, not solely because of lack of capital funds, as is usually alleged, but primarily because of appalling delays in selection of sites, failure to expedite plans and absence of two-fisted direction of work. On the other hand, one must make honest allowance for the tremendous and rapid subdivision of outlying areas, growth of population, influx of families from other states, strikes, high prices, increasingly high standards and expensive equipment. If it were not for our parochial and private schools New York would be in desperate shape. Bickering and red tape are serious obstacles to overcome in the public school system, but the Board of Education by and large, so far as the school plant is concerned, does a reasonably good job.

It may be cold comfort for those in the city who suffer from deficiencies in our schools to know that in the nearby suburban counties, within commuting distance, conditions are immeasurably worse, and that the state has fallen down miserably in giving real aid and direction to local districts too small, weak and unimaginative to cope with the deluge of new children for whom no preparation has been made. Our public schools are at least on a par. In the suburbs the tax rates vary to an astonishing extent, are staggeringly high in some places and ridiculously low in others. Our Board of Higher Education is an undistinguished body. Its membership could be cut in two without irreparable loss. It needs a vigorous chancellor over the college presidents, and more state aid.

PROTECTION OF LIFE AND PROPERTY

Safety in the usual sense means fire and police. As to fire, we have had excellent commissioners, in numbers a fairly adequate force, pretty good stations, and the need of reclassification of pay and pensions found everywhere throughout the city service.

I do not know what the people generally, young and old, conditioned by radio and television crime features and drug store who-dunits, want in a New York Police Commissioner—probably a synthetic character composed of equal parts of General Patton, Annie Oakley, J. Edgar Hoover, Dick Tracy, Nero Wolfe, the Shadow, and the Kindly Old Tracer of Lost Persons. I doubt whether there is any such amalgam available.

GANGSTERS AND POLITICIAN TIES

I would like to repeat a statement I made in resigning from the Management Committee. I do not want superfluous, lazy, clock-watching, easygoing employees, but we do require enough good ones armed with the best tools and materials to take care of our people and property. The so-called experts who slash budgets and the timid executives who think this is what the public wants at the moment do not realize that the average citizen may grumble a little but will pay the bill without too much complaint if he thinks he is getting his money's worth.

I am no more happy about crime conditions than the next man, but I see no good citizenship in magnifying the situation and undermining confidence in all law enforcement agencies. If anything is clear it is that there is no monopoly of virtue in any existing political party, that there is hypocrisy in all of them, and that only genuine leadership day in and day out, as distinguished from spasms of reform, will produce lasting good government. We have excellent district attorneys in the big counties primarily involved. They must have reliable prima facie evidence to ask for indictments—unless, like most special investigations, they just want to put on a show—and convincing proof if they expect to get convictions.

As to the much publicized metropolitan waterfront disturbances, we finally got around to the realization that this is an interstate, and indeed a national, problem. The Governors of New York and New Jersey established a machine which ought to work in spite of goon union leaders and cowardly and complacent shipping executives who had been playing footsie with them for years.

HEALTH, HOSPITALS AND SANITATION

New York's city hospitals are improving as to new buildings and construction, but suffer from poor repair, maintenance and operation, inadequate and grossly underpaid personnel. Great new medical centers do not produce doctors, nurses, supplies, and the care our wards should have. It is false economy, bad budget-making, financial starvation and not poor management at the top which has brought about the conditions widely complained of at hospitals like Bellevue. Moreover, the private hospitals which care for many public patients receive from the city much less than they spend.

Heaven help us if the private hospitals, lay and religious, should become discouraged and give up, and the city government, already overburdened, understaffed, bedevilled by the experts and financially embarrassed, should be compelled to take over the whole show. The Health Department suffers from the same troubles as hospitals and other essential services. They cannot be removed by false economy.

Progress in Refuse Disposal

Our Sanitation Department is undermanned, underequipped and harassed by slums, parking and other problems. Here again there is no quick and cheap way of getting results. This is not a case of man failure. The Sanitation Department needs more men and better equipment, but it has to deal with many newcomers in the worst areas who have not as yet been trained in cleanliness and who live under conditions which make it almost impossible. The streets are filled with parked cars and sweepers cannot get under them. Shifting from one side to the other is merely a palliative and no permanent answer. The disposal of garbage, ashes, refuse and other waste is a tremendous problem on which we have made great progress.

This problem began back in the days of reform administrations when incinerators were abandoned in favor of unregulated dumping and an embargo was placed on building new ones, all under the guise of economy. Today we are filling future park and reclamation areas with this material under careful safeguards and on the basis of plans which a few years hence will produce waterfront recreation and other benefits for the children of those who do not as yet understand what is going on.

The Great Water System

New York's great water system has for many years been under competent engineering direction. Patient building for the future has required activities outside of the city limits and recently the control of interstate streams. From time to time a plan has been put forth to cheapen our drinking water by purifying sewage and abandoning the Delaware upland supply. I am glad this problem is to be left with the reputable engineers who for so many years have been handling it successfully. Pending the arrival of Delaware water we need no rainmakers and cloud ticklers.

THE CITY PLANNING COMMISSION

A former director of the Citizens' Budget Commission has pontificated as follows on planning and capital programming: "The long-range planners must examine every important business and industrial activity of the community, its composite strengths and weaknesses, and forecast the economic future based upon present potentialities."

This is a good trick if you can do it. If we wait for the outcome of such examinations and forecasts before doing anything we shall be a century behind more aggressive and less confused municipal competitors in other parts of these United States. To get away from such maundering, I offered the following specific suggestions to improve the City Planning Commission:

The members of the Commission should give full time, except the chief engineer and any other member who holds other city office. The salaries of the members have been raised but, except for the chairman, the chief engineer and myself, the members still give part-time service.

By charter amendment, a simple majority vote should be required in the Board of Estimate on city planning items. Similarly, by charter amendment, assessable improvements, except for those wholly assessed on the local area, as well as other permanent improvements, should be included in the Capital Budget prepared by the City Planning Commission.

POLITICS AND RAPID TRANSIT

Transportation is a big subject. The suburban and railroad problems will require years to solve. As to rapid transit, it is perhaps too much to expect voters to make a calm and considered decision in their own interest. The five-cent fare was a sure-fire political contrivance for years. I remember when an eminent, cold-blooded Tammany strategist told me in 1924 that it would be good for just two more campaigns. He was conservative. It lasted through six campaigns.

Mayor La Guardia promised some of us in his administration to raise the fare in order to balance the budget and get started on improvements. He promised it in every one of his three administrations, but never got around to it. Meanwhile, costs rose, equipment deteriorated and the crisis came later under other mayors.

Mayor O'Dwyer had the nerve to establish a ten-cent fare and, contrary to predictions, got re-elected. The fifteen-cent fare across the board including buses, which I believe should all be privately operated, had been long overdue. Albany picked up this nettle when the Board of Estimate refused to touch it. I do not like the way in which the state did it, but that is a detail. No one likes to pick up thorny objects or hot potatoes, and there is no delicate and refined way of doing it even with kid gloves.

PROGRESS IN VEHICULAR FACILITIES

As to the vehicular phase of transportation, we have, contrary to critics, made great progress. This problem is by no means peculiar to New York. It is nationwide. It is unnecessary to stress the inconveniences and losses we suffer from traffic congestion. What we have accomplished so far and further remedies may be summarized as follows:

We need more drastic regulation. We have made considerable progress through the Department of Traffic with electrical and other devices, one-way streets, turns, etc. Before long we shall have to resort to night loading in certain districts whether the unions like it or not, and even if it costs more. We shall have to have better speed regulations, more police, more help from magistrates, and above all respect for law and cooperation by both pedestrians and riders.

Construction of expressways, supplementing parkways and channeling mixed through-traffic into rights of way free from access except at crossings will take express traffic off ordinary streets. We have made enormous progress on this program which before long will be understood and appreciated by the public.

Perhaps some idea of the magnitude of this work and of that into which Federal, state, city, Port Authority and Triborough funds are being poured can be obtained if it is understood that the average mile of such construction within New York City's limits costs over $5 million, and that a single mile of the Cross Bronx Expressway, half on each side of the Grand Boulevard and Concourse, is costing almost $12 million. We simply waited too long to begin this work. Further delay would make it impossible.

We must have not only much better regulation of street parking but ample provision for off-street facilities. Above all, we need a City Parking Authority Act with control over establishment and regulation of wholesale parking meters. Without the assured revenue from these meters, private investors would not buy the Authority bonds which would have no city credit back of them.

Plans for Future Projects

President Eisenhower's special Council of Economic Advisers, who are preparing a cushion of public works plans anticipating future economic blows, need not worry about New York City. We have computed plans for sound, necessary works running to a total cost of $460 million, and we have under way constructive projects aggregating $668 million. None of these represent boondoggling, Spanish air castles or dreams of crackpots.

Well planned and constructed public improvements are true economies, and can be built without any adverse effect on the tax structure. Public works must be built not only to satisfy the insistent demands of the rank and file of citizens but also to maintain and enhance land values and to provide the incentive to private capital so that it can keep abreast of the times, meet the competition of other cities and expand its investments.

It seems not to occur to some of our local candidates and critics that industry and the sciences and arts here in New York are the envy of ambitious and discriminating people on our own and other continents; that our public improvements are studied and admired; and that some officials in this despised government service are invited elsewhere as diagnosticians, consultants and advisers, presumably on the theory that we have learned something in this wicked and wonderful laboratory which may be profitable to others.

We have indeed been rebuilding the city. Fifty years hence when the horrid prophecies, the airy promises, the sawdust trail exhortations, the punks, pinwheels and other fireworks are mercifully forgotten, the benefits of the public improvements brought about in recent years—including their tonic effect on surrounding values and their stimulus to private efforts—will be recognized. Who knows, history may not record ours as an era of crime, corruption and despair. It may finally be known as our Augustan age.

The City's Financial Problem

Municipal finance is a complex business at best. The strident bickerings, charges and countercharges of special interests, pressure groups, politicians, reformers and pundits have so confused the simple basic issues that the public does not know who is telling the truth and what should be done about it.

The basic issues are simple. We have a growing population with more very young and very old people. Their needs increase steadily. Their demands for expanded and improved services must also in large part be heeded, because we are committed to the democratic principle that the good things, as well as the necessities of life, must be given to people all the way down the line, and not merely to the upper and middle levels.

These enlarged services cost a lot. The cost is paid out of our capital and expense budgets, out of city, borough and local assessments, out of aid from Albany and Washington and contributions from authorities and other public and quasi-public bodies. Our budgets, therefore, must increase unless we lose population and refuse services.

Cities Must Go Ahead—or Go Back

Many expenditures bring revenues directly or indirectly. Public improvements make the indispensable framework within which private enterprise can flourish. Private business borrows to expand its plant. So must public business. Private enterprise must compete. So do municipalities. Cities, like big business, cannot stand still. They advance or go back.

As to revenues, we can ask for more help from Albany and Washington. Washington contributes primarily to capital expenditures, Albany to both current and capital budgets. Neither the Federal government nor the state can be expected to return to New York everything collected here. Both have their own problems. We can only demand that our requests receive more sympathetic consideration in both places, and that urban areas cease to be discriminated against by rural statesmen. We should also demand that the state legislature pay some attention to the spirit of home rule and give New York City the tax and other bills we need to run our city business, especially those which cost the state nothing.

New York City and its government are not in bad shape. Our troubles can be cured, but not from outside by Federal or other evangelists, nor from inside by ambitious politicians who denounce each other, promising anything and everything, sound or unsound, and undermine respect for us throughout the country.

Nor does our salvation lie in charter changes, charts and government gadgets. We cannot have an adequate modern municipal plant and more and better service at less cost and with lower taxes and charges. Our big departments are undermanned. Under Mayor Wagner, better salaries are being paid to top officials but our public employees generally are still underpaid and many are discouraged. We need more aggressive leadership in administration to match leadership in business, and a framework of public improvements in which private industry can flourish and people live decently.

City government is not ordinary business, nor is it mass production and efficiency engineering. We are not going to be streamlined and made self-liquidating by faceless experts in red neckties. The city belongs not to its detractors, but to those who love it. The most we can ask is that those who are honored by high office rise above their promises, pretensions and rivalries to the statesmanship which New York City deserves.

10

Government's Role
in Housing

MY INTEREST IN HAVING GOVERNMENT DO something about the housing problem goes back to 1921, when I was secretary of the New York State Association and editor of *The State Bulletin*. At that time we urged amendments to the state Constitution to permit the extension of state credit and to enable cities to engage more extensively in housing activities.

Under Governor Smith a State Housing Board was set up and some low-rent dwellings were built by limited dividend corporations which received tax exemption. Tax exemption for a given period was also used to stimulate low-cost housing in the twenties. The depression in the thirties put the Federal as well as the state and city governments into housing.

By that time I had become a member of the La Guardia administration and served on a committee, appointed by the Mayor and headed by former Corporation Counsel Paul Windels, which drafted the housing amendment to the state Constitution adopted by the people in 1938. I was a delegate to the Constitutional Convention and no one could have been more astonished than I was at what happened to our brain child. Beginning with a broad grant of powers couched in the fewest possible words, the amendment was blown up in the convention into a verbose, turgid dissertation half as long as the original Constitution of the United States and composed largely of purely statutory matter.

It is futile to debate at this late date whether the complexity of the problem, the staggering sums and the novel economic theories involved contributed to this flood of words, or whether we should blame it on delegates who, in the words of the French wit, were too busy to write a short constitution. The fact is that this was the best we could get, and those of us who felt strongly that something had to be done by the state and its municipalities to supplement Federal work on this problem were glad that the people accepted the amendment at the polls.

Housing and Recreation

As Commissioner of Parks and head of other government agencies, my interest in low-rent housing in New York City requires no explanation. There is no such thing as a sound recreation policy for New York or other large cities which is not based upon close coordination with slum clearance, low-rent housing, and indeed, housing or rehousing of every kind. Practically all major public improvements are vitally affected by housing programs. The notion that housing experts can function in a vacuum is absurd. Housing programs are the major physical problems of cities, and should engage a considerable part of the energies of all public officials.

The housing amendment adopted in 1938 definitely stated in the first section that its major purpose was low-rent housing, slum clearance, and recreational and other facilities incidental thereto, and the power of eminent domain was granted not only for these purposes, but was extended so that excess property may be taken and used for other public purposes, or sold or leased with restrictions, to preserve and protect the housing improvements.

Up to that time it had been the practice of all government housing agencies to leave out entirely various recreation, street, school, police, fire, utility, and other costs which had to be taken care of by the municipality or otherwise independently. In the Red Hook housing development, for example, the City of New York contributed a great deal of land for recreation, and all park and play facilities were provided out of relief funds and were not reflected in the housing costs. In an early Harlem project the city provided land for an adequate play area to service the entire neighborhood as well as the new housing.

At Williamsburg Houses the city built an entirely new school. At Queensbridge, the state contributed the old Barge Canal Terminal for recreational purposes and the city, with relief funds, built a new bulkhead. The costs of such essentials were not included in the housing costs, although they belonged there. The same logic applied to the dedication by the city of streets incorporated in housing projects and to other expenses imposed by these developments.

There has been a great improvement since the first public housing experiments, but we still hear some of the old objections to using housing funds for other than actual construction of dwellings. Of course, the addition of such essentials costs more, but we should at least insist that all costs, direct and indirect, be published and be paid for out of new housing funds and not saddled on real estate or buried in false bookkeeping.

We should be honest with ourselves about subsidized public housing. The object is nothing more or less than to have the government give the family of low income rent at a third or less than the ordinary builder would have to charge. The subsidized tenant contributes not a nickel toward amortization, interest and taxes. The public pays for these so that the poor may have decent housing. Dress it up in any garments you please, deck it out in fancy phrases, this underlying fact remains unchanged, and we gain nothing by veiling it in transparent euphemisms. Still less is accomplished by the charge that the speculative builder and owner are wicked fellows who live on usury. This argument leads straight to Russia, where a benevolent government houses everyone miserably.

SELECTION OF HOUSING SITES

In the early days of public housing in New York a queer notion developed that the selection of sites should be a great mystery and that only a few insiders of unimpeachable honesty and vast knowledge in the most intimate official and unofficial housing circles should do the picking. Not only was there no sense in this notion, but it was positively dangerous. It is no doubt possible for shrewd and honest public officials to pick up, at prices far below assessed valuations, scattered pieces of real estate or options on them. They may even accomplish this without scandal. However, when a great municipal program is under discussion involving a number of large plots and many related public improvements, the only sensible procedure is to map these plots, invite full public discussion and acquire them by condemnation where the city does not already own, where it cannot foreclose and where it cannot buy the awards.

You cannot buy land to clear slums as though you were shopping for basement bargains. The future of entire neighborhoods is at stake, and there cannot be too much public knowledge of what is contemplated or too much airing of plans if general support is to continue and scandals avoided. The object in view, as I understand it, is to rebuild a large part of the community at great expense and under financial conditions justifiable only because of extreme emergency.

The new state housing amendment became effective on January 1, 1939. On November 22, 1938, I presented a proposed housing program before a gathering at the American Museum of Natural History, sponsored by the Citizens' Housing Council, the Park Association, the Metropolitan Association of Real Estate Boards, the New York Building Congress and architectural societies. The law permitted the State to make loans up to $300 million with subsidies up to $1 million a year. Cities were permitted to borrow up to 2 per cent of their real estate assessments and to grant tax exemption for public housing.

In a brochure, "Housing and Recreation," I proposed a city program that included ten projects to cost $195 million and five limited dividend projects to cost $90 million. All were genuine slum clearance projects and the sites proposed were later selected for housing.

SOME FALSE ASSUMPTIONS

Unfortunately, housing reform attracts crackpots and irresponsible enthusiasts almost as much as city planning, and sensible projects must run the gamut of hysterical attacks and insane criticism from perfectionists, day-dreamers and fanatics of a dozen breeds. In

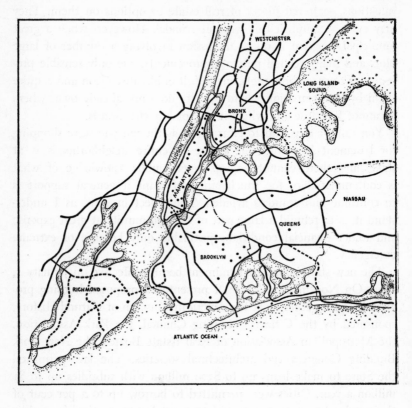

NEW YORK CITY METROPOLITAN AREA PARKWAYS, EXPRESSWAYS
AND MAJOR HIGHWAYS
*Dots show Major Housing Projects: Public,
Quasi-Public and Title I*

planning we need practical idealists who have roots in the soil, who know their town, who have limited objectives and can reach them without endless technical chatter.[19]

By 1945 housing and planning had become honeycombs which attracted the busy bees who look for a comfortable place to work and sweet pickings. Everyone wanted to become an expert over night. As a result, we were deluged with quick and easy remedies for age-old problems. There was a genuine emergency affecting the lives of many people, including homecoming veterans, but the housing shortage was neither overwhelming, nor tragic, nor beyond the capacity of well-balanced administrators. It called for intelligent, well-directed action, not for hysteria.

We were far in advance of the rest of the world in housing our people, and the standards we sought to impose were beyond anything which can be hoped for in 90 per cent of the rest of the world within our lifetime. We shall probably have to help to raise standards elsewhere if we expect to survive the jealousy and envy of millions of people who believe, rightly or wrongly, that we are committed to the policy of being our brother's keeper.

It was falsely assumed that everyone must have an absolutely modern house or apartment with all the latest plastics, gadgets, new materials, labor-saving and related devices. This may be the wish of many people, but it is not a necessity. There are many old-fashioned people who like their present homes, do not care to have them ultra-modernized, and who merely want to make the repairs and improvements which time and a somewhat higher standard of living justify.

The house in which I was born in New Haven was not new when my parents moved into it seventy years ago. It is still standing and apparently in good shape, and only a lunatic would think of tearing it down unless it is to make way for an apartment house or to disappear into the expanding Yale campus. There are houses, not only in the country but in suburbs and cities all over the United States, which are more than fifty years old and have close to a half-century of life before them on any reasonable assumption, and plenty of apartment houses twenty-five or thirty years old which will be neither decayed nor obsolete thirty years from now.

There are not enough of such dwellings, and the continuing housing shortage must be supplied by one or another of four forces or combinations of them. First comes public housing for persons of low income who cannot get decent homes without government aid, not only in the form of loans at low interest rates and partial or complete tax exemption but also in the form of direct annual subsidies. Generally speaking, such housing involves slum clearance directly or indirectly, by actually clearing substandard areas or by drawing people out of them into new suburban buildings.

The cheap money for slum clearance, tax exemption, subsidies, and for schools, parks, widened streets and other services may come from the Federal, state or municipal governments or from a combination of them. But many states have been unable or have refused to provide such funds and many municipalities cannot afford them because they are too near their tax and debt limits. In such a situation the burden is bound to fall mainly on the Federal government.

New York's Slum Problem

New York City's housing problem is, of course, a special case, because of the overcrowding in deteriorated areas, the high cost of land, the influx of population in the lower income brackets, and the difficulty of relocating slum tenants. Yet New York City has done more than any other community to improve housing. It has been helped by both the Federal and state governments, but the city itself has expended enormous sums for the same purposes.

Originally government aid to housing was supposed to apply only to the lowest income groups, but there is great need for rehousing large numbers of people who are not eligible for subsidized housing, but who cannot be provided with decent housing by private builders at rents they can afford to pay. To meet this situation, the city embarked on a program providing for non-cash subsidy housing. The city also sought authority from the state Legislature to permit it to lend up to 90 per cent of the cost of cooperative limited-dividend projects. This power was not immediately granted and, in lieu of this, the Mayor proposed nine projects to provide 10,425 units costing $154,307,000, to rent for fifteen dollars a room.

By 1955 the New York City Housing Authority had rehoused 80,000 low-rent families in seventy-one public projects, and twelve new projects with 16,920 apartments were planned, making a total of ninety-two projects with 110,823 apartments to house upwards of half a million people. In the process 55,000 slum apartments were demolished, 1,200 acres of slums and blight were redeveloped, at a cost of a billion dollars. From the foregoing it is clear that New York City has taken a long lead in dealing with the problem of housing. With Federal and state aid, and city funds, the municipality has, since 1934, subsidized public housing for half a million people, while thousands of additional families have been rehoused in projects that have received governmental help in one form or another.

The FHA type of government aid, which consists of guaranteeing a substantial part of bank or other loans for rehabilitation or construction, proved a sound method, despite some of the abuses that have since come to light. Obviously, if the Federal government will guarantee 100 per cent of a loan on a liberal appraisal, the local banks and loan associations will be less disposed to question the applicant closely.

The Role of Cooperative Housing

Cooperative housing also deserves recognition for the lasting contribution it has made to the practical replanning and rebuilding of New York City. The cooperatives have demonstrated that all urban slum clearance and redevelopment need not be 100 per cent publicly financed, subsidized, owned and operated. They ask of government the minimum needed to wipe out swollen assessments and fictitious values of deteriorated real estate, and have contributed generously and boldly to repair the mistakes, the selfishness and the inhumanity of earlier generations more concerned with profit than with healthful living.

The Amalgamated housing projects in New York City are outstanding examples of such cooperative efforts. The early success of Amalgamated dwellings was largely due to the personal interest and efforts of Senator Herbert H. Lehman and Mr. Aaron Rabinowitz. Mr. Abraham E. Kazan has been the working genius of these projects since their inception in 1926. The Amalgamated Clothing Workers of America, later combined with the International Ladies' Garment Workers, the United Housing Foundation and the Edward A. Filene Goodwill Fund have through their cooperative efforts constructed 12,310 dwelling units in the city, helping tremendously in clearing slums and providing decent homes for workers at low cost.

Here is a record of over a quarter of a century of steady, genuine, undeniable progress. The bright, eager critics of our slum clearance never mention such successes. Critics build nothing. They live on mud-throwing and false, garbled statistics. They claim the net result of all our housing works is fewer apartments, which is false; that we put too many people on an acre but not enough of them, that our buildings are too high, but too few, that we should build only on vacant land on the outskirts of the city and fix up the slums with rubber bands, scotch tape and violations, crucifying all landlords, tearing up mortgages, and reducing rents.

ALL SLUMS MUST GO!

At the dedication of Baruch Houses on the lower East Side of Manhattan, on August 19, 1953, I took advantage of the presence of President Eisenhower, Governor Dewey and Mayor Impellitteri to plead for the courageous, clean-cut, surgical removal of all of our old slums. By old slums I mean all the rundown rabbit warrens where unfortunate people are compelled by circumstances beyond their control to live in uninhabitable structures built by conscienceless speculators before we had adequate tenement legislation.

I am against phoney compromises, however labeled, which look to patching up a few buildings here and there, whether such schemes originate with landlords and realty operators or with tired reformers reduced to a counsel of despair. There can be no real neighborhood reconstruction, no superblocks, no reduction of ground coverage, no widening of boundary streets, no playgrounds, no new schools, without the unflinching surgery which cuts out the whole cancer and leaves no part of it to grow again, and spread and perpetuate old miseries.

New York City cannot do this job alone. We need further state and Federal help. This is no sidewalk problem to be solved locally. The annual Puerto Rican invasion alone proves this. We are still willing to make room for newcomers who seek a better life in a city which has traditionally been host to your "tired, your poor, your huddled masses yearning to breathe free."

Unfortunately, cuts by Congress in 1954 indicated a deplorable resurgence of hardboiled reactionaries to whom acreage is more important than people. For three centuries, as each wave of immigration has deposited newcomers on these shores, those inland and of slightly earlier importation and shorter memories have shrilled or muttered that the whole country is being engulfed by strange foreigners who cannot be absorbed. And yet we have absorbed them all, and there will somehow still be room for more.

There must, however, be limits to heavily subsidized public slum clearance housing. Many of us prefer aid to private capital through every legitimate device—federal guarantees of a fair return which enable builders to get bank loans; exercise of the power of eminent domain to assemble lots in many ownerships; writing down land costs to cover old buildings which must be sacrificed; partial real estate tax reductions and subsidies; and assistance on related public improvements. All these aids are better than straight public housing, but public housing will for some time also be required for displaced persons of low incomes.

Broadening the State Housing Laws

Following the state housing laws of 1938, initial efforts were made to induce private capital to enter the housing field. Legislation was enacted under which insurance companies, and later savings banks, could invest equity money in housing projects. It was under this law that the Metropolitan Life Insurance Company built Parkchester in The Bronx, and later constructed Peter Cooper Village in Manhattan. These projects pay full taxes to the city.

The Urban Redevelopment Corporations Law was enacted in 1941, but failed to attract lending institutions. This was followed in 1942 by the Redevelopment Companies Law. This legislation was later amended and paved the way for the construction by the Metropolitan

Life Insurance Company of Stuyvesant Town in Manhattan. As the representative of Mayor La Guardia, I had a part in inducing the Metropolitan to undertake this project.

Unfortunately, a controversy arose over the question of the owners' right to select tenants to be housed in a project that was to enjoy tax exemption and for which the city used the power of condemnation to clear the site. This controversy brought on a series of law suits, and passage by the city of an antidiscrimination law, the effect of which was to discourage other lending institutions from entering the housing field. This situation continued until Queensview, a cooperative project in Queens Borough, was built.

Having sponsored Stuyvesant Town, I found myself in the midst of this controversy. My conclusion about the racial issue is that while Mr. Ecker, then active head of the Metropolitan, was an exceedingly able, experienced, shrewd, hard-boiled, conservative gentleman, he had some poor advisers, and that the company management needed more of the milk of human kindness and needed also to keep abreast of the times.

While no tax exempt housing projects were built for several years, a number of large projects were constructed in New York by insurance companies and lending institutions, with incidental help from the city. Several of these developments were excellent in themselves, but did little to clear slums and redevelop blighted areas, or to rehouse people of low or medium incomes.

The Tenant Relocation Problem

Relocation of tenants in dwellings to be demolished for new housing, and for other public improvements, is one of the most serious problems relating to slum clearance, especially in New York City. There has been considerable discussion and some controversy over this matter. As a member of the City Planning Commission, I subscribe to the majority views of that body, as set forth in a report issued on January 20, 1954.

In the early stages of the housing shortage, tenants on project sites were merely given notice to vacate after the property had been acquired and were required to find new accommodations unaided.

Since that time various methods have been adopted to prevent hardship and the city has established the policy that tenants may not be evicted from the site of a public improvement unless and until quarters comparable to those occupied are available.

The New York City Housing Authority set up a Tenant Relocation Office to help residents and other tenants to find quarters. A first use of such an office was in clearing the site for Stuyvesant Town, where three thousand families were moved in nine months. Later legislation was secured which permitted the moving of houses to other sites acquired by the city. Still another measure was the payment of cash bonuses of $300 to $500 to families able to rehouse themselves. The New York City Housing Authority administers the relocation on all public housing sites—city, state and Federal.

Tenant relocation for privately financed slum clearance housing projects, authorized under Title I of the National Housing Act of 1949, is the responsibility of the sponsor. Residential tenant relocation for such projects is governed by a Federal law, in addition to the city policy, and tenants must be relocated in decent, safe and sanitary dwellings, reasonably convenient to their place of employment. Those eligible for public housing have a definite priority, equal to that of veterans, in public housing projects.

The policies and measures under which New York City has handled the relocation problem have been of interest to other communities and have served as a model in some cases. There has been controversy, and some well-meaning people have put forth impractical schemes, but no one has yet suggested a way to clear slums without dislocating people.

New Federal Housing Laws

While great progress was made in New York City in the decade following the first housing amendment to the State Constitution, the continuing housing shortage became even more critical following World War II. An increase in the marriage and birth rates, the demands of returning veterans and an increase in population, including the inflow of large numbers of families of low income, aggravated the situation.

As Chairman of the Mayor's Emergency Committee on Housing, I presented a report and recommendations to Mayor O'Dwyer which was sent by him to the Joint Committee on Housing in Congress on November 12, 1947. At that time it was indicated that there were some 140,000 families in New York City still housed in substandard dwellings. Two years later I became Chairman of the Mayor's Committee on Slum Clearance Plans, in anticipation of legislation then before Congress which later became known as Title I of the National Housing Act of 1949.

This legislation represents a realistic effort of the Federal and municipal governments jointly to attack large-scale slum clearance by private capital. The inducements offered are condemnation of land, writing down the cost of land and other aids. The "write down" is for the purpose of bringing the cost of land to a point where it is economical for private interests to build and in most cases represents roughly the cost of useless buildings that must be torn down, including their demolition and the orderly removal of tenants. The public gains by rebuilding of entire cancerous neighborhoods on the basis of forward-looking plans and high standards of construction and increased taxable values by reason of the new improvements. The Federal authorities initially set aside $16 million toward the write off and the City of New York allocated $8 million for its share in the first projects. The Federal government advanced the necessary funds for studies.

We promptly issued two short progress reports, and on January 22, 1951, presented seven booklets or prospectuses each describing in more or less detail a specific project in a definite area and outlining the kind of conditions to be imposed to invite definite offers by responsible private groups. We conferred with such groups and in several instances they agreed to bid on the sites selected.

THE FIRST TITLE I PROGRAM

This field was still new, untried and experimental and the initial procedure was necessarily slow and cumbersome. Neither Federal nor municipal funds were available in sufficient volume to do more than blaze the way for a larger future program. New York City's problem can be measured by the acres of recognized slums which cannot be eradicated by ordinary, private, speculative building. The slum acreage was then over nine thousand. Obviously, private capital, under the new Federal law, must be brought into the picture on a large scale if we hoped to escape a tremendously enlarged public housing program, with all its implications. Yet, for various reasons, those representing large reservoirs of private capital in banks, insurance companies, real estate and building enterprise were hesitant to take a lively interest in slum clearance by private capital. The risks as well as possible rewards are considerable.

Seven proposed projects were submitted by January 1951, and several others quickly followed. These were presented in separate, attractively printed booklets, with air photographs, maps, architects' drawings and technical material. By 1955, the Title I Redevelopment Program in New York City totaled nineteen projects, including four under way and six which had been approved. These projects will provide 27,614 units renting at from $20 to $45 a room and will cost $131,506,134. Other projects are being studied.

In the fall of 1955 the Federal Housing Administration, after long delays, made its first commitment for a government-insured mortgage for a private project under Title I of the Federal Housing Act. This was for Delano Village in north Harlem. It should mark the start of a billion-dollar urban renewal program which can be carried out in the next five years. With this kind of Federal cooperation we can go ahead with several large projects already well advanced and complete plans for many others. However, we were still waiting for further help from Washington and Albany on the subsidized public housing program.

Only Federal and state aid to cities, plus private and quasi-public credit and cooperation can possibly eradicate genuine slums and hopeless obsolescence and reclaim midtown urban decaying neighborhoods. The present administration at Washington, under incessant pounding by reactionaries in Congress, has failed to come to grips with this problem. The states, often dominated by rural interests and by groups fearful that government may become the landlord of increasing numbers of low-income tenants enjoying superior shelter at the expense of full taxpaying groups, are backing away from public housing.

Cities simply cannot afford to do the job alone. Private and semiprivate capital has been frightened away from this risky field by lurid windfall charges, often exaggerated, and by uncertainty as to the powers and responsibilities of private management. It is not a good picture, but one which can still be improved by statesmanship at all levels and aroused public opinion made manifest at elections.

11

Institutions and the City

AMERICAN CITIES HAVE NEVER RANKED WITH PARIS
and other foreign capitals as art and cultural centers, yet I think we
are making progress. The problems are partly, but not entirely, financial. Baron Haussmann replanned Paris not merely as the capital
of France but as the cultural capital of Europe. The great museums
in other capital cities are largely supported by national governments.
Our cultural institutions owe their existence to private initiative
and support, with what help the municipalities can afford.

There have been great men in the history of New York's museums.
The second and third generation of Morgans, Davisons, Osborns,
Roots, Rockefellers, Webbs, Fricks, Blums and others now appear on
the roster. The founders of the older museums were strong-minded,
opinionated, dictatorial men with a curiously one-sided sense of
public obligation. All the larger American cities had them—mostly
new millionaires determined to show that they could bid Duveen
more per square inch of canvas and cubic inch of marble or bronze
than any European competitor. We owe them much, however. They
bargained better than they knew, and we can now sift out and re-
arrange the loot. Those who inherit what they collected and hoarded
should never forget it. Nevertheless, it is a new day, and youth and
the times must be served.

Years ago, when many of her now famous institutions were
founded, New York's contribution was usually limited to providing

sites. These were mostly in parks or on land that was later put in that classification. The city remains the landlord, and that is why the New York Commissioner of Parks is ex-officio a member of the controlling boards of the public museums and other cultural institutions. The Park Commissioner also has more or less responsibility for the city funds that now go into construction, repairs and the maintenance of grounds. These sums, while far from adequate, are considerable. Each institution has its own method of handling endowments and gift funds, but the city contributes from one-fourth to three-fourths of the total annual outlays.

An Early Appraisal of Museums

When I became Park Commissioner, and ex-officio a member of a number of such public institutional boards, I soon learned that the city's representatives were not expected to attend board meetings. If they did appear they were supposed to be seen and not heard, and any show of critical interest would have been regarded as presumptuous. Such an intrusion was prevented by having the real business transacted by executive committees, from which public representatives were omitted.

In a report to Mayor La Guardia appraising the situation, I pointed out that it was a mistake for a public official to concede that there is something occult, esoteric or sacred about these institutions. In the atmosphere in which the trustees had surrounded themselves, not only public officials but the public generally had become intimidated by the vast treasure in their vaults and halls. When Napoleon told his soldiers in Egypt that forty centuries looked down on them, he intended that they should be impressed, not overcome.

My early report merely pointed out important tendencies and problems in language which a layman, thrust into the midst of experts and specialists, could write and the average citizen understand. The problems were obvious. Fewer and fewer philanthropists were appearing on the horizon, eager to further the cause of art and science and to perpetuate their names in stone, art, bronze, armor, ceramics, heads, loins, hoofs, century plants, or other more or less durable media.

As great patrons became scarce, expenses grew heavier, and tastes changed. All the institutional trustees talked about broadening the base of contributions. The broadest base, of course, is the public treasury. Realization of their greater ultimate dependence on the city treasury finally brought a change in outlook and policy. After some years the Park Commissioner was beginning to be accepted as a necessary evil.

The late George Blumenthal, distinguished president and generous supporter of the Metropolitan Museum of Art, actually invited me to his mansion to give me caviar and brandy and the glad tidings that a representative of the Park Department would be admitted to the holy of holies. As I left Mr. Blumenthal's Spanish Gothic palazzo, I walked on air in a daze. I was actually an accepted ex-officio member of the governing committee of the Metropolitan Museum of Art!

THE CITY'S INCREASING CONTRIBUTION

With a change of attitude on the part of those who represent our public institutions has come increasing popular interest, and a more responsive and constructive effort on the part of city officials to foster and support the great public institutions. With the city's aid, a program of physical reconstruction of plants has been carried out and a completely new approach to the problems of exhibitions and public education has been adopted.

Early in 1954, the Metropolitan Museum of Art, renovated, rearranged and reborn, but still recognizable, had an auspicious reopening with distinguished international representatives of the fine arts as its guests. No great museum can, merely by ingenious interior decorating, be converted into a cozy little home gallery, but the reconstruction at the Metropolitan has done much to relieve institutional fatigue and substitute comfort and convenience. Visitors are no longer lost in cavernous depths.

Americans are supposed in some highly vocal but not necessarily well informed circles abroad to be so busy, so competitive, so furious in the pursuit of money, place and amusement, so frightened of repose and leisure, so lacking in mental resources, that the traditional fine arts are neglected, excite little public interest and have become the exclusive concern of a shrinking group of tired intellectuals. Looking about this great museum, in one of our oldest public parks, owing its new shell and its magnificent collections to a fortunate union of public support and private munificence and its management to independent and unfettered trustees, one must conclude that if we are not yet an old nation, we have at least achieved some measure of cultural maturity.

I take pride in the fact that in the distribution of limited funds among many needed and worthy purposes, New York City has aided the Metropolitan Museum to house a magnificent history of man's achievement in art. Here there is no philosophy to vindicate, no program to sell, no school to propagandize, only an oasis of beauty where only the proven best is admitted. The city is beginning to appreciate the sources of our artistic inspiration. Our museums now realize that it is no disgrace to put on a good show, and that a museum need not be dry, tiresome and boring to be great. Smaller communities throughout the country must look to large cities for such institutions, because every village cannot house a first-rate collection of paintings, or a modern, barless zoo, or a vast exhibit of natural history, a fine library or botanical collection.

ANOTHER LIVE MUSEUM

It is a mistake, however, to think that all of New York City's great institutions are in Manhattan. The Brooklyn Institute of Arts and Sciences is one of the most notable cultural institutions in the world. It has four divisions, all of them distinctive. Brooklyn Museum makes no attempt to rival the Metropolitan's collection of old masters and classical material, but it has one of the finest Egyptian collections in the Western Hemisphere, and the finest collections of American oils and watercolors in the country. It is another museum that has become thoroughly alive and up to date in all its various activities. It serves the whole city as well as Brooklyn. Not long ago the representatives of twenty-five nations, meeting under the Educational, Scientific and Cultural Organization of the United Nations, held meetings there which continued for a month.

The Brooklyn Botanic Garden, is also outstanding and the Brooklyn Children's Museum is unique. The Brooklyn Academy of Music, which houses the Educational Department of the institute, was purchased and rehabilitated by the city and turned over to the institute, which is one of the greatest forces in adult education and cultural activities in any democratic community.

INTEGRATING RELATED PLANS

The city's aid to public institutions has, in recent years, been extended to the replanning of areas in which their plants are located, and the integration of related improvements. Plans for the New York Botanic Garden provide a good illustration of such integrated planning. In 1954 we dedicated the reconstructed Lorillard Snuff Mill on the grounds of the garden, which is now in use as a restaurant and meeting place. This needed facility was made possible largely by the efforts of Mrs. Harold Irving Pratt, and was financed by funds from Mrs. Pratt and other private donors, the Botanic Garden and the city. Construction was also started on a new research laboratory, financed partly by the city and private funds, as a part of the garden's program of improvements.

The New York Botanic Garden shares the major part of Bronx Park with the New York Zoological Society. Dividing the two institutions is Fordham Road, with Fordham University to the south of the Botanic Garden. What we call the Fordham Improvement includes a comprehensive arterial plan affecting all the major arteries in the area, Fordham University, the hospital, Botanic Gardens, the Bronx Zoo and park.

The New York Zoological Society, which, with the aid of the city, has helped develop and maintain the famous zoos in Bronx Park and Central Park, also has a large program of betterment. The most dramatic feature of this plan is the new Aquarium at Coney Island, which will house the most comprehensive exhibition of aquatic life in the history of man.

In aiding cultural and educational institutions in such area replanning and redevelopment as the Fordham Improvement, the city makes no distinction between those supported wholly or partly by public funds and others. Fordham University and Hospital are

Catholic institutions. New York University is private in the sense that it does not receive public funds, yet the city has cooperated in two comprehensive programs of expansion for this noted educational institution.

In 1943, the Board of Estimate and New York University reached agreement on the joint development of the New York University-Bellevue Medical Center on Manhattan's East Side, as a step toward developing teaching and research in the field of medicine and the extension of adequate medical care of all groups of the city's people. The site covered all the ground between Twenty-Third and Twenty-Fifth streets, First Avenue and the East River. Separate understandings involving the Federal government, the city and the center covered the new Veterans Administration Hospital on the south corner of the tract.

Within this area the city agreed to convey and exchange lands, close streets, remove encumbrances, build an elevated ramp of the Franklin D. Roosevelt Drive, rebuild Bellevue Hospital and provide an Institute of Forensic Medicine as part of the center. Both parties pledged themselves generally to construct as rapidly as circumstances would permit. The trustees of the Medical Center have spent or obligated a total of $28 million. The city appropriated funds for correction of the worst conditions at Bellevue and $14 million for a new Nurses Home and Residence. The city has since authorized the large sum of $35 million in future city capital budgets to rescue Bellevue from obsolescence and keep the city's part of the bargain. A progressive community has no other choice.

We are perhaps too busy and too close to the excavations and skeletons of buildings in this area to realize what visitors from afar marvel at—the transformation of the Manhattan shore of the East River. Harmony is absent, but there can be no charge of lack of variety in style, mass and composition. In this great reconstruction it is significant that only a scant half mile of commerce separates the Parliament of Man from the Pool of Bethesda, both dedicated to the healing of the wounds of a troubled world.

There is a close relationship in medicine between teaching and practice. It dictates that schools and hospitals shall be integrated in modern quarters. We already had promising examples here in the cases of Presbyterian Hospital and Columbia University, New York and Memorial Hospitals and Cornell. Bellevue and New York University have followed, and the practice is to be extended to new centers in Brooklyn and The Bronx. These new medical centers mark another advance in the indispensable partnership between philanthropy and government, between school and clinic, between private trustees and public officials, between doctors and laymen.

OTHER TITLE I PROJECTS

The Washington Square Southeast, Title I, Redevelopment Project is another which will permit the expansion of New York University's facilities as well as replace blight with modern housing, parks and other improvements and benefit other educational institutions in the vicinity. It will also be favorably affected by larger plans for the Washington Square section.

In Brooklyn, the first two Title I Redevelopment projects will permit the expansion of important institutions and enhance their environment while modern dwellings will replace obsolescence. One of these projects centers around Pratt Institute, one of the outstanding schools of the city, where a large area will be redeveloped, including new facilities for the institute. The Fort Greene project will permit the needed expansion of Brooklyn Hospital and Long Island University, replace slums with modern housing and enhance the Brooklyn Civic Center area, in which several other important educational institutions including Brooklyn Polytechnic Institute are located. All of our redevelopment plans, while providing modern housing and benefiting institutions related to them, will have community facilities which will serve larger areas and upgrade neighborhoods extending far beyond the boundaries of specific projects.

THE NEW YORK COLISEUM

The need for a commodious, flexible, modern exhibition hall in New York City has been recognized for many years, and in 1946 the state legislature assigned to the Triborough Bridge and Tunnel Authority the responsibility for providing such a structure. The facilities to be provided by this great $30 million structure are expected to encourage many new groups to schedule their expositions in New York where their members may take advantage of the unique cultural, entertainment and business advantages which can be found in no other place.

By agreement between the city and the Triborough Bridge and Tunnel Authority, the city agreed to acquire a two block area at Columbus Circle in the heart of Manhattan under Title I of the Federal Housing Act, and to transfer the easterly portion to the Authority. The Authority in turn agreed to pay the city $2,182,000 for the site and $42,000 annually in lieu of taxes plus all income in excess of a net of $1,225,000. The remainder of the master block will be improved with two modern apartment buildings constructed by private capital. Litigation initiated by an opponent of the clearance program on the westerly portion of the bloc, proposed for housing use, carried the case through the lower courts, the State Court of Appeals, to the United States Supreme Court, and delayed the acquisition of the property by the city until November 17, 1953. The site was then transferred to the Authority. The litigation held up all planning, the removal of tenants and other action by the Authority for eight months. However, demolition was promptly started when legal obstacles were removed and construction was soon under way.

THE UNITED NATIONS HEADQUARTERS

The successful effort in inducing the United Nations to locate their headquarters in New York, and the contribution of the city toward providing a suitable site are, of course, the most significant developments of their kind in our time. As a result, New York became the Capital City of the World, although its status otherwise is merely that of a municipality severely limited as to its borrowing, taxing and other powers.

The United Nations made its temporary headquarters within the borders of New York City and in neighboring Nassau County long before Manhattan was selected as its permanent home. The original Headquarters Committee of the United Nations considered several possible sites abroad and in a number of states here. Mayor O'Dwyer appointed a committee, of which I was chairman, to make a plan for a world capital to be located at Flushing Meadow Park.[20]

We appointed a board of design composed of distinguished engineers and architects to prepare a plan which called for the use of most of the park area formerly occupied by the World's Fair and a generously landscaped setting for the United Nations buildings. In submitting this plan to the United Nations, Mayor O'Dwyer offered to donate the site with all of its existing improvements, add others and provide contiguous ones without cost to the United Nations. He also assured the United Nations of full tax exemption and an international, extraterritorial status.

The Mayor did not instruct his committee to enter into a competition for the new world capital, although we believed that New York, with its extraordinary history as a melting pot and its many international interests, was the logical location. We were instructed to offer the best the city had, to present the advantages of our site without embarrassing pressure and undignified ballyhoo, to furnish temporary headquarters, if they were wanted, irrespective of the place of the permanent ones, and to supply housing for the United Nations' delegates and staff.

A remote, self-contained, residential world capital like Canberra, New Delhi or the Vatican, covering thirty or forty square miles of virgin territory, seems to have been the goal of the original United Nations' Site Committee. We presented the obvious practical objections to this idea, and apparently they were persuasive. The debate which ensued over locating the capital in Europe as against the United States, in the suburbs as opposed to the city, and over a working as against a residential headquarters, was educational and cleared the air.

MR. ROCKEFELLER'S FINE GIFT

With the dramatic acceptance of the twenty-two acre midtown Manhattan site on the East River, the necessarily urban character of the United Nations year-round operation was agreed upon, and I doubt whether today any serious person would challenge it. While I still believe that the original plan of establishing the United Nations at the site of the old World's Fair in Flushing Meadow Park would have been ideal, where many of the problems of congestion, traffic, parking and utility rearrangements could have been avoided, this question has been settled and no good purpose is served by laboring it further.

Mr. John D. Rockefeller Jr.'s offer to buy most of the land between First Avenue and the East River from Forty-Second to Forty-Eighth streets, at a cost of more than $8 million, and to give it to the United Nations was contingent upon the city's cooperation. Missing parcels of land which could not be purchased had to be condemned, and a number of other conditions met. Specifically these included the closing of the blocks between Forty-Second and Forty-Seventh streets east of First Avenue, a grant of the exclusive rights for the waterfront and land under water opposite the United Nations site, transfer of the city playground north of Forty-Second, widening and reconstruction of First Avenue—including a through-traffic tunnel—zoning changes, tax exemption, transfer of the City Housing Authority building to the United Nations at actual cost of construction, and granting of an easement over Franklin D. Roosevelt Drive. The total cost of New York City's initial contributions was estimated at $26 million.

In exchange, the United Nations agreed to pay for the reconstruction of Franklin D. Roosevelt Drive, to transfer to the city a strip of property thirty feet wide on the east side of First Avenue between Forty-Second and Forty-Seventh streets and forty-five feet wide between Forty-Seventh and Forty-Eighth streets and to construct its buildings in accordance with the general structural, safety and fire-prevention standards of the city. Adequate parking and garaging facilities on the site were asked by the city. It should be borne in mind that the $65 million spent by the United Nations within the site represents a loan from the United States. With Mr. Rockefeller's gift of $8 million and the city's contribution of $26 million, the United States' investment in the new world capital therefore amounts in all to $100 million. Even with these funds, the United Nations' strained finances forced postponement of the large Agencies Building planned for the northerly section of the site.

OTHER HELP BY THE CITY

In addition to its own work on the outskirts and on access and approaches, the city did everything possible to cooperate and assist the United Nations staff in carrying on work within the headquarters site. We have given our advice about the operation of places within the site where the public is admitted, particularly in those landscaped areas where proper design insures quiet and orderly enjoyment by delegates, staff and visitors, and prevents crowding, disorder and vandalism. It should be noted that there are peculiar but by no means insoluble problems involved in the limited use of an extra-territorial park in the heart of the city but not policed by municipal forces.

Help from the city came from many sources. The Borough President of Manhattan undertook to redesign and reconstruct, at the expense of the United Nations, a long stretch of the East River Drive in accordance with the United Nations' plan to build out over the roadways to the water's edge. This involved ripping out the former viaduct which was only a few years old, substituting a roadway closer to the water's surface and rearranging complicated access. During the organization and construction period, the city offered the United Nations its permanent City Building on the old World's Fair site for meetings of the Assembly and Council. The city also provided space at Hunter College in The Bronx which was used for the first meetings of the Council before transfer to the larger temporary quarters at Flushing Meadow Park, and persuaded a group of savings banks to build an entire low-rental housing project, known as Parkway Village, fronting on the Grand Central Parkway in Queens County for U.N. personnel. The city and the County of Nassau cooperated in parkway and highway improvements at the city line to afford better access to Lake Success.

THE FIRST AVENUE IMPROVEMENT

In addition to the work done directly for the United Nations, the city undertook on its own to build extensive improvements in the vicinity of the permanent site, the cost of which has been included in the $26 million previously mentioned. The United Nations is located between the East River Drive, which is restricted to pleasure vehicles, and First Avenue, which carries marginal Manhattan truck traffic. The roofing of the East River Drive shields the United Nations from riverfront automobile traffic, and in order to create a dignified and quiet plaza on the First Avenue side in front of the site, the city bore the whole expense of the new tunnel for through traffic. This tunnel occupies a place that was filled with every conceivable kind of piping and conduits, and the cost of moving these around before construction could start in earnest was almost $2 million. Subsequent tunneling cost about $5 million.

As a section of the park between Forty-First and Forty-Second streets was needed for tunnel construction, this recreation area had to be revamped. The old garages on each side of Forty-Second Street at the lower level of First Avenue were torn out and replaced by parks and the high walls supporting Tudor City covered with granite facing to make an attractive setting. The narrow tunnel between First and Second avenues on Forty-Second Street was demolished and a hundred-foot-wide avenue has taken its place. Half of the long block from Second Avenue to the United Nations was torn down to widen Forty-Seventh Street, thus creating an imposing approach.

SOME OF THE CRITICISM

A few critics, native and foreign, have charged that the city's approaches and adjacent improvements lacked scope, vision, beauty and generosity. Some of these criticisms, of course, came from speculators, some from perfectionists who are not concerned with budgets and costs, and some from disappointed architects and planners not officially identified with the project. We make no apologies for our plans, either as to scope or content. We strained our resources to the utmost, and we did not use the United Nations as an excuse to rebuild Manhattan.

It is easy for idealistic planners, homegrown or from abroad, to draw pretty pictures of a magnificent Champs Elysées approach to the United Nations site beginning at Park Avenue, replete with piazzas, arcades, tree-lined vistas and statuary, and of a great park across the East River in the Borough of Queens flanked by low-cost housing. Our own city officials and consultants made just such sketches, and they were abandoned because of the huge costs and the necessary dislocations and removals of people and business establishments. There is a serious constitutional question whether the taking of large, modern office buildings for a glorified approach is a public purpose.

New York has, of course, benefited greatly from its investment. Property values in the area have doubled. The United Nations has brought much color, life and intellectual stimulus to our city. It has helped to revive and rehabilitate a large blighted area. It is educating us in world problems, and lifting attention above our own. The problems of accommodation of foreign tastes, habits, needs and points of view are not serious here in New York. We are used to such things. Early fears that racial, geographical, ideological and religious debates in the United Nations would cause unpleasant repercussions among our numerous ethnic, political, evangelical and intellectual groups have been proven quite unfounded. New York is too humorous, too tolerant, too well balanced and too well policed to allow any disturbances which would be an affront to our United Nations guests who are already an accepted part of our great population.

If ours is indeed to be permanently the world capital, let it be remembered that we are not without education for this role. Our hope is that in this favorable soil the United Nations may survive and flourish.

SOCIAL AND PHYSICAL PLANNING

Those who listen to the reforming and driveling of uplifters and beady-eyed, long-range urbanists would think that we have never progressed beyond scattered, uncoordinated projects unrelated to any central or area planning. As I have tried to show, we have plenty of integrated projects in New York, perhaps not on an ideal basis, but certainly on a scale undreamt of in other municipalities in the democratic world.

Many of these large projects have involved decades of steady, stubborn, undramatic adherence to extraordinarily complex and widespread programs. We have been realistic but persistent. As obstacles have arisen, and have had to be knocked down, surmounted or circumvented, we have rarely had a helping hand from the critics, detractors and planning experts who talk and write about over-all plans, the good society, decentralization, dispersion, ideal subdivisions and the country in the city.

We are not concerned merely with planning ordinary public improvements which every community must have. New York City, with its status as a municipality created by the state, with its limited taxing and borrowing powers, is called upon to help meet the extraordinary demands of great national and international institutions serving a public that extends far beyond her borders. The problems thus created are tremendous, but not insurmountable, if we approach them realistically and with determination.

12

A Philosophy
of Parks

AFTER A CENTURY OF FRANTIC EXPLOITATION, without vision or thought of the morrow, Americans have made a start toward the *rus in urbe*, the parklike town, which was the aim of the Greeks and the Romans, and is still our great objective today.

Man is the creature of his environment. His outlook on life is conditioned by what he sees from his windows. Most of his spare time is spent outdoors. All the seven ages of man use city parks at different hours. At the beginning and end of the human age-scale are vast numbers of children and older people who are not cooped up in kitchens, offices, stores and factories, who virtually live in the park system, and get as close to nature there as life in a big city will permit. The field of urban recreation borders on and overlaps many others, including highways and traffic, housing, planning and zoning, policing, disorder and crime, buildings and public works of all kinds, disease and health, education and aesthetics, and finally the vague but tremendously important fields of citizenship and pride of birth and residence.

The increasing need for and appreciation of parks has resulted in a tremendous development of recreational areas, in the form of national and state parks and reservations. There is still need for expanding and improving these facilities, for preserving what we can of unspoiled nature, and for multiplying open spaces. This need is especially felt in crowded, overbuilt cities, which through lack of foresight failed to reserve such land for parks and when it could have been made to contribute to urban values.

Because of this failure, it has become necessary to provide more breathing spaces readily accessible to metropolitan areas. Most of our old communities, however, including some of only modest size, are badly lacking in such amenities, and it is shocking to find that many brand new suburban developments, which are supposed to make a special appeal to families seeking open space, are not making adequate provisions for future needs for parks, playgrounds and recreation.

OUT OF THIRTY YEARS' EXPERIENCE

The New York State Council of Parks was established in 1924 to carry out a state park plan I prepared in 1922. At the same time the Long Island State Park Commission was created. I became the unpaid head of these agencies and in 1934 I became Park Commissioner of New York City under a law which permitted me to act as head of the state park system and to hold other related unsalaried offices in order to facilitate coordination of city and state park, parkway, arterial, bridge, reclamation, housing and related public planning and improvements. During the years we have been guided by the following concepts of the purposes of state, county and municipal parks:

State parks should be large reservations where many people can go without elbowing each other, with natural recreational features, whether beach front, woods or mountains. These areas should be within driving distance of cities and towns where people can go for a day or stay overnight, spend a week or enjoy a longer vacation. Water for swimming, fishing or boating is a number-one requirement. The development depends, of course, on the type of area but should be planned for simple recreation. County and town parks are for example fairly well developed in Westchester County, just over the New York City line. Here acreage should be greater than in congested cities but less than state parks. More and more these will be restricted to local residents and outsiders will have to pay larger entrance and parking fees or be excluded entirely.

City parks on the other hand should be small and numerous to serve all neighborhoods for periods of play and rest measured by hours, not days. This has been our approach to New York City's problems. It is much better, if a choice is forced on us, to acquire one block in a congested part of Manhattan than ten acres in the open area of Richmond Borough. Larger parks also serve neighborhood needs. A perfect example is Crotona Park in The Bronx, ringed around with ten marginal playgrounds, ballfields, and a swimming pool, which in the future will also have an indoor recreation center.

There can be no uniformly accepted standards to determine the adequacy of parks and playgrounds in a community. Acreage is an unsatisfactory measure of park needs. The Bronx, where it was easy years ago to acquire outlying lands, has the greatest total park area, but this does not mean that it has adequate recreational facilities, since there are still neglected and congested areas remote from the big parks and not as yet served by nearby local small parks and playgrounds.

Similarly there is no such thing as a standard, fixed relationship of park area to population. In practice the answer depends upon good judgment and intimate acquaintance with every neighborhood. A readily accessible small playground in a congested section may be of vastly greater importance to the health and welfare of the community than a distant park of large acreage, although both may ultimately be needed to solve the entire problem.

In another chapter, dealing with conservation and reclamation, is a brief account of the State Council of Parks and its work in developing the New York State park system. It is the story of a thirty-year battle against odds, but I feel that the fight has been won and hope that we will soon come to terms with any opposition that remains.

My first concern on becoming City Park Commissioner was to salvage and restore the rich heritage of New York City's open spaces. Elsewhere I have emphasized the importance of restoring the waterfront areas which are the city's greatest asset, from an industrial and commercial point of view as well as for recreation. With the growth of population and the increase in leisure, open public space is as essential to city people as decent housing.

The three La Guardia administrations, with their twelve years of crowded effort, were as a watch in the night in the lifetime of a great city, bearing in mind that no extensive program can be carried out in an old, settled community without prolonged effort and conflict. Yet we were able to do a lot in a comparatively short time because we received Federal and state aid and could put large numbers of people to work under competent direction on realistic plans. During those years some new conceptions as to city parks were developed, along with new approaches to old problems, new men and an entirely new spirit.

Our first job was to rehabilitate the old parks, which were in deplorable condition. Practically all the buildings were in need of immediate repair. Twenty per cent of the comfort stations were closed because parts of the plumbing were missing. The zoos were filthy firetraps. Fences, playground equipment, benches, steel bridges and other iron works were rusty from neglect.

The parks in the five boroughs had been administered by five Park Commissioners. Before taking office I had insisted on a complete reorganization, bringing all the parks into a single department under one commissioner. We were in the midst of the depression and a small group of technicians were attempting to plan relief work in the parks for 70,000 Civil Works Administration men, who were being paid $8 million a month from Federal funds. They were assumed to be Federal employees and no one accepted responsibility for getting work from them.

Following La Guardia's election, but before he took office, we surveyed every park and parkway area in New York City and developed plans for 1700 projects to employ 80,000 men. We spent $90 million for relief work in the city parks in 1934. This was the beginning of the transformation of the city parks and the expansion of the system from 119 to over 600 parks and playgrounds.

SOME OLD CONTROVERSIES

Of course we had our difficulties, mostly growing out of shifts in the Federal government's administrative policies. The Civil Works Administration, a 100 per cent Federal agency, went out of existence on forty-eight hours' notice in the spring of 1934, and the Temporary Emergency Relief Administration took over with funds provided 50 per cent by the Federal government, 25 per cent by the state and 25 per cent by the city.

New York City was given the status of a Forty-ninth State, with General Hugh Johnson as local WPA administrator. I had to put up a stiff fight with General Johnson and his successors to direct the work under my department but in the end we managed to get things done. This was made possible by insisting upon definite plans, carried out under competent technicians.

All of our troubles did not stem from Washington. In the larger program undertaken early in the La Guardia administration we had to do battle over a farflung terrain. The only land we acquired without difficulty for the expansion of the park system was around the waterfront. This land was made by pushing out bulkheads and filling, but we had to get rid of a lot of obsolete structures and eyesores, such as abandoned ferry terminals, old state barge canal terminals and swamps.[21]

The public was glad to have us fill up and transform such areas into parks and playgrounds, but public reaction to the removal of landmarks is a fascinating and astonishing study. It is possible to stir up sentiment for structures which mean nothing at all to the average citizen. On Riverside Drive we had quite a time combating the machinations of the Columbia Yacht Club, coal pocket owners and the U.S.S. *Illinois*, which attempted to hold up the entire West Side Improvement and Henry Hudson Parkway so as to remain at their old waterfront locations.

The Columbia Yacht Club was a private club, in which, of course, the rank and file of citizens never set foot. It had no architectural merit, paid little or no rent and occupied valuable city land on a permit obtained from complacent city officials. The coal pockets did not belong where they were on any theory. The U.S.S. *Illinois* was a sort of club for the State's Swiss Navy, and had a berth in the center of one of the most important grade crossing eliminations. We moved this ancient hulk uptown to a place where the parkway is elevated and had the devil's own time with the land sailors in the process. From the hullabaloo in the press, an outsider would have thought that we were laying impious hands on the Liberty Bell or the Ark of the Covenant itself.

Preserving Historic Landmarks

Nowhere was opposition to change so vociferous as in the rehabilitation and reconstruction of the older squares and historic mansions. We had some fine rows over such places. I do not know yet how we got away with the Bryant Park reconstruction with so little difficulty. Perhaps it was because people were sick of the constant digging up and exploitation of this area, and because it was a shambles when we took office. Most of these old squares required improvement because their original design no longer met present-day conditions, because neighborhoods had changed and because overcrowding, neglect and decay had made them little more than mud and dust bowls.

At Stuyvesant Square we ran into the bitter opposition of certain adjacent property owners, including hospitals of several denominations. They wanted quiet, and objected to our setting aside certain patches for active play. All this led to a lawsuit, in which the city never had a chance, but which did not necessitate much of a compromise. We had similar arguments in a dozen other quarters, notably at Washington Square, where we simply struck the improvements off our list and left the field to local residents to battle over for the time being. We now have a comprehensive plan for redeveloping this entire area and part of it is under way.

At Bowling Green we had little trouble, but there was a long, bitter controversy at the Battery, first over a proposed bridge to Brooklyn, which I favored instead of a tunnel. We lost this fight and have long since completed and are now successfully operating the Brooklyn-Battery Tunnel. I favored a bridge at a time when there were no funds for a tunnel. The facts are simply that a bridge would carry twice the amount of traffic, cost half as much as a tunnel and could have been built in half the time, and I do not think a bridge would have defaced the area or spoiled the view from the bay.

In this game, you take what you can get and make the best of it.

The battle over saving the old Aquarium, or Fort Clinton, raged over a long period, and in my view the bitterness was all out of proportion to the issues involved. Instead of the obsolete Aquarium, we are building a new Aquarium at Coney Island, and the Federal government has jurisdiction over the walls of the old fort. Meantime, Battery Park has been greatly enlarged, redesigned and restored.

At Herald Square, removal of the Sixth Avenue elevated structure gave us an opportunity to restore the old clock and bell ringers which used to grace the front of the Herald Building, and to bring back a charming memory of Old New York. Even this was not without its difficulties, because of opposition from business interests who foresaw that their advertising signs would be less conspicuous under the new plan. At City Hall Park we had a grand debate over the restoration, in the course of which we were accused of substituting for a lovely old village green a rigid, formal design resembling a bath mat or a pair of suspenders.

Real and Pseudo-Antiquities

Historic mansions have also given us headaches. Most citizens know little about architecture and have no idea of the difficulties of restoring old buildings, providing authentic period furniture for them, and running them as museums. They are, however, easy prey for patriots, architects and antiquarians. The fuss made over the so-called Marshall Mansion in Pelham Bay Park was astonishing. This was a boxlike house built after the Civil War, to which an imposing Greek façade had been added. There was nothing in it, and it had no history of consequence. It was just a roomy country home of a family of some means, and was of no earthly use for park purposes. Nevertheless there was a great deal of moaning at the bar when, after vandals had broken in and smashed up most of the interior, we finally took the building down and substituted park facilities. At no time could we get from our lyrical opponents a coherent statement as to what should be done with this mansion. Something about the old firetrap roused the deepest and wooziest statements of patriotism, home and auld lang syne.

We completely rebuilt Gracie Mansion, at tremendous expense, as a home for the Mayor. It was a fine house, not as old as most people thought, because it was not the original structure. We were lucky to escape having the old Prince House in Flushing moved into Flushing Meadow Park. It had interesting associations, but would have had to be moved in pieces. We dug up the stone out of which the old Gowanus House in Brooklyn was made and built something on a smaller scale which is supposed to look like the original, and Aymar Embury and the others who worked on it did a splendid job in restoring the Jumel Mansion.

I have no responsibilities of any kind in the matter of the Hamilton Grange, but Alexander Hamilton was a great figure, and his Grange may serve to remind coming generations of the extraordinary group that founded this nation. I believe I was the first person to suggest that the city acquire the Manhattanville College site for the expansion of the College of the City of New York. It occurred to me that Hamilton Grange nearby might find a place on the extended campus. It could be used as the office of a professor of American history, politics or government, or for some other working part of the college. I am hopeful that we will soon reach an agreement on this matter, and that the money for the project will be provided.

MONUMENTS, GOOD AND BAD

As has happened in other cities, New York has inherited some monstrosities in the form of monuments. We are also the legatees of some fine things. All of them have been subjected to the ravages of time and more or less unrestrained vandalism. Restoration and proper maintenance is a tedious and difficult process. There are more than five hundred memorials in the City of New York. They consist of old buildings, monuments, fountains, tablets, commemorative flagpoles and ornamental sculptures, and are distributed throughout the park system.

We have restored the outdoor art we inherited and made it as attractive as patient effort and limited resources would allow. As to new monuments, we have attempted to establish and adhere to principles and standards not previously recognized in the city. It is often difficult and sometimes impossible to explain to groups who have a memorial in mind that what they propose is undesirable or inappropriate. We have met this problem in large part not merely by criticism but by actively helping to design the proper thing. The Art Commission has been helpful in this effort, but these schemes first come to the Park Department and it is our task to steer enthusiasts in the right direction, often along roads they do not care to travel.

Our most comprehensive plan for the restoration of a group of genuine historic buildings is that for Richmondtown on Staten Island. This project, which is part of a larger program for a planned development in Richmond Borough, is the last opportunity left in New York City to preserve a sizable reminder of Colonial and Revolutionary days.

Our critics apparently have little appreciation of what has been done toward preserving such assets. We have not only advocated but accomplished more in this direction than has been done in recent years in any other city here or abroad. These things have been accomplished in spite of enormous difficulties and in the face of strong opposition, in meeting which we received little help from the wisest and most articulate conservationists, traditionalists and upholders of the historic, the picturesque and the artistic.

USES, AND ABUSES, OF PARKS

An early problem in relation to park administration came from groups which sought to hold religious services in conspicuous, centrally located areas in our parks at times when they were most frequented by the general public. We could not allow such meetings. However, permits are granted for general religious gatherings in suitable areas for use at hours when they do not interfere with scheduled recreational programs, when no damage is caused, no money is collected or circulars distributed. Easter morning services and other meetings are permitted under park regulations.

The Bill of Rights is the unique American wing of our Federal Constitutional structure in which its choicest treasures are kept. It is the immediate jewel of our political virtue which must be jealously guarded. The practical difficulties in the way are, however, formidable and sometimes strike blind spots in the average eye.

Obviously there should be public places where outdoor meetings can be held to discuss anything which can properly be discussed without inciting riots, interfering with traffic and recreation or pre-empting space required for other purposes. The notion that oratory is a form of recreation which should be permitted in any park area at any time is preposterous. Half the parks in a city would be destroyed in a short time on any such theory. Incidentally, the enforcement of such a rule might result in complete denial of free speech everywhere.

When I became Park Commissioner, the only well recognized places where outdoor public meetings and discussions were held were Union Square and Columbus Circle in Manhattan. I established central locations in other parks in all boroughs where such meetings could be properly policed. The plan has worked well. Our regulations as to permits were upheld by a court decision in 1946, when thirteen persons were convicted for exhibiting hostile placards in City Hall Park while Winston Churchill was entering City Hall for an official reception. The court held that meetings were not prohibited through our permit procedure.

Parks are of various sizes and designed for many uses. To my mind, the most useful are those with playgrounds. These, too, vary as to size and uses, but they serve the same general purpose and are the best answer to what is miscalled juvenile delinquency. Keep youngsters occupied in their spare time, give them plenty of elbow-room for play, stimulate competitive sports and half at least of the youth problem is solved. Competition is still the rule of American life, and in youth if not later, most of us are either competitors or spectators.

Playgrounds and athletic fields may not be the sole answer to the youth problem, but they are surely among them. I do not minimize the contribution to be made by doctors, welfare agencies, police and courts to the task of providing, under difficult urban conditions, a normal and happy childhood for all who can enjoy it. Above all, there is no substitute for good parents, good homes, and helpful religious and school influences. All the efforts of all concerned are needed, and we should therefore dissipate none of our energies in petty differences over method and procedure. The philosophers who say that the ills and wickedness of the modern world are visited first upon luckless children, may prove to be partly right. All I know is that in recreation we have an ally of proven worth.

In athletics a professional is one who makes money and an amateur is one who doesn't. There is no crime in earning a living by physical prowess and likewise nothing insidious about competing for the sake of exercise and good, clean sport without making a business of it. Many justly famous and beloved athletes have proudly worn professional uniforms. Many have aroused wholesome enthusiasm and have been a fine influence to youth. But the best of them count for little in comparison with the millions of amateurs.

There is room for both, but in the American scene the amateur athlete means more to us than the professional. If there were no paid athletes—which I for one should regret—our world would somehow survive, but if all our amateurs turned professional it would be a tragedy too deep for words and too devastating to contemplate. Waterloo, said the great Duke, was won on the playing fields of Eton. Our great battles will be won by the boys and girls who carry the membership cards of the Amateur Athletic Union and similar organizations, and to their best ability live up to their standards.

There is, to put it bluntly, more to the spirit of amateur sports than can be measured by the jaded, pot bellied, cynical, sideline, grandstand and bleacher kibitzers who care about nothing but blood, slugging and world's records. I am supposed to be a hard-boiled fellow in administration, but I am not ashamed to be an idealist about recreation, the great outdoors, conservation of public and human resources, honest competitive sports and fun for its own sake without cash inducements.

Amateur athletic competition teaches boys and girls to fight fair, to recognize the gap between eligibility and victory, to accept defeat with a grin and success without swelling, and to realize that in the long run the race is not always to the swift nor the battle to the strong. What pursuit teaches more? Where else can you find the spirit of comradeship and sportsmanship which prevails at every amateur track meet? Where else do you see the unselfish, spontaneous delight of seasoned pole vaulters when a college freshman for the first time clears fourteen feet? Where else is there so little attention paid to race, creed, color, money, origin and the extraneous considerations which often mar our democratic way of life?

No professional sport, not even golf and baseball, does this. The best you can say of most professional athletics is that the performers are faster, more skillful and better trained. They have turned fun and exercise into serious business and a livelihood. On the other hand, professional sport rarely approaches amateur standards of conduct. Gladiators cannot waste much time on the niceties of life. I am not squeamish, but I still get a little nauseated when I read that a professional ball player has been sold down the river to another club. It reminds me faintly of Uncle Tom's Cabin.

If I were a trustee of one of the big foundations, I would endow institutions like Boys Clubs sufficiently to make their future secure, but not so generously that they would not have to pass the hat annually among thousands of supporters of relatively small means. That would be a lot better than pouring money into abstruse studies, fantastic research projects, global remedies and unreadable reports on juvenile delinquency, euthenics, Kinsey confessions and the incidence of flat chests in three-dimensional photography. Instead of contributing toward a research program in juvenile delinquency, why not give substantial sums for the expansion of healthy sports and to its allies such as the Scouts, the Y's, the K. of C., the 4-H clubs? This would accomplish immeasurably more in reaching the problems of youth at their source. A foundation could demonstrate that two hundred more city park playgrounds and a dozen indoor centers properly placed would do more for youth than all the police, courts, and probation officers put together.

A LAW TO CURB VANDALISM

One of our toughest problems in operating the New York City park and playground system and protecting the people who use it is vandalism by children. By this, I do not mean merely normal wear and tear of equipment and landscaping, but deliberate and wilful acts of destruction. Vandalism in our city has reached alarming proportions. Not only is damage done to city property, but lack of control over a minority of troublemakers makes many areas unsafe for the great majority of well behaved children and respectable parents. Vandalism is rampant not only in parks but in schools, where much property is destroyed, and it is conservatively estimated that the damage to public structures amounts to a million dollars a year. Teachers cannot replace parents. Vandalism goes way beyond healthy exuberance and the untamed spirit of 1776. There is a recognizable distinction between a Junior Hopalong Cassidy and an incipient Joe Adonis.

At my request the Park Association of New York City in 1952 retained Henry Epstein, former State Solicitor General and later Deputy Mayor, to draft the following law which we hoped would help to curb this growing menace:

The parent, guardian or other person having custody of a child under the age of sixteen years, who omits to exercise reasonable diligence in the control of such child to prevent such child from becoming guilty of juvenile delinquency as defined by statute, where such delinquency constitutes the wilful destruction of property of the City of New York, may be fined an amount commensurate with the damage done, but in no case to exceed the sum of $25.00.

Up to 1955, such a law had failed of adoption, and vandalism continued unchallenged because there are influential dreamers, inferior court judges who have read too many books, and pliant politicians who claim that the evil can be controlled by the police, the courts and the schools.

Neighborhood recreation facilities are now constructed as accepted parts of major public improvements. Our parkways are, in fact, shoestring parks with foot paths, bicycle paths, waterfront promenades, bordering active recreation areas. The new Federal-state-city expressway system for mixed traffic, under construction in Manhattan, The Bronx, Queens and Brooklyn, is patterned after the parkways and will provide additional parks and play spaces as well as landscaping along its borders. The Brooklyn-Queens Expressway, for example, in the short stretch from Battery Tunnel to the Navy Yard will have twenty-one parks and play areas. Similar incidental park and landscaped areas have been provided by the Triborough Bridge and Tunnel Authority.

Forty-one neighborhood playgrounds have been constructed as part of public housing projects. Others are under way. All are located so as to provide recreation for the surrounding community as well as for residents of the projects. It is now standard policy to acquire large enough playgrounds adjacent to public schools to be jointly operated by the Board of Education and the Department of Parks, by the former during school hours and by the latter for community use after school hours. The kindergarten section is open at all times for mothers and preschool children under Parks supervision.

AN EXAMPLE OF COORDINATED PLANNING

The Brooklyn Civic Center plan includes thirty-four separate and distinct projects. It was, however, a basic consideration in the over-all plan that open spaces add as much to the attractions and advantages of city life as the structures themselves. Each superblock of this tremendous development includes a park, or is parklike in plan. The north section of Cadman Plaza has been reconstructed as a setting for the War Memorial, which is used for recreation. The south section will be greatly enlarged in the construction of various civic buildings and provide focal points of many civic, housing and commercial structures.

PRIVATE AID IS NEEDED

Many needed facilities for which city funds were not available have been provided by generous private citizens. Outstanding examples are the Wollman Memorial, an artificial iceskating rink in Central Park, the gift of Miss Kate Wollman. The Loeb family provided a model yacht boathouse, and an anonymous donor gave the city a chess and checkerhouse, also in Central Park. The Friedsam Foundation donated two merry-go-rounds, one in Central Park and the other in Prospect Park, Brooklyn, complete with prancing horses and the traditional organs.

Anyone who preserves and adds to the city's open spaces is its benefactor. I was greatly entertained by a pronouncement of one of the candidates in a recent campaign that upon his elevation to City Hall there would be many more public concerts in and out doors, continuous picturesque carnivals featuring the costumes of romantic lands abroad, fiestas, general gaiety, dancing in the streets, etc. Actually there is no other city today which has as much public music and dancing, largely contributed by generous citizens, not to speak of private and semipublic theaters, concert halls and similar entertainment.

There may be nothing more beautiful than sweeping, well-clipped lawns and handsome background planting, but people today more and more require and demand active recreation areas. Athletic fields have been constructed in a number of New York parks, including 530 baseball and softball fields and many football, soccer and cricket fields. There are eighteen running tracks in various parks. Large areas have also been developed for picnicking, with fire places, tables, benches and concessions for food and charcoal. Many miles of bicycle and bridle paths have been laid out, and we have golf links and tennis courts.

INDOOR RECREATION CENTERS

Next in importance to small neighborhood playgrounds are adequate neighborhood indoor play centers for year-round organized recreation. Many outdoor areas are not usable in the late fall and winter, and their program has necessarily been curtailed because of the limited space available in buildings primarily designed for other purposes. Detailed plans have been completed for eight new year-round indoor centers located in congested sections of the city where facilities provided by other agencies do not meet community needs. The first center, opened to the public on March 30, 1951, in St. Mary's Park, Bronx, has an indoor swimming pool, gymnasium, game rooms, domestic science rooms and space for manual training and arts and crafts. Other centers will be built as funds are available. The City Building in Flushing Meadow Park, Queens, having served as a meeting place for the United Nations pending completion of their own permanent headquarters in Manhattan, has been restored to its former use as a popular indoor ice and roller rink.

In spite of a variable climate, our people of all ages spend more and more time outdoors. They can stand some overcrowding in their living and working quarters if they can find healthy public outdoor recreation nearby. Our recreation systems are operated by several agencies without overlapping, duplication or conflict. We have developed our city park system in close coordination with the state system in the suburbs, on the basis of small parks and playgrounds near home, larger ones not far away, and great beaches and open places in the suburbs for those who can get away for the day.

The bays and sandy barrier beaches of Long Island, running east to Montauk, from Coney Island to Rockaway, Rockaway to Long Beach, Jones Beach and Fire Island, are all one continuous natural resource, destined, and in recent years planned, for recreation. In this effective process, begun in the nick of time and fanatically adhered to without regard to political lines, one can see genuine as distinguished from academic planning, the real thing as contrasted with the chatter of amateurs.

We have no interest in irresponsible, revolutionary schemes for wholesale dispersion of population, decentralization, satellite towns, green belts and the like. A vigorous, progressive park program need not be revolutionary to be the most significant single contribution to intelligent city planning. Parks are not second even to modern housing in their beneficial influence on city growth and change, and they are no less dominant than health and schools in their effect upon civic morale.

Needed Six Park Improvements

The New York City park system still badly needs six things, all of them costing money: (1) An adequate maintenance budget. (2) Decent wages for grossly underpaid personnel. (3) Adequate policing. (4) Construction in crowded neighborhoods of scores of additional playgrounds for which we have land and plans, but lack building funds. (5) More indoor recreation centers in strategic slum areas for year-round use and to prevent the neglect which is improperly called juvenile delinquency. (6) Early development of reclaimed beaches.

Much remains to be accomplished, but we may without egotism and hyperbole boast that no great city with comparable problems has done more in a similar period to make highly industrialized urban life not only bearable but healthy, happy, interesting and attractive.

13

Recapturing
Natural Resources

CONSERVATION AND RECLAMATION OF OUR NATURAL
resources are as important as building. To me this has been self-
evident ever since I entered public service. By 1919, when I became
Chief of Staff of Governor Smith's Reconstruction Commission,
conservation had become something more than an abstract principle.
Since then I have devoted as much effort to recapturing and developing our natural heritage as I have to anything else.

Governor Smith's program for reorganizing the state government
was fully prepared during his first term, but his defeat at the next
election caused most of the proposed reforms to be postponed for
two years. Meantime, as secretary of the nonpartisan New York State
Association, I wrote a report for one of the association's subcom-
mittees entitled, "A State Park Plan for New York."

This brochure, published in 1922, proposed a plan for a unified
state park program to meet the needs of an increasing population
which was concentrating in cities but was otherwise becoming more
and more mobile. The New York State Council of Parks, set up in
1924, was an outgrowth of this effort to focus attention on the problem of conserving the natural resources of the state and developing
them to meet the growing needs of the public.

At that time the oldest and best known recreational area in the
state was the Niagara Reservation, which had been acquired in 1885.
Palisades Interstate Park had been created in 1900 to preserve the

scenery of the Palisades, at that time threatened with destruction by quarrymen. The initiative and most of the land and money for this park came from private individuals—Harriman, Rockefeller, Perkins and others. George W. Perkins was the first president of the Palisades Park and was also head of Governor Smith's special committee on parks whose report led to the creation of the New York State park system.

We are greatly indebted to the generous, farsighted men who made these timely gifts. The beneficence of Mr. John D. Rockefeller, Jr., in this instance was especially notable. His gift of Fort Tryon Park and The Cloisters, in upper Manhattan, and the miles of Palisades across the Hudson to serve as a setting, ranks high among acts of private munificence. The acquisition of this strategic promontory in New York City, the preservation and enhancement of its natural beauty and historical associations, and the magnificent setting given the Gallic fragments in The Cloisters—these were things which the city could never have done for itself, at least not in our time. This was no conventional donation. We must go back to the Renaissance to find its equal.

After the acquisition of the Palisades in New Jersey, the park was extended northward into Rockland and Orange counties in New York State, to include the mountainous lands along the Hudson River. The total acreage of the park is about 47,000 acres and embraces the entire beautiful Palisades, with numerous beaches, boat basins, camping sites and other features along the Henry Hudson Drive.

Hook Mountain is a geologic extension of the Palisades and Tallman Mountain. Bear Mountain Park has become a popular all-year center, where, in addition to facilities for recreation and sports of all kinds, the park authorities cooperate with the American Museum of Natural History in maintaining five museum buildings, with a zoo and outdoor collections of animals, reptiles, birds and flora of the region, several miles of marked trails and the remains of Fort Clinton, the Revolutionary War earthwork.

Bear Mountain is the eastern gateway to the largest section of Harriman State Park, named for the late E. H. Harriman, whose widow made its creation possible by gifts of acreage and money. This was in 1910. By 1955 we had completed more than thirteen miles of the Palisades Parkway from George Washington Bridge to Bear Mountain, and were progressing on the entire parkway, with additional recreational facilities along the way.

INTEGRATING THE PARK REGIONS

East of the Hudson, the Taconic State Park Commission has steadily developed parks and advanced construction of Taconic and Sprain Brook parkways, as well as the Bear Mountain parkway spur, which will carry motorists from the east side of the river to Bear Mountain Bridge. These parkway extensions are typical of the work that has already been done and of future plans for making the various parks in the different regions accessible to the motoring public and integrating them into a fully coordinated system.

It is impossible, in limited space, to list and describe the numerous parks and other features of the various regions of the state, as developed by the Allegany, Genesee, Finger Lakes, Central New York State park commissions, as well as the Niagara Frontier, Thousand Islands, Taconic and Long Island commissions, whose work covers the entire Empire State outside of the five counties of New York City. The unpaid members of these commissions have performed an invaluable service of tremendous importance to this and future generations.

The public is becoming increasingly appreciative of these services, and millions are now using the facilities of the state park system, stretching from Montauk Point on Long Island, to the Niagara Frontier, where we have redeemed, with private and public funds, vast open spaces which will henceforth be enjoyed by the public. At times this has been quite a battle: against nature, against all manner of obstructions; against indifference and inertia, neglect, selfish private interests and shortsighted legislators and officials—but I think it has been worth while.

Following Governor Smith's re-election, in 1922, one of our first battles was against a proposed amendment which would have opened up the forest preserve to power interests. We won this battle and

Governor Smith became an advocate of a Power Authority Bill, which was enacted in 1931. I became chairman in 1954 of the Power Authority created by this bill, but meantime a lot of water had gone unvexed and unused, to the sea.

I have always been active in opposing invasion of the state's 2 million acres of forest preserve by private interests, but I believe that the public should utilize the recreational potential of some of this vast area. The Council of Parks has for many years advocated a reasonable relaxation of the Constitutional limitations and interpretations which have arbitrarily prevented all but the most restricted recreational use of the preserve. Such an amendment was passed by the Legislature in 1946 but was held in committee during the next session and was not submitted to vote of the people.

This Constitutional amendment would in no way break down the safeguards against exploitation by power, lumbering or other private interests. Only a small part of the huge acreage could ever conceivably be used for recreation purposes, and that only with the simplest improvements in the form of access, shelter and sanitation—the minimum needed by the average urban residents, including women and children, in order to enjoy vacations safely and comfortably in the great preserve. The locking up of this preserve, on a basis imposed by fanatical conservationist minorities, is the most conspicuous void in the New York State park system. Because of heavy usage and overcrowding in most state parks, camping has necessarily become more and more curtailed or restricted. The only logical areas for additional camping facilities are in parts of the forest preserve.

In 1924 there were only two glens and three historic sites with any recreational facilities in the center of the state. There was nothing on the east side of the Hudson River. Letchworth Park, on the Genesee River, was the only recreational area of any appreciable size between the Palisades and Buffalo. The only state "park" on Long Island was a patch of two hundred acres of sand on Fire Island which had been acquired in 1893 as a quarantine station during a cholera scare.

The growing recreational needs of the state were completely ignored in this curious, irresponsible, administrative hodgepodge of scattered monuments, scientific, historical and occasional scenic spots which through accident, private gifts or temporary enthusiasm of local people had become more or less serious concerns of the state. These scattered places were administered by dozens of boards, societies and ex-officio and other commissions, some reporting directly to the Governor, others to state departments, still others functioning with public funds with little or no governmental control and co-ordination and all of them operating without analysis of regional recreational needs and anticipated population growth. Mass production of automobiles, shorter working hours and an enormous increase in outdoor activities, sports and recreation marked the end of the age in which parks could be considered exclusively municipal functions.

The State Council of Parks

With the enthusiastic support of Governor Smith, an amendment to the conservation law was adopted establishing the State Council of Parks, in 1924. This Council is made up of the unpaid members of the various regional commissions. The state is divided into natural and logical park regions, and the Council acts as a central advisory agency for all lands, parks, and places of historic, scientific and scenic interest supported in whole or in part by State funds. Historic sites were later transferred to the Department of Education, and some other adjustments have been made from time to time, but the Council, of which I have been chairman since 1924, formulates and suggests plans for the management, improvement and extension and use of lands under its jurisdiction in conformity with a unified park policy.

The Council also acts as a clearing house for information on park planning and administration; prepares and adopts annual budgets; makes information available to counties, towns and villages and advises as to connections and relations between state and local parks; recommends construction of new state and county highways and connections between parks.

In 1924 a bond issue of $15 million was voted to acquire more land and develop state parks under the new unified plan. Most of the proceeds of this bond issue went to the newly established regional

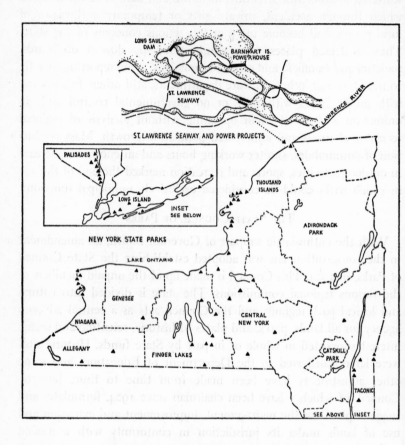

THE NEW YORK STATE PARK SYSTEM

*Above are the St. Lawrence Seaway and Power Projects,
including the new St. Lawrence State Park*

commissions, including the Adirondack and Catskill Forest Preserves, but an initial sum of one million dollars was allotted to the Long Island State Park Commission, of which I had become president. The five counties of New York City are not included in the state regional park system, but the park and parkway programs were later closely integrated.

THE LONG ISLAND PARK PROGRAM

As soon as the Long Island park and parkway program was launched, serious opposition developed. Owners of large estates, who opposed the Northern State Parkway, joined with those in opposition to Deer Range Park (later Heckscher State Park), on the South Shore, and with representatives of real estate promoters who aimed to acquire all of the Montauk Peninsula and to exclude the general public.

Litigation promoted by opponents of Heckscher State Park was the subject of actions in every possible tribunal, from the County Court of Suffolk County to the Supreme Court of the United States, and lasted more than five years. The bitterness engendered by this opposition is now almost impossible to understand, especially as many of those who were most vociferous at the time have since become convinced that they were always supporters of the park and parkway program.

The opposition was successful in holding up the entire program for a year. Finally, in 1926, supporters of the program succeeded in effecting compromises under which the Long Island plans began to go forward. I have no desire, at this late date, to stir the dead ashes of old conflicts. The story of those fights has been told many times: As a result of the battle over Northern State Parkway it had to be replanned and made a long loop to avoid certain estates in Wheatley Hills. We are now straightening out this loop. The legal and other battles over Heckscher Park, named for the late August Heckscher, who contributed $262,000 to buy the Islip property when the Legislature refused to vote the money to take up the option, were especially violent.

The fight to secure control of the almost inaccessible sand bar now known as Jones Beach State Park was followed by a struggle to salvage this isolated strip of sand, but was merely a part of the larger task of conserving and reclaiming vast stretches of the Long Island waterfront which had either been neglected, were being exploited by speculators, or were being monopolized by a few privileged persons to the exclusion of the public.

On Long Island, the original parkway program is virtually completed. Only the Sunken Meadow spur and Heckscher State Parkway are unfinished. We have completed the widening and improvement of the Southern State Parkway, and the two original causeways to Jones Beach as well as a third, the Captree Causeway. We will further expand and develop Sunken Meadow and Fire Island parks, and will provide new facilities at Jones Beach, in addition to the renowned Marine Stadium. We have comparable programs for the other park regions of the state.

It is never popular to charge for public facilities, but the State Council of Parks has from the beginning followed the policy that the user should pay reasonable charges for services such as parking, cabins, bathhouse lockers, games and other like facilities. Park officials have found that the public treats facilities for which a charge is made with more respect than free ones.

Another principle has been the exclusion from state parks of strident and jarring catchpenny, mechanical amusement devices. The advertising sign—with its ubiquitous allies, the mobile loudspeaker and the airborne blurb—has been strictly controlled. Enforcement of this policy has not been easy. Commercial invasion of scenery, restful relaxation and active recreation has become a curse. We have exercised every ingenuity in keeping it out of the state park system.

New York City's Waterfront

Recapturing and restoring to public use the splendid waterfront areas within New York has, in many ways, been the city's most dramatic achievement in recent years. New York is a great world port. The largest vessels afloat come and go through The Narrows and dock near the heart of Manhattan, while thousands of smaller cargo ships find berths around the great harbor. Yet only a small part of the city's waterfront is used for shipping. Through the years much of it was not used at all or was misused. During the past three decades our efforts have been directed toward the conservation and reclamation of this waterfront area, New York City's most valuable asset.

This work was initiated in 1926 when I became chairman of the Metropolitan Conference on Parks, in which city officials participated in developing a program to extend the city parks and to integrate them with the new state park and parkway plans. An immediate result of this movement was the acquisition by the city of some 2650 acres of wooded land, mostly in Queens and Richmond boroughs. This marked the most conspicuous progress in park and recreational work within the City of New York for more than a generation.

By 1930 this program had been greatly expanded. Thus, nearly a quarter of a century ago, land was acquired for many major projects that later came into existence. These include the Riverside Drive extension, the Hutchinson River Parkway connection, Whitestone and Flushing Meadow parks, Grand Central Parkway, La Guardia Airport, Marine Park extension (Great Kills, Richmond), and other parks that have long been in use. The state owned a lot of unappropriated land, scattered through the various counties and municipalities. When the state park plan was adopted, legislation was passed under which such unused land as was suitable for parks and playgrounds could be transferred to municipalities. In this way we acquired additional park areas.

A partial list of extensive areas of lands under water granted to the City of New York by the state since 1925 includes large holdings in and around Jamaica Bay, the ocean front at Rockaway, Flushing Bay, and a public beach and 412 acres for Great Kills Park, the largest in the city.

For over twenty years the New York City Park Department has been reclaiming these and other waste lands, swamps and land under water to create new parks, parkways and other improvements as part of a long-term program. Impetus was given the reclamation program by a decision of the United States Supreme Court in 1934, which held that New York City created a public nuisance by dumping refuse and garbage at sea, which floated ashore to litter the New Jersey and Long Island waterfronts. The court ordered the practice discontinued.

SEWAGE AND GARBAGE DISPOSAL

Meanwhile, the sewage and garbage disposal problems had become serious. The condition of the harbor and river waters had been getting progressively worse. The Health Commissioner, Park Department and the Interstate Sanitation Commission attested to this health menace, to the imminent dangers of infections and epidemics and other objectionable conditions. To meet this problem and abate pollution of the waters in and around the city, we established a ten-year program of scientific sewage disposal plants. As a result of this program, our beaches and waterfront are now clean and many recreational and residential developments dependent upon removal of pollution have been advanced. At the same time an incinerator construction program was launched to dispose of combustible refuse.

Incinerators are expensive and take a long time to build. This compelled the city to dispose of much of its refuse on land within the city limits and to establish or expand vast dumps, which were badly controlled and offensive. The first step toward orderly and decent control of dumps was on the Bronx River at Sound View Park. Here reasonably adequate facilities under Park Department supervision were established as a basis for reclamation, and neighborhood nuisances were guarded against. The 1939 World's Fair ended the notorious Corona dump with its mountain of refuse, which, with the material from the Riker's Island dump, was used to fill the swamps and low land and create new ground for what is now Flushing Meadow Park and La Guardia Airport.

Complaints of residents in the vicinity of landfill operations forced the city to adopt a definite program, long recommended by the Park Department, for the construction of incinerators and the placing of waste material only on city-owned lands to be developed as parks or for other public purposes. With suitable equipment, stock piles of earth for cover, and with proper supervision, temporary fill areas are now operated without neighborhood nuisances and produce constructive results.

Converting Dumps into Parks

In converting land fills and dumps into parks we were confronted by the difficult problem of securing at reasonable cost the topsoil required to sustain lawns, shrubs and trees. A few years ago our estimates showed that topsoil to cover the landfills then planned would cost some $8 million. No such sums were available, and the Park Department employed Clarence C. Combs, a landscape architect, to study and report on economical ways and means of making topsoil artificially.

Conditions varied in different landfills under our jurisdiction, but we were convinced that Mr. Combs' recommendations were sound, and that by following the methods he proposed the total cost of this essential phase in the development of new recreational areas the cost would be about $2,784,500, as compared with $8,550,000 for natural topsoil.

In 1953 we issued a technical progress report on our long-range program. If this report did nothing else, it served to illustrate the time, effort, money and cooperation of many agencies required for the kind of long-range planning so glibly and lightly recommended by those who have no knowledge of the work involved and little sustained interest in getting it done. It is most difficult to enlist and sustain public interest in these long-range programs, whose complexity is little understood, which are primarily meant for the future and not the immediate present, which necessitate some inconvenience to those living near by and which are necessarily in competition with other more dramatic, more pressing and more popular demands for shrinking city funds.

The Jamaica Bay Development

The most comprehensive plan of conservation, reclamation and redevelopment for recreational and residential purposes in New York City is in the Jamaica Bay area. We are constructing a great recreation and conservation area where natural wildlife will flourish. It will be the only one of its kind on such a large scale within the limits of any large city in the world. Its unique value is that it will be easily accessible to school children and adults by bus, subway, boat and car, and that its size insures an atmosphere of space, privacy and unspoiled nature in which men as well as fish, birds and other wildlife will find endless enjoyment. I put this program well up toward the head of all the many projects we are working on.

The entire city-owned north shore of Jamaica Bay, from Floyd Bennett Field to Idlewild Airport, will be devoted to park developments, including, at Canarsie, a mile-long bathing beach where the Park Department has for many years operated a fishing and boating center. At Spring Creek Park a boat basin, picnic areas and playfields will be constructed on land partially reclaimed by landfills.

Linked by Shore Parkway and easily accessible from interior sections of Brooklyn and Queens, these park lands will serve the private home-owner as well as residents of public and private housing projects and numerous visitors from all sections of Brooklyn and Queens. Bay-view Houses, a 1600-unit project of the City Housing Authority, is located on a site bounded on the south and east by Shore Parkway and the Canarsie Beach developments. Farther inland, the Glen-wood, Linden, Boulevard, Breucklen and Cypress Hills housing projects will benefit from their proximity to Jamaica Bay.

While the park properties along the bay's south shore are more scattered and limited in extent, there have been important additions in the Far Rockaway area through the transfer of property to the Park Department at Mott Basin, and between Norton and Sommerville Basins, a 270-acre tract is being reclaimed by landfill operations. These park areas, when reclaimed and developed, will be within easy reach of Redfern, Hammel, Arverne and other housing projects in the Rockaways.

The entire Jamaica Bay region presents a dramatic example of realistic planning for the future of New York. Here can be seen the beginning of large-scale planning—not merely on paper and for the record, but actually on the ground—for early use by the present population and for increased enjoyment by future generations. We have begun here a coordinated program of urban conservation, reclamation, housing, transportation, sewage disposal, recreation and many related and incidental public works.

The Fresh Kills project on Staten Island is another comprehensive reclamation and development plan, which includes the reclamation of 2,741 acres, where 6 million cubic yards of ashes, incinerator residue and refuse are being used to fill mostly salt marsh. This is not merely a means of disposing of the city's refuse in an efficient, sanitary and unobjectionable manner pending the building of sufficient incinerators. We believe that it also represents the greatest single opportunity for community planning in the city, not only for recreation but for residence and industry.

Spectacular Shorefront Highways

One of my first tasks as a member of the La Guardia administration in 1934 was the Westside Improvement. The Henry Hudson Parkway Authority, of which I was the sole member, was set up in that year. The Henry Hudson Bridge, built by the authority, was opened in 1937. Coming down from the north, the parkway leads to Hudson Memorial Park, where the bridge crosses the Harlem River to Inwood Park in upper Manhattan. From this point the highway follows the shore of the Hudson River to Battery Park, at the southern tip of Manhattan Island. This project, above Seventy-Second street, involved clearing the river front of railroad tracks and other unsightly encumbrances. This, with the redevelopment of Riverside Drive and incidental parks, provides a wonderful scenic highway.

At Battery Park, where the Brooklyn-Battery Tunnel continues the arterial route, fill from the tunnel excavation was used to enlarge the redesigned park. In Brooklyn, the tunnel emerges at Hamilton Avenue to connect with Gowanus Parkway and continue to Shore Parkway, which follows the water's edge almost to Coney Island, where we have recaptured large beach areas and restored them to public use.

After passing Sheepshead Bay, Shore Parkway touches Plumb Beach, Marine and Canarsie parks and skirts the north shore of Jamaica Bay until it reaches Idlewild Airport, which, with the parkway, rests almost entirely on filled land. Cross Island Parkway carries motorists to the reclaimed waterfront at Clearview Park, on Little

Neck Bay. Across Whitestone Bridge there is Ferry Point Park, on made land, and Orchard Beach, near the city line is still another man-made beach. The extension of Hutchinson River Parkway involved the transformation of large areas of marsh into a ribbon park.

MANHATTAN'S EAST SIDE

The most spectacular transformation that has taken place in Manhattan in this generation—more important than the skyscrapers concentrated in the center of the island—has been the reclamation of the East River waterfront. For almost the entire length of this river front, from Battery Park to the Harlem River, the East Side has been converted from notorious slums on dead-end streets into modern housing developments, institutional buildings and parks, including the United Nations headquarters. Franklin D. Roosevelt Drive and the expressway extension to the Battery, built by the borough presidents of Manhattan, completes the encircling of Manhattan with expressways and connects with the Brooklyn-Battery Tunnel and the circumferential arterial system.

This is not the place to discuss the tremendous effects upon living and working conditions of such developments, or to go into details regarding the enhancement of real estate values which is reflected in the increased tax revenues accruing to the city. The main point is that conservation and reclamation, which are frequently considered as having to do primarily with natural resources in wide open spaces—with saving forests and soils, etc.—are quite as essential in crowded areas, where every tree is a valuable asset and space is at a premium. With the growth of cities and metropolitan areas, I am inclined to believe that conservation and reclamation must start in our cities and their immediate environs.

THE THREAT TO STATE CONTROL

Having for many years been closely associated with the problems of reclamation of submerged lands and the planning and development of recreational and other waterfront facilities and improvements,

I was naturally alarmed when a controversy arose between the states and the Federal government over the ownership of oil found under certain coastal waters. For a time this issue threatened to stop filling and reclamation operations, projects to arrest beach erosion and other shorefront developments in which ownership and control would be placed in doubt.

The story of the Federal government's attempted grab of the states' submerged coastal lands began one day in April 1937, when President Franklin D. Roosevelt, Secretary of the Interior Harold Ickes and WPA Director Harry Hopkins lunched together at the White House and the President raised the question as to the ownership of the oil found under these coastal waters. For more than a century virtually everyone, including public officials, lawyers and all the courts that had considered the question, believed that the individual states were the owners of the lands under the bays, ocean and other navigable waters within their state boundaries. Shorefront and harbor developments proceeded on this basis through the years.

As late as 1933, Mr. Ickes had refused to grant Federal oil leases in California's submerged coastal lands, informing the applicants that "title to the soil under the ocean within the 3-mile limit is in the State of California, and the land may not be appropriated except by authority of the State."

The controversy broke into the open in 1938 when Congress was asked to declare all tidelands to be part of the public domain of the United States. This Congress flatly refused to do and reiterated its refusal again in 1939. The dispute remained quiet through the war years until late in 1945 when President Truman, picking up the cudgels where Roosevelt had dropped them, issued a proclamation that oil and all other resources of the subsoil continental shelf were under the jurisdiction and control of the Federal government. This proclamation was followed by the commencement of a suit against the State of California to establish the Federal government's claim.

Congressional resentment boiled over and the Senate and the House promptly passed a joint resolution declaring that the individual states were the owners of the submerged coastal lands within their borders. With equal promptness, President Truman vetoed the bill.

THE SUPREME COURT DECISION

In June 1947, the Supreme Court decided the California case. Without flatly saying that the Federal government owned these marginal lands, Mr. Justice Black declared that it had "paramount rights in and power over" California's marginal coastal belt with "full dominion" over the resources of the soil, including oil. In December 1950, similar rulings were handed down in cases involving Louisiana and Texas, despite the fact that in the Texas case it was shown, and admitted by the court, that Texas had been an independent republic and had ceded no lands to the United States upon its annexation. Vigorous dissents were written in each of the cases.

In its 1952 session Congress started all over again to break the stalemate that had brought the development of offshore oil reserves to a standstill because neither Federal nor state governments had clear authority over leasing arrangements, and retarded shore and harbor improvements by State and local officials who did not know where they stood in this confused picture.

Bills were introduced by both Federal and state adherents and hearings and debate flourished. Again, as in 1946, "compromises" sponsored by the administration were rejected and a joint resolution, commonly known as the Holland "quit claim" bill, was passed by large majorities in both House and Senate. This bill, in clear and simple language, confirmed the titles of the individual states to their submerged lands.

The vote in the House was an overwhelming 247 in favor, with only 89 against the states' ownership bill. Here was a most courageous and encouraging demonstration of the desire of elected representatives in Congress to protect the rapidly diminishing rights of the states against the excessive concentration of power in our bureaucratic Federal government—a concentraton rapidly reaching a point where the continuance of our states as independent, sovereign political entities was threatened.

THE FIGHT FOR STATES' RIGHTS

On February 17, 1953, I appeared before the United States Senate Committee on Interior and Insular Affairs, in support of S. J. Resolution 13, referred to as "The Submerged Lands Act." The purpose of this legislation was to correct the intolerable condition created by the decisions of the Supreme Court. The bill would release to the states and their grantees all title and interest of the United States to lands beneath navigable waters within the boundaries of the states, and the natural resources within such lands. The Federal government's constitutional right to regulate navigation and to provide for flood control, and its title to lands or improvements specifically acquired, were expressly excepted from the operation of the proposed act.

It was my contention that Mr. Justice Black's ruling in the California case, holding that the Federal government rather than the state has paramount rights over the three-mile marginal belt along the California coast, meant that all such titles derived from the state were voided. In New York that ruling had cast a cloud on the city's title to the submerged and reclaimed lands on which its piers, many of its recreational facilities and other waterfront improvements stood. This cloud threatened to destroy the work of years.

I had prepared a map of New York City showing the overall situation. It traced the original shoreline of the city in colonial times and up to the present, indicating some of the major waterfront developments. I called attention to Coney Island, originally a small island; to the Rockaway Peninsula, which was originally a thin sand bar. Nearly all of New York's fifty miles of commercial waterfront development stand on reclaimed land. I also presented data relating to developments on Long Island, and some details of the transfers of state lands, with which I was familiar.

As Secretary of State under Governor Smith, in 1927-28, I was a member of the Board of Commissioners of the Land Office, which has had general care of all state lands since 1784, and I know some of the problems arising in connection with titles, ownership and rights to the submerged and reclaimed areas in the state. I also know of the good use that New York and other Atlantic states and cities are making of these submerged lands beyond the low-water mark. As I said in a letter to The New York Times, the Federal government ought to be able to handle its problems of oil conservation under its war and commerce powers without taking title to New York's submerged coastal lands.

The real objective of those who talk about the Federal character of so-called tidelands oil, which does not even exist in states such as New York, is manifestly to transfer control to the hands of arbitrary and ill-informed Federal bureaucrats without regard to the cost in terms of invasion of states' rights, established titles and proper development and use of these great natural assets by those who have traditionally controlled these assets and are best equipped to do so.

Happily, this controversy was ended and the problem resolved by the passage of the Submerged Lands Act of 1953, which vested title to these lands in the contiguous states. The Supreme Court, in the case later brought by Alabama and Rhode Island, upheld the law. However, the fight to conserve, reclaim and develop the rich heritage of the state's natural resources for the use of the public continues on other fronts.

14

The Niagara Frontier
Battle

As chairman of the State Council of Parks, I have had a direct and active interest in the Niagara Frontier and St. Lawrence River areas since 1924. Two years before that we defeated a proposed amendment to the State Constitution which would have opened up the Forest Preserve to private power interests. At that time, Governor Smith became an advocate of a power authority law, which was enacted in 1931. In March 1954, Governor Thomas E. Dewey appointed me chairman of the New York State Power Authority.

The state park system, as originally set up, included the Niagara Frontier and the Thousand Islands regions. More recently St. Lawrence County (outside the Forest Preserve) was added to the latter regional division. We propose to develop both, following plans made more than a quarter of a century ago, greatly augmented by our programs for waterpower development.

Our Authority has the battle of the Niagara frontier to fight over again against five embattled utility companies of considerable influence and supported by powerful allies, but without much of a grasp of public relations and public opinion as they are today. I think we can lick them to the ground. If not, they will be in the courts for a long, long time with no hope of ultimate victory. Our program is a park and parkway program also. I have waited impatiently over thirty years for progress in developing the great international escarpments on the St. Lawrence and Niagara rivers, and have had no truck with the power interests in all that time.

The History of the Falls

Niagara has presented us with two gifts: beauty and power. Through much of its history these have been in conflict. Today they complement each other and it has been proved by our Canadian neighbors that the power of Niagara Falls to generate electricity can be used to protect and beautify the whole of the Niagara River.

As a great spectacle Niagara Falls became famous throughout Europe more than two and a half centuries ago. Father Hennepin, a French missionary, had seen the Falls in 1678 and had written about them in books that were bestsellers early in the eighteenth century. The Falls had been recorded even earlier by Champlain in his *Voyages*, published in 1613. The Falls had simply awed and terrified Father Hennepin, as well as the explorer La Salle who was with him and who in turn took the Niagara River in the name of France. There was no thought of power in their minds, yet water was diverted by another Frenchman, Chabert Joncaire, about 1757, to run a sawmill in connection with his "trading house" established at Lewiston in 1719.

Both the power and the majesty of Niagara were for a time forgotten in the wars that followed. In the French and Indian War the border passed to the British. The brutal Devil's Hole massacre of 1763, in which nearly a hundred British were killed by the Seneca Indians, was an aftermath of that war. Devil's Hole State Park marks this site today. After the American War of Independence the east bank of the river became part of the State of New York. The War of 1812 was fought over both banks of the river and some famous battle sites are now preserved.

After that war a final frontier boundary was established through the Niagara River, and since that time Americans and Canadians have looked across the river with ever friendlier eyes. Today the scenes of struggle on both sides—Fort George, Fort Niagara, Fort Erie and others—are commemorated not as reminders of war but as landmarks to peace. The Province of Ontario and the State of New York have dignified them with parks to mark a border unfortified for over a hundred years.

Historically, New York State pioneered in establishing the first state park in the nation when the reservation at Niagara Falls was opened to the public in 1885. For forty years this tiny parcel of land at the edge of the Falls was the sole public recognition of Niagara's importance, but it did provide enjoyment for millions of people who came to view one of the world's greatest spectacles and to find rest and recreation in surroundings of stirring beauty.

It seems strange to us today that this pioneering effort met with determined opposition. It is even stranger that, once a beginning was made, a system of parks did not develop along the whole of the American side of Niagara River. Throughout the country there is probably no frontier more exciting or more naturally belonging to the people for their enjoyment of scenic splendor, or as dignified by historic landmarks which take us back to the turbulent beginnings of the nation.

EARLY IDEAS OF PRESERVATION

In the early days the park idea occurred to no one. The frontier was a wilderness. The important things were the fight for survival, the cutting of forests, clearing land for farms, building homes for settlers and eventually hastening the progress of commerce. In the half century after 1825 both the beauty and power of Niagara Falls were exploited not for the benefit of the people, but for the profit of the few who owned the adjacent land. The Erie Canal opened in 1825 and the railroads that followed brought hordes of "pilgrims" from all over the world to the shrine of the Falls.

After the midcentury manufacturers began to use the water power. In 1861 the Hydraulic Canal for water power was completed, soon followed by blast furnaces, a grist mill, a paper mill, an open hearth furnace and dye works. This was in the American tradition. Industry in this country began along the rivers and long after steam was turning the wheels of factories abroad Americans were still using direct water power. Hydroelectric generation had not yet come, so it was necessary for the mills to cluster along the rivers and to obtain their power from water applied directly to water wheels.

All this industrial growth defaced the scene. Factories obscured the views and, close by the Falls, hotels and diverse commercial ventures lured the visitor. By 1887 there was hardly a foot of American soil from which a tourist might look at the Falls without paying a fee. The American town of Niagara Falls swarmed with peddlers and barkers.

The thought of reserving and dignifying land about the Falls had been in the minds of men on both sides of the river for about ten years when Lord Dufferin, Governor General of Canada, made the first official move in 1878. He suggested to Governor Lucius Robinson of New York that the governments of New York, Ontario and Canada acquire existing property rights and "form around the Falls a small public International Park." It was not to be fancy and "sophisticated," as he expressed it, but restored insofar as possible to its natural state as originally "laid out by the hand of nature."

Governor Robinson was immediately impressed. In his 1879 message to the New York Legislature he echoed Lord Dufferin's thoughts and recommended that since Ontario had appointed a commission to look into the plan, New York State should do likewise. Within the year both legislative bodies had taken action and the New York Legislature asked the commissioners of the state survey to report.

The plan was vigorously opposed. To adopt it took five years of battle against armies of lawyers, landowners and commercial interests. The state—so they said—was proposing to halt progress, to defeat industry and to violate the sacred property rights of American citizens for mere sentiment.

The "Memorial," which turned the tide, was a famous document in its day. In effect, it was a petition addressed jointly to the Governor of New York and the Governor General of Canada. Appealing on grounds of religion, education and "the union and peace of nations" for the joint guardianship of the Falls, it was signed by some seven hundred distinguished American citizens and British subjects. It was probably the signatures rather than the language that made it effective. No legislature in the eighties could ignore such names as Thomas Carlyle, John Ruskin and John Lubbock, or our own Emerson, Longfellow, Whittier, Holmes, Parkman, Agassiz, and Phillips

Brooks, not to mention a Vice President, Supreme Court Justices, Senators, Congressmen, and other governmental notables across the land.

A CONTINUING FIGHT

A bill passed in March 1883 and signed by Governor Grover Cleveland authorized "the selection, location and appropriation of certain lands in the village of Niagara Falls, New York for a State Reservation to preserve the Falls of Niagara," but made no appropriation. What of the cost? Over the anticipated expense there was new and angry controversy as to the impoverishment of the state by increased taxes and the claims of property ownership with riparian rights.

What was a park? In many minds of the time, according to a commissioner's report, it was "an area of land laid out with neatly trimmed lawns, formal pathways, geometrical flower beds, statuary and cast iron benches." Nothing could better convey the popular notion of the period than this definition, and today's visitors to the Canadian parks will note that to some extent the idea once prevailed there. Also, nothing shows the advanced thinking of the New York sponsors better than their counterplan: to restore rather than to construct; to go back to nature rather than away from nature. This, they insisted, would cost comparatively little, and so it proved.

The first step was demolition. Hotels, mills and factories at the river's edge were torn down. Except for a few concessions, the whole practice of individual profit was eliminated and in due time the adjacent property increased in value. The throngs of visitors increased, the visits were longer, and more and more profit accrued to the town's hotels and shops.

Visitors to Niagara Falls, New York, today are sometimes disturbed by the size and continuity of the Canadian park system compared with ours. There is a parkway all the way from Lake Erie to Lake Ontario near the river's edge. In the parks there are elaborate gardens, an amphitheater—presented by the late Sir Henry Oakes—from which to see the Falls, large automobile parking areas, and wide scenic vantage points, restaurants, and other facilities for public enjoyment. But much of the land was acquired at an early date, mostly as undeveloped or farm acreage. The acquisition cost little in money, effort, legal battles or conflict with property owners when compared with the comparable costs on the New York side. Much of the property was dedicated and money for development came not from direct taxes but eventually from the sale of electric power.

The New York State areas were thickly settled and built to the shoreline. Sizable towns ran to the water's edge, blocking the way. The big and growing population of the state, thoroughly engrossed in industrial progress, had to be convinced of the need of parks before the Legislature could successfully act. In Ontario, settlement was thin and scattered. The population of the Province was small, rural and more amenable to legislative changes. The only difficulty came in obtaining from such a population sufficient money to develop and improve the land so cheaply acquired.

PAYING FOR THE CANADIAN PARKS

By 1890 immense strides had been made in the development of water-driven electrical generators and in electrical transmission. Between 1889 and 1892 English and Canadian power companies negotiated for the right to install generators on the Canadian side. The "water rental" for these rights was paid directly to the Canadian Park Commission to be used for riverfront development. That is the way our Canadian friends paid for their fine park development. But since a large percentage of the power, in the early days, was sold on this side of the boundary, the initial Canadian park development was paid, in part, by American money.

Meanwhile, on the American side, the Niagara Falls Power Company began delivering electric power, derived from the state's Niagara water, without being required to pay anything whatever. Over a quarter of a century later rentals were imposed, but they were paid into the general revenue funds of the state, and not to the Reservation Commission for park development as had been done in Canada. The urgent industrial needs of the period and the enthusiasm for industrial development naturally influenced the Legislature.

The history of private exploitation of the Niagara Frontier is one of outrageous effrontery. The record shows that the private companies have never had any genuine interest in the preservation of this public asset. Before the turn of the century the escarpment had been practically ruined by mills, factories, power installations, bazaars and hideous advertising signs. Several private power companies had been incorporated to take unlimited amounts of water from the Niagara River. Had these companies been equipped to use all the water at their disposal, they would ruthlessly have drained the river, denuded the Falls and completed the destruction of this great natural spectacle.

This early exploitation was finally curbed by aroused public opinion, which resulted in the establishment of the State Reservation and the park and parkway program, governmental control of the Falls and river, and limitation of the amount of water which could be diverted for power production by the provisions of the Boundary Waters Treaty of 1909 between the governments of the United States and Canada. Since that time development of the water power of the St. Lawrence and Niagara rivers has been the subject of various international agreements and legislative acts, and numerous controversies.

THE FIGHT FOR STATE DEVELOPMENT

Until 1948 intensive efforts were made to secure Congressional approval of a combination power and Seaway project. In that year the New York State administration determined to secure a license to develop the International Rapids of the St. Lawrence separately from the Seaway. The two projects are closely related, but financially and otherwise separable. The Niagara River power project has no direct relationship to the St. Lawrence development, but I happen to be involved in both, as well as in expanding the state park and parkway program in the entire Niagara and St. Lawrence regions.

In recent years, the utility companies which have attempted to prevent the state from developing Niagara power have interfered little with the state and provincial Canadian development of the St. Lawrence Rapids. Back in 1907, however, private power and industrial interests made one grand drive for all the potential energy from falling water at Long Sault where, in partnership with the Hydro-Electric Power Commission of Ontario, we are building a great dam.

The early efforts of private companies to grab this St. Lawrence power were scandalous. They procured legislation and got themselves a license at the modest rental of $25,000 a year, but the process was so outrageous, the public clamor so great, the grant so clearly improvident and against public interest, that the infamous act was repealed in 1913 and the Court of Appeals, in a sweeping decision, sustained the repeal. There the matter rested for forty years.

In 1952, the Federal Power Commission reopened hearings on the State Power Authority's application for a license to develop the St. Lawrence Rapids. The license was granted in 1953, but work was held up by litigation. Meanwhile, the battle for state development shifted from the St. Lawrence to the Niagara Frontier.

DANGER ON THE NIAGARA FRONT

Under the 1950 amendment to the treaty with Canada, additional amounts of Niagara's waters were available for power production and private utility companies began seeking by every means at their command to defeat the State Power Authority's proposed development of Niagara and to grab this state-owned water for themselves. Since 1900 every Governor of the State of New York, with one exception—Governor Miller—has advocated keeping the state's water power resources inalienable and their development a prerogative of the state. This well-established policy was again in serious danger of being reversed.

The first task confronting me as chairman of the New York State Power Authority was to appear before the Senate Committee on Public Works at hearings on four bills having to do with Niagara power development. The so-called Miller-Capehart bill, which had already passed the House, would designate the Niagara-Mohawk and associated utilities as the companies to develop and distribute the power. A bill by Senator Herbert H. Lehman and Representative Franklin D. Roosevelt, Jr., would provide for public development, but give preference to municipal plants and cooperatives. The Ives-Becker bill, sponsored by Senator Ives and Representative Frank Becker, designates the State Power Authority as the agency to undertake the development. Finally, a bill sponsored by Senator Case, Republican of South Dakota, leaves the question of what agency should develop the power to the Federal Power Commission.

The issues are quite simple, but they were grossly and unfairly represented by the five utility companies, which wanted the Federal government to hand over to them for private exploitation waters of the Niagara River which are owned by the state and declared to be inalienable under its laws. These companies conducted a campaign of skilful misrepresentation with cries of "socialism" and slogans about "the free enterprise system."

THE FALSE CRY OF "SOCIALISM"

The question here is not one of socialism, nor does it involve Republicanism versus New Dealism. It is whether Congress should turn over the Niagara River to private exploiters. The alternative is to have this great state-owned resource in the custody of the Power Authority for development of additional hydroelectric power under international treaty in an orderly and businesslike way, with assurance of protection and preservation of the scenic beauty of the Falls and the river for the continuing benefit of the public.

By the Power Authority Act of 1931 and the amendment of 1951, the Legislature had declared that the Niagara and St. Lawrence rivers are natural resources of the state; that such natural resources, including the river beds, water, power and power sites, shall always remain inalienable; and that they shall be developed by the state through its designated agency, the Power Authority of the State of New York. Granting a license to the private companies to develop power at Niagara would therefore be in direct violation of the established policy and the law of the State of New York.

So far as I know, this was the first time Congress had been asked to interfere with or obstruct the operation of Federal and state laws on licensing power development where no direct Federal project was involved. Under Federal law the New York State Power Authority had been granted a license to develop power on the St. Lawrence River and President Eisenhower, by executive order, had authorized the Authority to proceed with the project. This license was being attacked in the courts not by the utility companies, but by a land development concern and beach protective association, on the grounds that their members would be damaged by raising the level of Lake Ontario.

Of the bills pending in Congress at the time only two were desirable and consistent with Federal and state laws. As I told the Senate Committee at its hearing, all my experience as head of the state park system has reinforced the conclusion that the state should never turn over the control of Niagara at the source to private companies. We had the experience over thirty years of recapturing and reclaiming much of the Niagara waterfront, including the protection of the Falls. In all that time power development in Canada was subordinate to the park development and the Canadian Hydroelectric Power Commission, which is exactly like our State Power Authority, got its money, its licenses and its power to operate through the Park Commission.

I make no bones about the fact that I am a park man. I have devoted a large part of my life to that kind of work and make no apologies for it. We inherited a shambles at Niagara and have been laboring for three decades to reclaim what the power companies left us. The Falls themselves were protected to some extent, but had the companies been successful in the early days in obtaining the rights they wanted to divert water, there would not be any water at Niagara Falls. There would be nothing to look at! That is a matter of history.

The Tactics of the Opposition

During this controversy I was personally resentful of the charges in magazine articles, handouts, page advertisements and so forth, by the utility companies, as well as indirect advertising that represented us as Socialists. I am no Socialist and had never before been called one. It is a name that is tossed around rather freely by these power companies.

The State Power Authority plan for Niagara is not a "socialistic scheme." It is a fair and reasonable business arrangement to be financed by private funds. The Authority must sell its bonds to prudent private investors. There is no state credit back of its bonds. The Authority is a business organization, owned by the people of the state, it is true, but using private funds and answerable to its bondholders who will insist upon revenues from fair and reasonable contracts for the sale of power at the source, largely, if not wholly, to private interests.

There is no attack upon private enterprise or any threat to private utilities in the development of the Niagara power by the Authority. The project will aid and strengthen private utility operation. The Authority will see to it that the scenic beauty of the Falls is protected and preserved. At the same time the private utility companies through purchase contracts with the Authority will have the benefit of more business and continued access to large power supplies, insuring saving to consumers. Our Canadian friends are developing far more power than the private companies on the American side. The Canadian consumer obtains this power at half the cost to the American consumer, in spite of the fact that the Canadians have built and are supporting with power revenues a park system which puts to shame the meager park facilities on the American side.

Today a real opportunity is presented to adopt the Canadian plan of financing park development, which can be realized with the least possible direct tax burden. The plan is simply to establish a rental based on a unit of water diversion for power. A percentage of the revenue from such power development would thus be returned to furthering the protection and the development of the area and to better promoting the health and recreation needs of our citizens.

The Enlarged Niagara Program

The Niagara Frontier State Park Commission has had a definite program for regional development since 1924. It has been expanded from time to time to meet new needs. In the 1920's the modern parkway was only a concept, and received less attention than it does today. Basically, however, the program dates from 1924. For many reasons this program has lagged. On Long Island the program adopted at the same time is 90 per cent completed. At Niagara the program is about 20 per cent completed, but much has been accomplished and it is now moving. It is our hope that it will soon be further accelerated.

The reservation itself has been expanded. Adjacent lands were acquired as a result of the collapse of the Falls View Bridge in 1937, and the new Rainbow Bridge was built with the bridgehead adjacent to the park. The site of the famous Cataract House was added and slum clearance begun. Whirlpool State Park, Devil's Hole State Park and the Lewiston Heights escarpment were acquired. Finally the historic Fort Niagara area, returned to the state by the Federal government after occupation as a regular army post for over a century, was added to the park system. A group of civic-minded citizens formed the Old Fort Niagara Association, Inc., a nonprofit corporation, for the purpose of restoring the old French fort to its original form. Commencing their work over twenty-five years ago, this association is still operating the Old Fort under agreement with the Niagara Frontier State Park Commission.

During this period the Commission looked up-river to the south and to Buffalo and began to acquire lands and to develop parks on Grand Island. This island, situated above the Falls in the Niagara, divides the river into east and west channels. Larger than Manhattan, it is the largest inland island in the United States. At the south end the development of Beaver Island State Park, with its attractive bathing beach, was begun. Along the West River, lands were acquired for a seven-mile riverfront parkway which connects Beaver Island State Park with Buckhorn State Park at the northerly tip of Grand Island.

The Niagara Frontier Bridge Commission and its successor, the Niagara Frontier Authority, constructed the North and South Grand Island bridges, later transferred to the New York State Thruway Authority. In cooperation with the Thruway Authority we have plans for traffic interchange at both ends of the North Grand Island Bridge. A waterfront parkway is proposed to connect Buckhorn Island State Park with the City of Niagara Falls on the mainland and to extend the parkway to the reservation on a route outside the industrial plants. This parkway will make it possible to drive from the South Grand Island Bridge to the Rainbow Bridge and thence to Ontario, bypassing the cluttered mill area.

Other proposals include the conversion of Rapids Boulevard, connecting Whirlpool and Devil's Hole state parks, into a parkway; and a continuing parkway between Lewiston and Youngstown, terminating at Fort Niagara State Park, which will be fully developed, in addition to preserving the historic old French Fort area. The Commission is also cooperating with the Niagara Falls City Planning Commission and the Rainbow Bridge Commission in beautifying the areas immediately adjacent to the river, as well as the existing state parks.

This program, which has many other features too numerous and detailed to list in limited space, cannot go forward unless a share of the profit from power development is allocated for the purpose. Our friends on the Canadian side of the boundary have shown us the way to develop the vast power and recreational resources at Niagara. All we have to do is to follow their example.

Niagara power, added to that of the St. Lawrence, will be a tremendous asset to the entire section. As a by-product we have the unique opportunity of developing to its full the most magnificent recreational area in the East, if not in the entire country. If our plans are carried out, the millions who come to see the Falls can be more adequately served. The traffic approaches can bypass the blight which is a holdover from the old, haphazard days. The most beautiful parts of the river, above and below the Falls, will be made accessible to all.

There will be broad parkways paralleling the river and additional and improved facilities for the public are planned, such as automobile parking areas and conveniences near the scenic points. Historical sites along the frontier will be marked and restored and incorporated in the regional park plan. To me, this Niagara-St. Lawrence development seems to be the most prodigious project of its kind which public agencies can undertake at this time. It is much needed conservation and reclamation and building—for industry, commerce, recreation and the enjoyment of our natural resources. At any rate, it is the most challenging job I have ever undertaken.

When the Congress acts favorably on legislation to delegate to the Federal Power Commission the authority which is normally theirs to issue a license for the development of Niagara power with state preference, we shall promptly submit an application to this Commission for this license. We shall be prepared to complete detailed plans and specifications, obtain necessary financing and start construction. Our engineers have shown that after both St. Lawrence and Niagara have been completed, an additional 3.8 million kilowatts will be required in New York State by 1965. The question is, how long do we propose to argue this case in the light of the critical shortage of power, while the flow of Niagara continues 365 days in each year and twenty-four hours in each day? Our Canadian neighbors will continue to enjoy the benefits of this flow while we argue among ourselves.

New York State will never allow its greatest natural resource, declared inalienable by our legislature and courts, to be handed over by Congress to five private utility companies. We shall fight through every court to the highest tribunal against this grab by the utility and electric companies. They can perhaps obstruct but they can never win. The most they can do is to tie up our share of additional Niagara power in politics and litigation for another twenty or thirty years, in the course of which Ontario Hydro will use all the water including ours.

There is a great principle involved here and no banking system, no utility lobby and no political party that is wrong about it can escape public condemnation and reprisal. We of the New York State Power Authority are conservatives. We intend to control our state power at the source, to develop hydroelectric plants with funds raised from private investors and to sell our kilowatts to existing private and public plants, companies and groups of all kinds at fair rates determined by contract. There is nothing socialistic about this.

15

St. Lawrence Power
and Parks

HARNESSING THE INTERNATIONAL RAPIDS OF THE
St. Lawrence River got under way on August 10, 1954, with impressive ceremonies on both sides of the Rapids, when Canadians and Americans blew up the bottom of the St. Lawrence, and great columns of water were lifted toward the sky at the spots where the mighty stream will be held back by the Long Sault dam.

The last obstacle to the St. Lawrence project was removed when the Supreme Court refused to hear an appeal from the lower courts, which upheld the license granted the New York State Power Authority by the Federal Power Commission. State legislation clarifying the Authority's right to condemn property and to issue notes for temporary financing was provided at an extraordinary session of the Legislature on June 10, 1954, and the Authority obtained a temporary loan of $40 million to start construction.

We had moved rapidly since March, when I became chairman of the Authority, but our partner, the Hydro-Electric Power Commission of Ontario, had proceeded at the same pace. Our joint schedule aims at the first sale of power in 1958, and completion of the project a year later, barring unforeseeable emergencies. This will mean fast work, for the St. Lawrence project is exceeded in size only by the Grand Coulee Dam, on the Columbia River, and its generators will produce 700,000 kilowatts of power, more than all the hydroelectric plants of the Tennessee Valley Authority. The total cost is estimated at $561,730,000.

An issue of $335 million of revenue bonds to finance the New York part of the project was put on the market in December 1954. The major part of the issue, $267 million, is on long-term bonds, due on January 1, 1995. The balance of $68 million is in serial obligations maturing in annual installments from 1965 to 1976.

While the power companies which would like to get control of Niagara River power have not opposed our plans for the St. Lawrence projects, certain newspapers, organizations and individuals were extremely critical during the state campaign because I did not hand out premature reports and promises. Some of these statements were slanderous, politically inspired and not in the slightest degree calculated to produce power and a Seaway. Charges that our Authority was involved in a huge, crooked "give-away" to power interests was gratuitous and irresponsible. We borrowed $40 million on character from the banks so as to keep up with the Canadians and so as to shorten the construction time from seven to five years. This was necessary to avoid a breakdown in construction schedules which would affect all of the power and Seaway work along the St. Lawrence.

The Authority has no public credit back of it. We must sell revenue bonds to the conservative investing public. Our Ontario partners have provincial credit and are in a totally different position. The sale of a bond issue of over $300 million for power purposes is a complex affair. As to contracts for the sale of that energy which we are about to generate to consumers of one kind or another, we had conducted no negotiations whatsoever leading up to such contracts except in the case of the Aluminum Company of America. Alcoa has rights and responsibilities, has been on the St. Lawrence for over fifty years, is the largest employer of labor in the area and cannot be flooded out by fiat.

We had conducted no negotiations with the five companies which are applicants for the Niagara License, including the Niagara-Mohawk and Consolidated Edison. No one has opposed their application for this license more actively than we have or more effectively. As to contracts for the sale of power to customers of various kinds, these are subject, under our law, to advertised public hearings both by the Authority and the Governor. The question before the public was whether we would proceed to develop power in accordance with international agreement, Federal and state laws, a Federal license and our oaths of office in an orderly businesslike and honest way, or whether this subject was to be thrust back again as it was for years into demagogy and political gestures.

I was confident that Averell Harriman, as Governor, would acquaint himself quickly with the facts as to the power projects, as distinguished from the guff circulated by irresponsible people toward the end of the 1954 campaign. I did not have the slightest doubt as to his support, because we have a clean program which follows the law, which involves no state credit, which makes no sacrifice to expediency, and which protects fully the greatest of all the remaining natural resources of the Empire State.

These are precisely the principles Governor Harriman had enumerated. He, too, is an old park enthusiast. He comes by it by inheritance. His father and mother antedate me as conservationists. Governor Harriman had been a Park Commissioner even longer than I have been, having served as a member of the Palisades Park Commission since 1921. Such service represents a great tradition and one I am glad to share with the new Governor.

In his first annual message to the New York State Legislature, Governor Harriman said:

My administration will firmly adhere to the policy of the inalienability, conservation and further development under public auspices of our great basic natural water resources on our international boundary rivers. . . . A major battle is now shaping up on the Niagara River. There five private utility companies are seeking by Federal legislation to seize the states water power. I cannot emphasize too strongly the importance of a unified, determined effort to persuade Congress to reject the plan of the five utility companies.

What is essential and imperative is that Congress enable the State Power Authority to develop the power at the Niagara for the benefit of the consumers of our state and not for the benefit of the five utility companies. In addition, our Niagara Frontier park and parkway program, established more than thirty years ago and largely held back by the private power interests, must no longer be neglected. As Governor of the State I shall do all in my power to attain these objectives.

Tax-payers Are Not "Menaced"

The utility companies seeking to oust the State at Niagara and their allies have characterized the Authority not only as socialistic but as a menace to taxpayers generally. Nothing could be further from the truth. Our Authority has no intention of attempting to put private utility companies out of business. We propose, within the framework of our law, the Canadian treaty and our license, to market power by contract with existing private utility companies where they have or can establish adequate facilities, maintaining, however, proper safeguards to assure that the benefits of cheaper power are passed on to the consuming public. Although the Authority has the right to build transmission lines, we do not propose to exercise it unless we cannot proceed promptly, adequately and equitably through the facilities of existing private utility companies. The same logic will apply later at Niagara in the event that the Authority is granted a license to construct the Niagara project.

The Power Authority, like other successful authorities in New York State and elsewhere, combines, we believe, the best features of public ownership and private operation. We have a minimum number of first-rate full-time executives. We use competent engineering and other consulting firms for design and supervision, and reliable contractors—selected, whenever possible, by open competition—to carry out plans. The Authority is a nonprofit organization. We have every incentive but the profit motive, and this has no place in the protection of basic inalienable natural resources.

When I was persuaded, somewhat reluctantly, by Governor Dewey to take the chairmanship of the Power Authority and to add this tough chore to other heavy responsibilities, I did so with certain understandings as to my methods. So long as I am chairman of the Authority the methods will be no different from those I have followed in other public agencies for thirty years. There is no mystery about them. They are an open book, often criticized initially, but in the long run respected by the majority of fair-minded people.

I believe the head of an authority, as distinguished from an ordinary government department or commission, must be its executive officer, but that all trustees are equal in deciding policy, that they should be fully acquainted in advance with the important subjects requiring their vote, but not bothered with administrative detail. I believe the chairman should work through his top administrative aides, giving them general direction but not interfering in technical matters and never discouraging initiative, absolute frankness and professional independence.

I believe in delegation of power, but to the right people, not to stooges, clockwatchers, trimmers and incompetents. We can afford to pay for real talent and we shall do so. Our men have to be able to cope with the best in the utility, manufacturing and business establishments with which we must deal.

Ours is an exceedingly complex business, run strictly on business principles, but under public auspices. It is international. It is closely related to the Seaway. It is supervised in one aspect or another by several agencies, national and international, too many in my opinion. Many personalities enter into these things, some of them with bureaucratic pride of position and some not without what Mr. Shakespeare called the insolence of office. We can only hope that as we move on, most of them will be as helpful, cooperative, friendly, sympathetic and quick on the trigger as Lewis Castle, administrator of the Seaway Development Corporation, and his associates, the late Robert Saunders, chairman, and the other members of the Ontario Hydro-Electric Corporation.

We had some trouble with contracting groups, such as the dredging and towing interests in the Great Lakes region, which attempted to dictate policy by obstructionist tactics based upon legal technicalities governing work along the international boundary. These groups did not show a sufficiently lively interest in friendly relations between us and Canada, and seem not to realize that our Canadian partners pay half the bill. Needless to say, we have made it clear that we will not be dictated to, that we do not consider the St. Lawrence the private domain of the Great Lakes dredging interests, that there is enough work for all, that we expect the entire industry to cooperate, and finally that our understanding with

Ontario Hydro provides for open and free competition regardless of whether the work is let by us or by them.

This job has its humor. In addition to those who supervise the supervisors, execute the executives and watch the watchmen, we have to contend with St. Regis Indians, who ask the tidy little sum of $34 million for their pre-Revolutionary interest in Barnhart Island, and assorted characters who are steaming up distant owners on the Great Lakes shorefront to sue us for the rise and fall of the tides. These are merely little incidents that brighten our days.

We cannot make flat promises that all of the St. Lawrence power will stay in the north country. A great part of it will in the end remain there. A lot of it will go into waterside manufacturing. Some of it will go elsewhere in the Adirondacks and nearby areas, possibly in part serviced by our Messena-Taylorville transmission line, some to rural electrification and municipally operated units which are within reach, places like Plattsburg, possibly over the state border. Some of it may provide small yardsticks for power costs. We want customers, all kinds, and all will be treated fairly. We cannot wait until the St. Lawrence Valley gets built up. We must sell power as it is produced to pay off our indebtedness.

None of our St. Lawrence kilowatts, in my humble opinion, will ever reach New York City. Existing private transmission lines are inadequate, transmission losses would be too great and the cost would be prohibitive. No one in New York City would save a nickel on such transmission. All this, of course, applies to St. Lawrence, not to Niagara, power, which is still in dispute and presents problems of a different character.

No one can as yet foretell how many new workers, families, business establishments and other enterprises will be attracted to the St. Lawrence area by the power and Seaway developments. A great deal of misinformation has been peddled about the probable loss of taxable values in the area of improvement, and the adverse effect on the budgets of local governments. I have listened to such prophecies of woe, in similar contexts, for thirty years, and time has shown over and over again that substantial, well-planned, well-built and well-operated public improvements create taxable values far in excess of those lost by condemnation of land for the stimulating public purposes in view.

Water Power and Atomic Energy

In the course of our planning it was inevitable that we should be confronted with the question: When will atomic power be competitive with steam-generated and then with water-generated power?

There is more to this question than persuading underwriters, bankers and investors that loans and bonds for water power development are unquestionably good for the next thirty years. Our entire industrial civilization is involved. We asked a committee of distinguished experts, consisting of Henry T. Heald, Thomas F. Farrell and William L. Laurence, for an opinion on this fascinating subject. Their analysis, based on the latest and most reliable information available, shows that none of the present estimates indicates that nuclear power will compete with St. Lawrence power during the next thirty years, by which time its cost will be largely amortized.

Treatment of Local Residents

In a project of such magnitude some local residents must be discommoded. Those whose property must be acquired will be compensated fairly. Where, through flooding of lands or otherwise, families who must move may suffer some hardship, reasonable allowances will be made. Those who have genuine rights and interests will be treated in a decent, orderly and humane way. No large undertaking can be built without dislocation and other community problems. In this instance, the seriousness of the impact will depend to a great extent upon the willingness of the community to accept temporary inconvenience and to cooperate in the face of some hardships, anticipating an era of expansion and prosperity along the St. Lawrence.

The St. Lawrence Power project and Seaway will, we believe, attract much permanent business to this area. The Authority stands ready to help the local communities within reason. On the other hand, it cannot assume extravagant expenditures for improvements which represent legitimate local ambitions not closely related to power development.

The power development will consist of a control dam in Long Sault Rapids at the end of Barnhart Island, with adjoining power houses, one on either side of the international boundary. The impounded waters will flood a number of small communities on the Canadian side, fewer on our side, and there will be other physical changes in the area. We have agreed with Ontario Hydro to build the Iroquois Dam at a new location, to help the Ogdensburg International Bridge Authority with advice as to the early financing of their vehicular toll bridge, and to refrain from building a road on the Iroquois Dam until the Ogdensburg bonds are largely retired.

OTHER PLANS FOR THE SECTION

After the power house and other construction is completed it is planned to erect an administration building, garage and residential facilities for key operating personnel on Barnhart Island. The rest of the island, about one thousand acres, will be a park, with picnic areas, parking spaces and other facilities for the public. Across from the island, on the southern shore, there will be another thousand-acre park, with a roadway and railway access to Barnhart Island and the Long Sault Dam. The Authority proposes to acquire an additional thousand acres on the shores of the lake to be created, which will be turned over to the Thousand Islands State Park Commission. Many other improvements are planned, including bridges, and relocated and improved highways. The Authority is cooperating with local officials and bodies in stimulating permanent housing, in zoning and in dealing with other problems growing out of the power development.

The Thousand Islands have, from Indian days, been justly celebrated as one of the great scenic and recreational areas of the country. Since 1924, the regional Park Commission has made great progress in developing parks and expanding recreational facilities there. The section has long been extensively developed by palatial summer homes, and diversified water sports attract thousands. Improved highways have tremendously increased the number of visitors in recent years. As chairman of the New York State Emergency Public Works Commission in 1933, I recommended an internationl bridge to Canada, to be constructed as a self-liquidating project by a public authority. The Thousand Islands Bridge was opened with an impressive ceremony in 1938 and has since been a great success.

The public parks in the area are mostly on the mainland, starting at Wescott Beach and the historical battlefield at Sacketts Harbor, southeast of Watertown, and following the St. Lawrence to Chippewa Bay. More recently we acquired Wellesley Island State Park, in the river opposite the American channel span of the Thousand Islands Bridge. In 1953 we obtained legislative authority to add St. Lawrence County (outside the Forest Preserve) to the region and have since acquired land for additional parks. The power development will provide still more parks and recreational areas in the region, which will be integrated into the existing system and made accessible by improved highways, bridges and parkways.

Recreational and living facilities on the riverfront, now enjoyed by local residents, which must be flooded, are to be replaced insofar as possible on substantial vacant land properly planned and located, and provided with public docking and other facilities. Large numbers of tourists can confidently be expected to visit the St. Lawrence Valley once the power and Seaway projects are completed. Our Operations Building at the end of the power house will provide, in addition to space for the maintenance and repair of the power equipment and for administration offices, ample facilities for visitors to watch operations and to enjoy from the observation penthouse on the roof the large lake to be created upstream from the power house.

Highway, path, picnicking and other recreation facilities on Barnhart Island, and on the mainland opposite the Island between the Seaway and the St. Lawrence River, will be provided. All the land between the Seaway and the St. Lawrence River will be acquired, and park facilities in this area will cover approximately 2700 acres. This area, to be known as St. Lawrence River State Park, will be turned over to the Thousand Islands State Park Commission for operation and maintenance, reserving, however, to the Power Authority those areas necessary to operate the power house, dams and other hydro facilities, including housing for key operating personnel.

Recreation will be one of the great by-products of the St. Lawrence Power and Seaway developments. We shall construct a direct landscaped entrance to Barnhart Island from Route 37, involving a bridge across Grass River and an underpass to be built by the Seaway Development Corporation under the Seaway lock. Arrangements will be made among the Seaway Development Corporation, the State Department of Public Works and the Federal Bureau of Public Roads for the connection to Roosevelt Bridge leading to Cornwall, Ontario. Route 37 is the main artery along the river leading to the power project. We shall reconstruct the highway in the area east of Waddington where it will be flooded out. Here we shall build a scenic riverfront boulevard. The State Department of Public Works has announced an arterial plan for Messena, providing for a by-pass around the village. We are coordinating our work with theirs.

We are also providing means whereby cottages and the better movable permanent homes can be moved to new sites. We propose to acquire an area of land large enough to accommodate homes that can be moved, and to request legislation to make it possible for the Authority to move homes and sell them back to the original owners. The program will be somewhat similar to that adopted by the Jones Beach Parkway Authority and used successfully on the widening of the Southern State Parkway and the extension of Meadowbrook Parkway on Long Island. Boating facilities will be planned for this area as well as local recreation facilities.

Our park plan will give the Thousand Islands Commission what it was created for and what it has hoped for for years. The dream of thirty years ago is moving to reality. St. Lawrence River State Park, including areas on the mainland and Barnhart Island, will be one of the great park and conservation attractions of the state, rivaling Niagara. There will be no more dramatic panorama to glorify the works of nature and man working in harmony for the common good. In the immortal words of Walt Whitman, we are the pioneers who stem the rivers.

16

The Car and the Road

IN EVERY CITY THROUGHOUT THE COUNTRY AND IN the sprawling suburbs surrounding the larger cities, traffic is piling up in swollen gasoline gullies, throttling industry, commerce and business; blocking street cleaning, fire and police apparatus; endangering the lives of men and women going to work, of mothers pushing baby carriages, and of children going to and from schools and playgrounds. Parking facilities are inadequate almost everywhere. Regulations are badly drawn, conflicting, confusing and spottily adhered to or enforced. Only the most drastic remedies will alleviate the pain and it will take major surgery to cure the disease. Apparently in most places press and public, politicians and administrators, drivers and pedestrians are not yet prepared for a sedative, not to mention surgery.[22]

The most serious aspect of the problem, of course, has to do with conserving human life. Somehow, we must check the killer—speed—which is costing more lives than all our wars, to say nothing of the army of cripples it produces every year.[23]

The wheel, perhaps man's greatest invention, which lifted him from the mud and gave him mobility, now turns by spark and explosion without human sweat but with plenty of blood and tears. Again our genius has outrun our character and control. A motorcar is a heavy, largely metal conveyance powered by an internal-combus-

tion engine and controlled by delicate mechanism to transport people
and goods over roads which should be good but mostly are not.

Such a machine is bound to be dangerous at best, especially when
it is turned out by assembly-line techniques in enormous quantities
by manufacturers who, until recently, showed no lively interest in the
road system on which it depends. The head of one of the largest of
these corporations wrote me several years ago that cars should be
made year in, year out and year round, but that roads should be built
only in depressions! He has since changed his mind.

What would anyone but a lunatic expect to be the gruesome results of such a concatenation of circumstances, when added to it is
an almost complete absence of uniform, adequate official controls?

REGULATIONS AND ENFORCEMENT

We have insufficient traffic police on foot, on motorcycles and in
cars. The job is dangerous, tiring and thankless. The mechanical aids
are much less ingenious than these enforcement officers have a right
to expect. Too many magistrates and justices have their own curious
ideas of what constitutes cooperation with the police. The majority
supports them, but some quibble, some unfortunately can be reached,
some say safe driving rather than speed should be the test, and some
are just naturally "agin" the whole idea of enforcement. An officer
who has wasted hours in futile or humiliating court proceedings becomes less anxious to do his duty.

I do not say that the average cop is complacent or discouraged or
the average local judge lenient, venal or hostile, but the percentage
of poor ones is too high and there are too many superiors in the
stations and courtrooms who are unable to command obedience.
Too many newspapers are sympathetic to speeders, demand higher
limits and play up every hard-luck story. The result is that weak
intellects come to believe that every driver is entitled to be his own
policeman and judge.

THE RESPONSIBILITY OF STATES

The states have the prime responsibility for registering motor
vehicles, for licensing drivers, for providing standards of safe perform-

ance, for adequate maintenance and periodic inspection of vehicles, for insuring financial responsibility of owner and driver, and for establishing the rules of the road, including the regulation of speed. Some of these functions, particularly those having to do with the regulation of traffic, are properly delegated to cities, towns, villages, counties and other regional or municipal agencies.

Lack of uniformity in traffic laws, however, and failure to resist demands for high-speed limits have been responsible in large part for the increasing tendency to flout and violate the most reasonable regulations. Progress is being made in the gradual adoption of a uniform code, but at a slow pace. There must be no letup in the program of adopting a basic uniform code covering all forty-eight states, and the establishment of reasonable and safe regulations by the states and their subdivisions.

Cars More Dangerous Than War

Fully half of all traffic deaths are due to speed. Cars have become more dangerous than wars. In the last fifty years more than a million Americans have been killed by the motor car. By comparison, in all of the wars in which the United States has participated since the Revolution, we have lost some 600,000 men in battle.

Records compiled by the New York Good Roads Association a few years ago show the close relation between traffic deaths and the speed limits set by various states. At limits of from 40 to 60 miles per hour, the death rate climbed steadily from 4.2 per 100 million vehicle miles to 8.2. The Pennsylvania Turnpike, with a speed limit of 70 miles per hour, had a death rate of 8.0 per 100 million vehicle miles. The New Jersey Turnpike, with a speed limit of 60 miles, had a death rate of 6.5. New York State, with a legal speed limit of 50 miles per hour, on state highways, had a death rate of 6.0. On the Long Island parkways, where the speed limit is 35 miles in Brooklyn and Queens and 40 miles in Nassau and Suffolk counties, the death rate was 1.5 per 100 million vehicle miles!

No honest mind can escape the significance of these figures. Fatalities increase as speed increases. Not all speeders are caught. Increased patrolling is necessary. Mechanical gadgets, radar, automatic speed controls and timing devices may be practical in certain areas, but these also require policemen to operate them. Our entire highway system cannot be protected from speed maniacs by mechanical robots. Thorough police work with sufficient patrol cars and adequate equipment is a prime necessity.

Most drivers using parkways and expressways in urban areas are on trips involving short distances—ten, twenty or thirty miles. The maximum time saved by driving at 60 instead of 40 miles an hour for such distances is only a few minutes. Are they worth a life? The tragic record of weekend and holiday accidents raises the question whether the lives and limbs of innocent people should be allowed to be endangered so that someone can have a few more precious minutes to waste, after burning up the roads in a mad rush toward a cocktail, kaffeeklatch, or the evening pinochle game.

VARYING SPEED LIMITS

A county judge on Long Island reversed a decision of a local court which had convicted a motorist of violating the 40-mile-an-hour speed limit on the state parkways. This motorist, a lawyer by profession, was a self-styled champion of the speeding underdog and claimed to be vindicating a great principle. The county judge held that there was a defect in the basic state parkway law and that, as a result, the 40-mile-an-hour parkway speed ordinance was invalid and was, in effect, superseded by the 50-mile-an-hour limit set by the state for ordinary highways.

In arguing the case before the Court of Appeals, the Long Island State Park Commission reminded the court of the appalling death rate on the highways of the United States and of the high percentage of fatalities due to speed. It was pointed out that both traffic policemen and the courts allow a tolerance of at least 5 and more often 10 miles an hour before an arrest or fine.

It was brought out further that the state parkway speed regulations follow a logical pattern which recognizes differences in the conditions prevailing in various localities. Thus, in New York City, where there is a great concentration of traffic, the speed limit on the parkways is set at 35 miles an hour. As the parkways radiate into the

surrounding counties, the speed limit is increased to 40 miles an hour
in Nassau, western Suffolk and Westchester counties and to 45 and
50 miles an hour in Putnam and Dutchess counties to the north.

In summarizing its case, the Park Commission argued that an increase in the speed limit from 40 to 50 miles an hour would increase
the number of fatalities from 1 to 5 per 100 million vehicle miles.
This would have raised the average of 5 deaths per year to 25 on the
Long Island parkways. The Court of Appeals reversed the decision
of the county judge and reaffirmed the Commission's 40-mile speed
limit.

Parkways were designed, built and protected for pleasant, careful
driving. Cross traffic has been eliminated by attractive stone-faced
bridges. Wide rights-of-way have been landscaped with native trees,
flowering shrubs and evergreens. They have been developed as shoestring parks with pavements for passenger cars only. All this is a useless
expenditure for the speeders, who, at the rate they travel, cannot
distinguish a rosebush from a bale of hay.

On the older sections of parkways, built over twenty years ago,
center dividers have been installed to separate opposing lanes of traffic.
This device has effectively stopped head-on collisions. It was originally suggested to me by the late Dr. Foster Kennedy, distinguished
neurologist, that brain injuries accounted for most auto fatalities and
that most of them were head injuries due to head-on collisions involving high speed.

The traffic accident cost to the nation is almost beyond belief. It
is estimated that the price of injury, property damage and insurance
exceeds $3 billion per year. Insurance, still inadequate, becomes
steadily and alarmingly more expensive. The inescapable conclusion
is that speed makes the difference between major and minor accidents
—that is, between injuries and deaths—and that only drastic regulation of speed plus other controls can materially change the present
horrible picture.

Let Us Have Safety First!

The automobile has brought many problems, which cannot be
solved quickly. There is much to be done to deal with the various

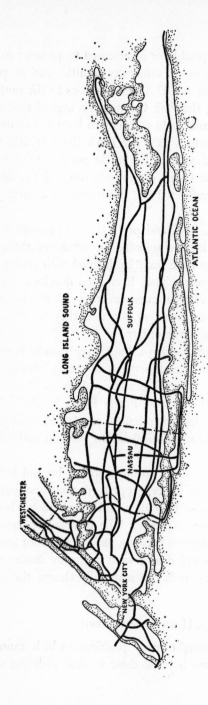

LONG ISLAND PARKWAYS, EXPRESSWAYS AND MAJOR HIGHWAYS

phases of the matter in towns, cities and the nation. It is my suggestion that we put first things first and deal directly with the most serious aspect of the problem, which is safety. It is my contention that speed is primarily responsible for the appalling death rate from automobile accidents.

This statement has been challenged by no less an authority than Mr. David M. Baldwin, Director of the Traffic Division of the National Safety Council, of which I was a member of the Board of Trustees. Mr. Baldwin wrote that while many people feel that speed is a substantial causal factor in motor accidents, "there are others, equally sincere, I am sure, who feel that there is no direct relationship between speed and accidents and that a reduction in speeds would not reduce accidents. We are to some extent in the position of an arbiter, and we are looking for facts. Frankly, there are few facts available."

As I wrote Mr. Baldwin, I am interested in safety, not in the interpretation of statistics, and have no use for people who see no relationship between speed and accidents and believe that reduction in speeds would not reduce accidents. Having as an administrator planned roads, built and operated them for many years, and having almost daily seen, studied and carried responsibility for gruesome accidents, and having by structural and regulatory methods successfully guarded against speed, I know from first-hand experience that speed is the biggest factor in serious accidents and frequently the sole reason of fatal ones. My resignation as a member of the Board of Trustees of the National Safety Council followed.

Specifically I advocate:

1. More drastic regulation of speed without regard to unrealistic, theoretically designed limits and political pressures for higher limits.

2. Stopping the senseless advertising of high-speed motors as a basis of sales.

3. An unrelenting campaign to acquaint the public with the cause and effect of accidents and especially the terrible danger of excessive speed.

4. Continuance of efforts to obtain uniform laws and regulations governing the speed of motor vehicles on our highways and streets with reasonable local control.

5. Closer cooperation among all regulatory agencies, including the various administrative officials, the police and the courts, in the rigorous and impartial enforcement of proper speed limits.

RAILROAD CROSSINGS AT GRADE

An important factor in assuring greater safety in motoring is the elimination of railroad crossings at grade. The separation of highways and railroad tracks by elevation, depression or by substituting parallel side lines, is in many ways a special, complicated and costly matter. Here basic responsibility is fixed beyond dispute by fundamental law. It is the highway, not the railroad—the car, not the train—which creates the hazard and must be primarily responsible for its removal. The prevailing opinion of Justice Brandeis, speaking for the Supreme Court of the United States in the case of Nashville, Chattanooga & St. Louis Railway v. Walters, *et al*, handed down in 1934, states this principle clearly:

> The railroad has ceased to be the prime instrument of danger and the main cause of accidents. It is the railroad which now requires protection from dangers incident to motor transportation.

The laws of the several states which are supposed to give force to this opinion vary widely, and still reflect a disposition to penalize the railroads and to make them pay for construction which in most cases benefits them little and cannot be capitalized by them.

Up to 1925, the New York State Constitution fixed the railroad's share of cost at 50 per cent and the state's and municipality's each at 25. Other changes were made from time to time, but the program developed under Governor Smith lagged, largely because the railroads did not have available 50 per cent of the costs.

In the Constitutional Convention of 1938, a new and somewhat complicated formula was proposed and adopted. The amendment placed the entire cost of the elimination squarely on the state and provided that it should include incidental improvements rendered necessary or desirable because of the elimination and reasonably included in the engineering plans therefor. The state, however, was to be reimbursed by the railroad for the entire amount of railroad improvements not an essential part of elimination, as well as the amount of the net benefit to the company or companies from the elimination exclusive of such railroad improvements, the amount of such net benefit to be adjudicated after the completion of the work as prescribed by law, and in no event to exceed 15 per cent of the expense of the elimination, exclusive of all incidental improvements.

The new amendment, in spite of its complexity, has worked well. The railroads no longer spar for time. What constitutes a direct railroad benefit is, of course, debatable and subject to later determination, but immediate financing is now assured. Moreover, in most cases new highways, and especially expressways, thruways, turnpikes and so-called freeways automatically provide over- and underpasses at rail crossings as part of their own independent financing.

During the depression there were limited Federal funds available under Federal highway laws involving no railroad participation. These were later discontinued except on a matching basis on Federal highway routes. Federal appropriations for crossings, including reconstruction of existing crossings and the opening of new ones on other than Federal highway routes should be resumed, because many cities and states cannot afford adequate appropriations for this purpose. The present restrictions should be liberalized as to grade crossing expenditures on the urban, secondary and primary systems.

Obviously, design standards of rail crossing eliminations should be as high as those of other crossings, and provision for maintenance of train schedules and car movements by temporary devices and detours must be carefully worked out by the most intimate cooperation of railroad and highway engineers. In most instances the railroad must let and supervise contracts since it assumes the major risks.

CONTROL OF BILLBOARDS

Any program of highway expansion and improvement, especially one involving new routes and rights of way, which does not face frankly and firmly the menace of indiscriminate billboard advertising will not have sustained public approval. Intelligent women in particular have profound convictions on this subject. Honest public officials of long experience are increasingly fed up with glib assurance of cooperation from billboard companies and advertisers who have little regard either for safety or for the preservation of the landscape. Parkways are already more or less protected by wide rights of way, state laws, and local zoning ordinances and easements, but most laws governing new mixed traffic arteries including toll roads have been rigged with weak sign and billboard provisions or stripped of all such regulations.

The billboard companies have shrewdly sought the aid of farmers and other adjacent owners who seize the opportunity to pick up a few fast dollars, and of unions engaged in putting up and painting signs, to defeat regulatory bills and prevent effective administrative rulings. Since there are many other more promising media, advertisers seem much less interested in plastering the highway system with appeals for their wares than the billboard companies claim.

In terms of safety and public support, it is essential to curb the billboard interests from the start. Road building at best brings with it some undesirable features. If every highway is to become just a gasoline gully, those who live and work nearby and those who drive for pleasure and with some respect for scenery, are going to be more and more in favor of putting the new roads somewhere else or drastically limiting their construction.

SOME ADDITIONAL REGULATIONS

The maximum size and weight of vehicles vary throughout the nation and there is too much pressure for huge trucks, buses and trailers and too little appreciation of the benefits of small, light taxicabs and passenger cars in cities. Inspection of cars and drivers is good in few areas, poor or undependable in others, and nonexistent in some of the largest states. These states should penalize careless owners and the courts should impose heavier penalties on flagrant offenders.

Reliable interstate records should be established on a uniform basis covering registration, licensing, inspection and financial responsibility. These records would, among other things, catch violators of laws who acquire licenses and registration certificates in other states. The results of such laxity are scandalous and higher standards must be generally established and enforced as an integral part of the program. There is altogether too much selfish visible and hidden opposition to effective remedial state legislation. Effective regulations might well be made an indispensable condition of receiving Federal aid.

We need many additional regulations and restrictions governing the use of motor cars, not only to make them safer but to facilitate their movement and increase their usefulness to the community. Tighter zoning requirements would be enormously helpful. These cannot constitutionally be made retroactive, but they can be extended and enforced on new structures and the rebuilding of old ones, so as to require offstreet loading and unloading vehicular facilities and parking spaces for a reasonable number of cars on the premises. We must begin actually to enforce loading, unloading, parking, and double-parking laws, restrictions on the movements of oversized trucks during peak traffic hours in congested areas, and regulations covering parked and cruising taxis and other practices which block intersections and disrupt traffic.

In the field of regulation, we also need more well-planned one-way streets, more efficient synchronizing of lights, more liberal use of painted lines, better illuminating devices and signs, and much better pedestrian controls and safeguards. We must stagger business hours and thereby cut down peak loads. We must make some traffic, which now runs in the daytime, run at night.

Such regulations will be opposed by ultra-conservatives and by employees and unions that will either refuse to work on new inconvenient and unaccustomed schedules or demand exorbitant overtime rates which business cannot pay. When, however, the majority of the people realize that such rules are required, the minorities, no matter how vociferous, well heeled and threatening, will have to yield. In the meantime it is not to be expected that office seekers and holders will be enthusiastic about sticking their necks out, and those who depend most on catering to organized minorities will be the least inclined to take the lead.

These expedients, though tough, are infinitely preferable to the desperate remedies proposed by extremists who would destroy property values and the real estate and business tax systems on which our municipalities depend for their existence. These extremists demand that in city centers, including residential as well as business districts, all private cars be kept out, that we cut in half the present number of taxis, that no parking, even with meter regulations, be permitted, and that we abandon all tall buildings for low horizontal structures on large garden plots. Dull, worn-out officials and irresponsible planners join in such proposals. But the process of change must be evolutionary and in charge of those whose aim is to modernize not revolutionize, to preserve values, not destroy them.[24]

17

Relief from
Traffic Strangulation

GLOOMS AND GROUCHES DECLARE THAT THE URBAN traffic disease is incurable, but few, if any, urban illnesses requiring physical construction and honest regulation are hopeless. When articulate, influential city people finally get around to accepting drastic operations, strong medicine, diet and a certain amount of regimentation, this disease too will yield to treatment but the cures are slow, distasteful and expensive, and the field is full of plausible quacks and medicine men with instant painless salves, ointments and incantations. We need reliable practitioners for deepseated troubles, and the general practitioner, the family doctor, is more to be trusted than the average medicine man from far away. There are, to be sure, some good diagnosticians, but very few. At best, they analyze. They do not operate or cure.

The remedies are modern expressways right through and not merely around and by-passing cities; offstreet parking facilities of all kinds supported by wholesale metering; marginal parking fields coordinated with rapid transit; staggered working hours, higher zoning, which prevents overbuilding and excessive population; smaller taxicabs, better buses, better traffic lights and other control devices, more police, lower speed limits, more enforcement, more courageous magistrates, adequate compulsory auto insurance, much more effective inspection of cars, licensing of drivers and revocation of licenses. There will be widespread approval of these remedies in principle and howls of rage from groups and individuals against their application. The pressure for exceptions will be enormous. Compromises simply aggravate the disease.

The big problems in solving urban traffic strangulation are cost, which runs from $1 million to over $15 million a mile; moving people out of the way, demolition, maintaining services and, last but not least, offstreet parking. Offstreet parking facilities, subsurface, surface and above surface, are expensive and, if they are to be self-supporting, must be tied up with arterial construction, metering and capitalized revenues from meters.

Public municipal parking authorities, which sell their tax-exempt revenue bonds to private investors and do not depend on public credit, continue to be the best means of financing offstreet parking, but authorities and other municipal agencies responsible for traffic solutions must have cooperation from those who plan, lay out and prepare land-taking maps and designs for arterial construction. It is a mistake not to include in modern arterial rights-of-way land for offstreet parking which otherwise will congest service roads and make them virtually valueless.

Practical solutions of the traffic problems in cities should be coordinated with slum clearance, street widening, parks and playgrounds, utility modernization and other improvements which go with up-to-date city mapping and planning. These incidental features of traffic projects are often neglected by narrow-minded administrators at all levels who can only see one problem at a time.

Cities must not be forgotten or neglected in our national highway planning. The strategic, military and evacuation aspects of arterial construction are vital in cities. Stimulation of employment when defense and other spending is cut down is more important in urban centers than elsewhere. The reduction in cost of goods and food by first-rate truck facilities is a top problem in big municipalities.

The needs of cities must not be minimized because they require relatively little mileage. This is strategic mileage of vital importance to both interstate and urban systems. It is the hardest to locate, the most difficult to clear, the most expensive to acquire and build and the most controversial from the point of view of selfish and shortsighted opposition. Without attempting to override local opinion and dictate from distant capitals, the Federal and state governments can help immeasurably to overcome local pressures by establishing engineering and other standards which can only be departed from at the risk of loss of Federal and state aid of all kinds.

APPROACHES TO THE PARKING PROBLEM

There is no one easy answer to the offstreet parking problem. It depends upon the community, its needs, practices, traditions, politics, economic and social outlook, leadership in business and numerous other factors. Additional offstreet parking can be provided in the planning of major new arteries, including widened streets, boulevards and expressways as a necessary incident in their building and as an added source of revenue. We must build adequate offstreet parking facilities directly through the municipal government, and indirectly by inducements, exemptions, aids, subventions, and other Santa Clauses easily recognizable or thinly disguised.

New York City's attempts to provide offstreet garage facilities in cooperation with private enterprise thus far have not been eminently successful. For example, the New York Life Insurance Company was persuaded by the city to agree to construct a two-story public garage with a park on the roof just south of one of its housing projects at East Sixty-Fifth Street between Second and Third avenues in Manhattan. The agreement provided that the city assemble the plot and sell to the highest bidder for the purpose of building a garage to be operated under these conditions. The New York Life Insurance Company agreed to bid for the land the sum paid for it by the city in condemnation and to finance the entire project. The matter was taken to court and the city was restrained from condemning the site pending what would have been a long trial to prove that it was for a public purpose. The project was then dropped.

There have been any number of suggestions that we rip up public parks, such as Central Park and Bryant Park, to provide underground parking. The advocates of underground parking point to the Union Square undertaking in San Francisco on the assumption that this unusual project proves that all underground garages must be successful.

The fact is that underground garages have been studied for Central Park and Bryant Park in New York and found wholly impractical. Bryant Park is surrounded by subways and contains an underground maze of utilities. It would be virtually impossible to get in and out of this area without disrupting traffic on the surrounding streets and interfering with recreation. In addition, Bryant Park has been rebuilt in recent years after being continuously torn up as the result of subway construction. To tear it up again and reduce its size and usefulness would be unthinkable. It would also break the bank.

The southerly end of Central Park, where garages have been recommended by uninformed geniuses, is solid rock. An underground garage here would be prohibitively expensive and would promote traffic congestion. There is an erroneous assumption by some persons that public parks exist primarily to afford cheap, convenient, and easy locations for every conceivable use from garages to opera houses, incinerators, and supermarkets. If they prevailed, our public recreation system would disappear. Progressive communities do not dump traffic into their parks. They even protect them by zoning against garages on adjacent private property. In Manhattan it is much more economical to acquire separate sites for multistoried or open-deck garages built above ground.

ARCADED SIDEWALKS ARE HELPFUL

There are endless opportunities open to ingenious traffic experts for quaint devices, to use an old Greek term, to expand our shrinking streets without invading our parks. One of them, in which I have great hopes, is the arcaded sidewalk. For years every time we took a crack at it we were stopped by owners who would not listen to such plans and timid officials who feared exorbitant awards in condemnation. Finally we got our chance while building the underpass and plaza at the United Nations Headquarters. Tudor City, an apartment project in the neighborhood, had no shops of value on First Avenue and the new ones made accessible by the arcade were a godsend to ungrateful landlords, second in value only to the removal of the slaughterhouses to make way for the UN headquarters. The awards were reasonable. The experiment, example, precedent, guinea pig, guide post, or whatever you choose to call it, is now manifest. It should be followed widely throughout other cities. The New York Coliseum, at Columbus Circle, is to follow this plan.

Private capital alone without government aids of one kind or another and supplementary government building cannot solve the parking problem in the average congested urban area. Obviously all new large buildings, residential and commercial, should be required by law or zoning regulations to provide reasonable offstreet parking and loading facilities, but these rules cannot constitutionally be made retroactive. Sufficient additional offstreet facilities at reasonable prices cannot in many areas be made self-supporting without inducements and subventions, open or disguised. Wholesale metering is the logical helper. It provides revenue, regulates and cuts down unnecessary and prolonged parking, discourages overnight standing, and drives those who use the streets as garages into offstreet parking lots and garages built and operated for this purpose. There should also be Federal aid for parking along main highways on the Federal system.

A parking authority or other agency, if it has the power to install and collect revenues from meters, can in many instances raise enough funds over and above reasonable offstreet charges to finance all the facilities that private capital, with or without tax and other aids, cannot furnish. Both meter and public parking charges must be within the means of car owners and users.

Another requirement which only government can supply is the power of eminent domain, that is, condemnation to assemble offstreet plots, and garage and terminal building sites at suitable locations close to meter installations. In the larger cities with rapid transit facilities, increased use of fringe parking on main arteries at the outskirts of the city and close to rapid transit stations should be encouraged. Such parking lots, if properly planned, constructed and operated, furnish all-day parking at comparatively low cost, thus relieving traffic congestion in the central areas.

There are locations where a city may get bids to acquire land and

lease it to private capital for long terms on conditions which will
insure construction of garages without public appropriations. Such
construction may include other uses. These projects will be upheld
within reason by the courts as a public purpose. Here again the public
authority device is an excellent one, especially where municipal budgets are tight and the debt margin is shrinking.

Until we get a parking authority we are never going to solve the
offstreet parking problem in New York City. The Traffic Department is doing a good job painting white lines, regulating traffic,
installing signal lights and attending to other details, but this agency
can never provide the big solution. A parking authority that installs
meters wholesale, wherever they are needed, and builds offstreet
parking facilities financed in large part by the revenues from parking
meters, is the answer.

The Budget Director in New York now favors using all meter
revenue just to finance the Traffic Department. The Traffic Commissioner can never finance offstreet facilities. He is not familiar with
that kind of operation. We had a Parking Authority, but when we
tried to get the law changed so that we could make the system work,
we were beaten by the oil people and the garage people. The law
is still on the statute books, but the commissioners resigned. Until
we get the right kind of an authority, we will not take care of offstreet
parking in New York City.

NEW YORK'S GREAT AUTHORITIES

In New York we have two great authorities which have a vital role
in dealing with traffic problems, vehicular and air. The Port of New
York Authority is interstate; the Triborough Bridge and Tunnel
Authority is intracity but has covered the five boroughs of Greater
New York and reached out into the suburbs.

The Port Authority owns and operates Idlewild, La Guardia,
Newark and Peterboro airports; Holland and Lincoln tunnels; the
George Washington Bridge over the Hudson; three bridges between
New Jersey and Staten Island; an inland freight terminal in Man-
hattan; a grain elevator in Brooklyn, and a splendid new bus terminal
and airlines terminal on the west side of Manhattan.

Triborough owns and operates Triboro, Henry Hudson, Whitestone, Marine and Crossbay bridges and the Queens-Midtown and Brooklyn-Battery tunnels. We built the East Side Airlines Terminal in Manhattan and are building the New York Coliseum, which will have parking facilities for two thousand cars. We are also spending $80 million of Triborough bondholders' money to build parts of the Federal-state highway system, which would otherwise suffer long delays and perhaps, through preemption of the right of way by private building, become entirely impossible of accomplishment at any reasonable cost.

In 1954, the Port of New York Authority and the Triborough Bridge and Tunnel Authority joined forces and authorized an expenditure of $750,000 on a joint study of vehicular congestion in the metropolitan area. Some of the major projects proposed are:

An elevated expressway connecting the Holland Tunnel with the Manhattan and Williamsburg bridges; an express crossing in midtown connecting the Lincoln and Queens Midtown tunnels; an expressway across The Bronx linking the George Washington Bridge with the Whitestone Bridge, a second deck on the George Washington Bridge; and a bridge across The Narrows, at the entrance to New York harbor. We must have another bridge at Throggs Neck paralleling the Whitestone span, also, to take care of increased traffic using the Narrows Bridge.

There are, of course, many secondary projects all related to the integrated arterial system serving the entire metropolitan area. The most dramatic and costliest of these projects is the Narrows Bridge. It will be the longest suspension bridge in the world—4400 feet— and the tallest—with a clearance of 237 feet. The cost, without all the necessary approaches, will run in the neighborhood of $280 million.

This span will be the most important single piece of arterial construction in the world. When it comes to describing it it is all superlatives. Biggest, highest, most expensive, and the great metropolitan bypass for Westchester, New England and Long Island traffic bound for New Jersey, Philadelphia, Washington and points south. It is the natural north-south route, and the shortest by many miles. It will contribute immensely to alleviating congestion in Manhattan.

The greatest single problem in connection with these various proj-

ects in New York City is that relating to the relocation of owners
and tenants who will be displaced. It was never easy to move houses
and people, business establishments, plants and utilities, especially
in old settled communities. The housing shortage has enormously
aggravated this difficulty. Public sympathy at the start is usually with
the fellow in the path of the improvement, no matter how generous
the offers to purchase, how high the awards in condemnation, how
fair the substitutes proposed in public housing and the sums paid
to people to move themselves.

The press alternately screams for traffic relief, exaggerates the
plight of those who are displaced, denounces the lag in construction
and curses with Old Testament ferocity heartless administrators
who remove neighborhood landmarks. Elected officials are sensitive
to such confusing advice and figure that their best bet is to play safe,
do nothing, and postpone everything controversial until the atmosphere clears and they can see who is likely to win the argument.
All this makes for cowardice, delay, and, of course, finally much
higher costs.

To avoid uprooting families in connection with the Narrows Bridge
we propose to use as much land as we can in the Fort Hamilton
Military Reservation in Bay Ridge, Brooklyn, and Fort Wadsworth
on Staten Island. When people must be moved, it will be done in an
orderly way. Families eligible for public housing can be relocated
more readily than others. Intermediate income people must be dealt
with at great lengths. Their resistance is terrific. We must employ
ingenious means and a good deal of determination to do what
needs to be done. When there is any sign of weakness—the minute
a politician says we can move a highway over a bit or curve it
around a group of apartments—that is when trouble starts.

We had that kind of trouble with the Cross-Bronx Expressway.
Plans were approved years ago, and for more than two years we tried
to move families out of a section they would not leave. Unfortunately,
when Mayor Wagner was campaigning in The Bronx, he told these
people he would move the Expressway.

When he told me about it I said, "I am sorry, Bob, but you will
have to tell them you can't move it. The city is not going to make

this decision. The city pays only half the cost of land. It is Federal and state money that's involved and I represent these officials. If you try to move this Expressway you'll never get another nickel from us. You will have to explain that it was all a mistake." The Board of Estimate finally voted for the route, unchanged.

One solution to this problem in New York is to buy boarded-up tenement houses and rehabilitate the buildings. It will cost money, it is not economical, but all major improvements in congested areas are expensive. It took me four years to persuade the Federal, state and city governments that we should pay tenants to move, even if they own nothing. We started out paying them $100 a room—for decorating and other expenses. Now we pay them $200 a room. It is well worth it, however, when you are dealing with arterial improvements that cost as high as $5 million a mile.

18

For a National
Highway Program

THE HIGHWAY DILEMMA IS A MAJOR CONCERN
of every man, woman and child in the country. Our problem is to
keep pace with a motorized civilization and to keep it civilized.
How to accomplish this within our abilities and means is the task
before us.

In 1953 the General Motors Corporation offered some $75,000 in
prizes for the best essays submitted on better highways. Having a keen
interest in the subject and some experience in dealing with the
practical problems involved, I submitted a paper on "How to Plan
and Pay for the Safe and Adequate Highways We Need," for which
I received the main award.[25]

The plans submitted in the competition were, of course, original in
the sense that they had not been published before. But this did not
mean that the successful contestants were artists improvising alone
in some obscure attic. Whatever of value emerged represented experience for which many earnest, thoughtful, enthusiastic and loyal
workers severally shared the credit. "No man," as John Donne said,
"is an iland intire of it selfe," and in good fortune as well as bad we
must never fail to acknowledge our debt to others.

The purpose of the General Motors contest, and my purpose in
entering it, was to stir the interest of motorists and the public in
the vital problem of highways. With this objective still in mind, I

would like to draw upon my essay to restate the problem, and to summarize its conclusions.

We have some 60 million cars of all sorts in use today. At the present rate of production, estimates indicate that by 1964 we will have upwards of 70 million cars of all sorts, including more than 13 million trucks and buses. The highways on which these vehicles run are by and large inadequate in mileage, location, width, capacity and durability. They are unsafe, of inferior, dated design, and poorly lighted and policed.

Over a period of years, the makers of cars averaged a gross income of some $10 billion a year on their products. By way of startling contrast, the average outlay for new construction on roads of all kinds was only about $2.7 billion a year. The discrepancy becomes greater and the gap yawns wider every year. An adequate road system, if we could get it in, say, ten years, would cost $50 billion or more.

WHY WE CANNOT BUILD FASTER

At first blush, a ten-year program may seem unduly long, but a glance at the practical difficulties in the way will show why a faster schedule is impractical. We have limited trained and competent engineering and contracting personnel, equipment and material for the program from planning to construction and finally inspection. Only so much work can be done at one time without overburdening the construction industry, raising prices and contributing toward inflation. Too much and too rapid construction would paralyze urban areas and make their daily functioning almost impossible.

We must carefully observe and gauge urban and suburban growth, housing construction and other trends to be sure that we are building in the right places and on the proper scale. In moving tenants out of the path of highway construction we must proceed in a humane, decent way and help them to find other homes and business places. Moreover, the minimum schedule of major highway building in urban areas runs to at least three years for each large project—a year to design and sell the plan to those who support it is needed to lift it from idea to reality, and at least two years to clear and prepare the site, build on it and landscape it.

STANDARDS AND PLANS

All states have urban, primary and secondary highway programs of some sort, in one way or another eligible for Federal aid. State laws usually fix routes but only in the most general way, that is, by designating the starting and finishing points with occasional intermediate locations. The more important arteries meriting Federal aid are placed on the official map of the Federal Bureau of Public Roads in the Department of Commerce.

State programs differ widely in scope, detail and reliability and run all the way from ill-defined sketch lines on large-scale general maps to routes which represent real study and in some instances accurate right-of-way and first-stage, preliminary and even final specifications. Postwar shelf planning with Federal or state aid or both has produced many useful preliminary and final plans. Some of them, to be sure, suffer from obsolescence and require considerable changes to bring them up to date.

While standards are well established in most branches of highway construction from the simplest three-rod road to the most modern and sophisticated expressway or parkway, there must still be types which have not been seriously studied, much less tried, and endless variations of the best we have in use are possible. For example, the combined vehicular express rail and rapid transit road has not been thoroughly canvassed. We have only a few successful experiments in increasing the efficiency of parkways and expressways where full additional lanes are impractical because of inadequate rights of way and the excessive cost of rebuilding bridges. Here narrow center dividers separating opposing traffic lanes, accelerating and decelerating lanes, space for disabled cars and other similar devices are required.

We do not have anything like complete information free from prejudice on the types of elevated highways and parkways which do not depress the value of surrounding property. We also lack reliable graphic reports on increases in adjacent and neighboring values due to building roads, parkways and crossings. Elevated parkways and expressways, contrary to uninformed opinion, need not blight the areas through which they pass. If properly designed and lighted, the space under these structures can be used for recreation facilities, parking and other useful and attractive purposes. Decisions as to tunnels and against bridges at important water crossings are often settled on the basis of prejudice instead of fact.

In New York City there have been substantial increases in neighborhood values adjacent to parkways and expressways due largely to the fact that they were properly designed. Parks, playgrounds, walks, bicycle and bridle paths have been constructed as incidental improvements on their borders. In many cases they have been located along waterfronts and streams of natural beauty and have been coordinated with beaches and other recreation facilities. In some places, particularly along the ocean and bay fronts, overlook parking strips have been built.

We should do much more advance mapping of arterial rights of way to anchor routes and prevent building. These should include actual vesting of title by purchase or condemnation as well as official notice to owners to prevent building in mapped streets. Manifestly, there is much to be done to improve highway planning and standards to make the experience of more progressive states and communities available to those which are lagging.

There is altogether too little research in the highway field. The Federal government does a little but not nearly enough. Some states go in for limited research either separately or in cooperation with the Federal government through such agencies as the American Association of State Highway Officials, the Highway Research Board and the Automotive Safety Foundation. Municipalities do almost nothing. Considerable study of value is made commercially but, of course, with a bias in favor of the product of the company which does the laboratory, field work and publication.

The automobile industry, in all its ramifications, the designing and inspecting engineers and the road material men and contractors do not work together enough, do not pool their information as much as they should, tend to stick too closely to their own limited fields, depend too much on occasional conferences, conventions, dinners, casual meetings and trade and professional publications and too little on formal, well directed and financed, day in and day out cooperative working arrangements.

We still lack simple, generally understood language and terminology to replace obscure gobbledygook and code words in describing the various types of roads, streets, highways, boulevards, parkways, mixed traffic, limited and controlled access arteries, freeways, thruways, turn-pikes, expressways, interchanges, cloverleaves, dividers, access drives, accelerating and decelerating lanes, "origin and destination" statistics, etc. We need simple Anglo-Saxon words used and interpreted in the same way by everyone.

Again, in the field of design and inspection of construction we have no consensus as to the relative merits and usages of regular, salaried civil service or governmental forces compared to outside con-sultants who work for a fee or percentage and we have the most astonishing variations as to salaries, fees and percentages. In some instances, particularly on large new projects, the best solution is a combination of civil service employees and consulting firms, where the former supply intelligent supervision, set standards of design and exercise general control and the latter furnish the manpower and service required to get out the plans and specifications expeditiously.

For both public and private work we must have an assured supply of well trained young men. The engineering colleges are not supply-ing enough of them. Corporations involved in the motor industry should contribute more liberally out of corporate earnings under the Federal 5 per cent exemption rule to enable the universities to meet this demand. We must have better salaries, less red tape, faster promotion of capable people and better incentives in the civil service.

All of these subjects require a free exchange of views, more facts, and more standardization. On the other hand there is such a thing as too much standardization. This is a big country with extremes of climate, people, traditions and practices. The process of raising standards must necessarily be aggravatingly slow, but it should be steady. Standards must be adapted to local conditions.

THE MULTIPLICITY OF AGENCIES

To those unfamiliar with our unique federation of sovereign states and our inherited conceptions of limited Federal powers, states' rights and municipal home rule, the administration of highway building and maintenance must seem incomprehensible. And yet, somehow, it can and must be made to work. It requires many evolutionary modifications but not by any means a revolution. We must get away from fixed ideas about the exact boundaries of each jurisdiction, from dogmatic assertions and political chestnuts, to a practical approach based on what will most quickly and smoothly get us to our objectives.

Traditionally our Federal government from the beginning and under its great founders has sponsored and supported national highways and other transportation. Washington and Jefferson were both national planners in the broadest sense. Washington was vitally interested in this subject. From his early manhood his aim was to penetrate the wilderness and link the Ohio country with the Atlantic seaboard. To checkmate the French he conceived and hacked through Braddock's Road following an old Indian trail, Namocolin's Path, from Fort Cumberland to the Forks. As President, he limited his recommendations for public improvements to post-offices and post-roads and additional Cross-posts because the new Federal government had no money, but he continued to press his transportation program when he left office, concentrating on the canal to connect the Potomac and Ohio rivers.

Jefferson was in complete agreement with Washington's arterial concepts. He favored internal improvements but was also held back because of lack of funds. Gallatin worked out a program of internal improvements which Jefferson approved. By 1806, there was an increase in national revenue to almost $15 million. After meeting all current expenses and paying off millions in interest and principal on the funded debt, Jefferson had a surplus of $4 million in the Treasury. He recommended keeping up the tariffs so that this surplus could be spent on proper roads, canals and other improvements of value to the nation.

"By these operations," he said in his message of 1806, "new channels of communications will be opened between the States; the lines of separation will disappear, their interests will be identified, and their union cemented by new and indissoluble ties."

Today the Federal Bureau of Public Roads is at the apex of the triangle, the head of the hierarchy. It sets standards, determines what routes shall have Federal aid, gives advice and help, and is responsible for integration of state systems, continuous travel, military and emergency needs and the encouragement of a nationwide program. Over the years this agency has functioned well. It has not been bureaucratic at the top. It has generally been intelligent, persuasive, diplomatic but incorruptible and reasonably firm as to standards. Without it we should have no national through routes uniting all sections of the country, few comprehensive long-range state programs, no uniformity of design, no progress in the less populous and prosperous states and municipalities, no official leadership, no continuing Congressional support and no formula for Federal aid. Nevertheless, the Bureau has lacked adequate authorizations and appropriations and the power to prevent the lag in road building. We must now make up for this. The Federal machinery is there. It has public respect. It needs to be amplified and implemented.

There are forty-eight state highway departments. Some have matched the Federal aid, to which they were entitled, only fast enough to ward off redistribution elsewhere. This must be corrected. Municipalities of all kinds also have their separate highway and street jurisdictions. Their claims upon Federal and state funds only began to be recognized when we scrapped the untenable theory that financial support stopped at the boundaries of urban areas. This more than any other obstacle was responsible for the present road congestion and traffic strangulation.

Much more Federal and state money is made available in some municipalities than in others. The tendency everywhere continues to reflect the habits of mind of legislative majorities usually dominated by rural members who believe in acreage as against people, as though both are not entitled to fair consideration. A larger share of state as well as Federal funds should be allotted to cities, especially large cities, where problems are most intricate and arterial costs are highest.

To these jurisdictional units must be added the special regional bistate bodies, the state and municipal public authorities and turnpike commissions, which depend for their financing upon tolls usually without involving general public credit, but in some instances backed by public credit to reduce interest charges.

Our new toll roads are simply a logical extension of strategic public crossings, which in comparatively recent years took the place of the old privately owned bridges, tunnels, viaducts, plank roads, turnpikes and ferries created by special bills, franchises and permits of unsavory history. There is no difference in principle between a toll over a bridge or through a tunnel and one on a modern express route, provided these facilities are publicly established, owned and operated. It may be easier to collect charges on a short crossing than on a long parkway or thruway with several points of access, but they are essentially identical devices by which we capitalize anticipated earnings to build superior facilities not otherwise immediately attainable.

We must assume that there will continue to be a complex administration of highways, that the Federal government must set the pace, that it must contribute a proportionately larger percentage of aid to routes of more than local significance and that it must continue to raise and enforce standards. Extensions, amplifications, improvements and innovations in financing this complex system will be more effective than attempting to introduce a complete revolution in administration.

Beyond the boundaries of our country, the Federal government should take a livelier interest in the Pan-American Highway—that is, in finishing the main Central American route without further inexplicable delays. An eastern spur should be studied with a ferry from Key West to Havana where it would split, one fork westerly with a ferry to Yucatan and a connection to the main Pan-American artery, the other fork easterly to Haiti and eventually through the Dominican Republic to Puerto Rico. This Pan-American project will not be justified by traffic alone for some years, but it has enormous hemisphere significance as a unifying bridge to the Caribbean Islands and South America.

THE PROBLEM OF FINANCING

How to pay for a modern safe system of highways needed to keep abreast of the demand for and the output of cars—that is the crux of the question. We have at last recognized the problem. We have the technical know-how. We have the plant and materials. We have the ambition. Have we the courage to finance the needed program and then keep up with current requirements? Given a disposition to use every tried and promising expedient and to keep away from engagingly simple panaceas, I believe the job can be done without dislocating our economy, competing unfairly with the satisfaction of other needs, or tearing up so much of the landscape and streets that ordinary business cannot function.

Let us consider the debated slogan—"No more diversion of highway user taxes." There is an increasing number of well informed people who honestly believe that every dollar of gasoline and oil and even license taxes should, in the constitution of every state, be segregated and usable only for highway construction and maintenance. As the matter stands, twenty-four states have constitutional auto segregation provisions of some kind.

In some states little thought has as yet been devoted to capitalizing these revenues to insure sufficient funds for rapid and uninterrupted progress. We must, of course, concede that even if all of these revenues were thus impounded, the total would still be insufficient to build and maintain an adequate highway and street system unless we omit policing, the traffic courts and some other costs. If we were to charge all traffic police and enforcement officers of all our cities and villages to gas, oil and even license receipts, there would be a totally different picture. There is strong evidence that in some states the segregation of all gasoline and licensing taxes would result in a smaller total than is now spent annually on highway construction and maintenance. The New York State Budget Director, for example, claims that the total expenditures for highways and streets in New York State since the war have been nearly twice the amount of highway taxes and fees collected in that period.

There is, indeed, a strong argument in favor of the old established principle of putting all government revenues in a single general fund, not in a number of separate sealed boxes labeled for specific purposes on the debatable theory that he who pays shall get the benefit. Those who hold to this principle point out that segregation of revenues might also be claimed by users of parks, establishments which pay business taxes, private carriers which are subject to franchise taxes and patrons of racetracks. This line of reasoning is taken seriously in several large states. The argument for gasoline revenue segregation, perhaps including license-plate receipts, may therefore be said to be persuasive in many but by no means all states. It is not a sine qua non. It should not be worked to death. There are too many paid secretaries of automobile associations who make a living by exaggerating the diversion argument, opposing all tolls and generally holding back construction by insisting that it must be on their terms and no others.

Here again, there is no one formula which will be adopted immediately throughout the nation. The idea must win its way. There will, for some time, be states which are wedded to the general-fund principle and not ready to adopt auto diversion amendments. Moreover, it takes from three to four years on an average to get an amendment through with a statute and machinery to make it effective. The highway program should not be held up awaiting unanimous action on segregation in all states. We must also remember that the segregation of auto taxes in states which as yet have no constitutional requirements to this effect will create shortages in their general funds which must be made up by other taxes. This cannot be done with mirrors or solved by a slogan. Construction costs money, and the expenditure of public money means taxes.

THE "PAY-AS-YOU-GO" FALLACY

The next slogan to consider is "pay-as-you-go," as against bond issues and borrowing. Governor Alfred E. Smith shrewdly remarked in his first term that the trouble with the pay-as-you-go policy is that you don't pay and you don't go. Private industry faced with the need of expanding its plants and other facilities does not proceed on the pay-as-you-go basis. It issues securities or borrows the capital required to plan and build extensions promptly, instead of adding a wing or addition here and there with current operating balances as they become available. It must be admitted also that borrowing involves interest as well as amortization.

Properly controlled borrowing, that is capitalizing anticipated future earnings or receipts, is precisely what distinguishes a free enterprise society from a socialistic or communistic one. There is no sound argument in principle against borrowing to give us an adequate highway system in an automotive age. Borrowing can, of course, be overdone. It can be poorly planned. It should not be used exclusively, but it has its place and it is an increasingly important one where we are so far behind, and where the pay-as-you-go slogan has been so ineffective.

It is apparent that if we are to raise billions of dollars for a highway program, we must have more Federal aid for main and subsidiary routes, more state and local bond issues involving the general credit, and more special bond issues supported by capitalized auto revenues. Finally, we must float more bonds of regulated public, regional, bi-state, state and municipal authorities dependent upon the revenues they collect and with the right to pledge the credit of the subdivision of government in which they function only where it is necessary in order to reduce interest rates.

A reputable public authority can confidently issue a million dollars of 2.5 per cent twenty-five year income-tax-exempt bonds with no state credit, if it can prove to prudent investors that it has in prospect $60,000 annually in net revenues. The great advantage of this procedure is that work begins promptly, is uninterrupted, is not dependent on protracted annual arguments about appropriations, is not in competition with other desirable public works and purposes, and preserves a sound relation between tolls and costs.

THE CONTRIBUTION BY AUTHORITIES

Another advantage of authorities is that as their bonds are paid off they can refinance to build better and more extensive highways as the need is demonstrated by actual usage. This assumption is, to be sure, attacked by those who claim that authorities tend to perpetuate themselves, never go out of business and resist turning their facilities over to ordinary government departments for free use. There is some truth in this, but the authority toll idea must be increasingly used in the absence of sufficient funds from other sources, at least as long as the emergency continues and until we have an up-to-date highway system. Contrary to the general public belief, it is not necessary for an authority to have title to the land and facilities it operates. Title may be in the state, municipality or other public subdivision in which the authority operates. Authorities can and do sell revenue bonds to investors who have rights to revenue but not to the facility itself.

Critics have opposed toll facilities on the basis that the conditions in metropolitan areas, where the problems of congestion are greatest, are not solved by these facilities, and on the theory that revenue bonds carry a rate of interest greatly in excess of bonds backed by the full faith and credit of the government.

Issue must be taken with this point of view. If the facility is designed to be of greatest benefit to traffic it will go through rather than bypass the cities. To date, many of the most important links in the arterial highway system are the strategic river crossings, generally in urban areas, upon which tolls are charged. These toll river crossings have done more to remedy mounting traffic congestion in urban areas than any other factor. They have furnished new facilities many years in advance of the time in which they could have been built out of normal governmental construction appropriations. Until recently, water crossings were built from bridgehead to bridgehead and tunnel plaza to tunnel plaza and the approaches were left to others to worry over. Traffic massed at the focal points. Crossings must from now on extend far inland and merge into the general traffic pattern.

As to the question of interest rates, these depend upon anticipated revenue and upon the character and reputation of those responsible for administration. As an illustration of low interest rates, the Triborough Bridge and Tunnel Authority in New York City refinanced its bond structure in 1952 when it sold a $215 million revenue bond issue at an average interest rate of 2.02 per cent.

Much has been written about the 40,000 miles of main arteries called the "interstate system." The construction of this system, comprising about 1 per cent of the road mileage of the country and estimated to carry 20 per cent of the rural traffic, would cost at least $11 billion. Included are highways potentially wholly or partially self-liquidating. The former policy of the Congress and the Bureau of Public Roads, which prohibited the expenditure of Federal highway funds on toll highways, must be revised.

Pennsylvania Turnpike, the first of the modern toll highways, as distinguished from river crossings, could not have been financed without a 45 per cent Public Works Administration grant and a loan from the Reconstruction Finance Corporation. There are many projects on the interstate system other than those which have already been proposed for toll financing which could be built if some Federal and state subsidies were made available.

In New York City, the Triborough Bridge and Tunnel Authority is using its excess borrowing capacity to build $80 million worth of approaches and arterial connections on the Federal aid urban system. It would be equally proper to reverse this procedure and use public funds to subsidize projects which can be shown to be self-supporting to the extent of, say, 75 per cent of the cost. In an all-out attack upon the highway program, public and quasi-public funds from a number of sources must be considered. Henry Hudson Parkway in New York City was built by using money from seven different sources.

As to "Excess Condemnation"

A financial device often suggested and rarely applied in this country to reduce or rather recoup some of the cost of new highways—particularly wide thruways, expressways, turnpikes, freeways and parkways—is the use of excess condemnation on a large scale to acquire strips of land adjacent to rights-of-way for purposes of resale at higher prices when the improvement is finished and the surroundings have become valuable. There are powerful, and I believe unanswerable, arguments against this.

Most state constitutions rigidly limit excess condemnation to rounding out plots so as not to leave odds and ends of unsalable land and to avoid consequential damage. The amount of money which might be recouped by a wide extension of this power has in most instances been greatly exaggerated. Increased surrounding values in any event result in higher assessments and taxes. Last but not least, speculation in land for ultimate public benefit by even the most reliable public officials should not be encouraged. It would certainly lead to widespread suspicion and, human nature being what it is, to irregularities. For all these reasons, this device should not be considered as an important or promising factor in highway financing.

The answer to the big problem of financing the proposed ten-year program seems to me to be to raise gas taxes in a number of states, particularly the larger ones, increase truck taxes, probably on the ton-mile method, capitalize considerably more of the present 4.9 cent average state gasoline tax, and segregate a Federal 3 cent gasoline tax (1 cent above the present 2 cent tax) together with the present 6 cent per gallon oil tax, so as to double the existing Federal aid program.

Federal excise taxes on automobiles, tires, parts, gasoline and oil amount to over $1.5 billion per year, most of which is diverted to other than highway uses. Taxes on gasoline and oil seem to be the only practical ones to recommend for segregation. It has been urged in some quarters that the Federal government give up all gasoline taxes and thereby leave this field of taxation to the states. It seems unlikely that Congress will do this in view of the fact that there would be no assurance that these funds would go into highways, and because of the adverse effect on Federal aid, regional planning and ample construction in the less wealthy states. It is essential, however, that highways, because of their present conspicuous inadequacy and their increasing importance in the economic life of the community, be exempted from the economy drives in Congress which rightly have for their aim reduction of unnecessary Federal expenditures.

My proposal for a $50 billion ten-year national highway program, made in 1953, may have seemed unrealistic at the time, but with the tremendous increase in the production and use of automobiles the plan began to receive serious attention. It certainly helped to focus attention on this major national problem.

My proposal was followed by President Eisenhower's even more ambitious program for the expenditure of $101 billion for a comprehensive national highway system. The stalemate in Congress resulting from the rejection of the President's program left the country in a desperate condition. The road is more than ten years behind the car. The tremendous output of cars goes on at an accelerated pace while the highways become more obsolete and more congested.

An indispensable national program, about the need of which there is no dispute, bogged down owing to obscure and obscene fights over financing, pride of opinion and legislative weakness. The regional, transcontinental, military and defense aspects of the program were ignored. Those opposed to borrowing, as against pay-as-you-go, have lacked the guts to impose the taxes they advocate. Those proposed to be taxed, notably trucking and auto accessory interests, have taken full advantage of this stalemate. They are tough, two-fisted, well-heeled and represented by a skillful lobby without inhibitions. Meantime, our motorized civilization has suffered an enormous setback. The bills we shall have to pay for congestion, delays and stoppages will run into billions. This is the price of selfishness, poor leadership and political ineptitude and weakness.

A program of this size and complexity cannot be realized without widespread, continuous and undeviating public support. Differences in Congress, in state legislatures and in local bodies, over methods of finance, routes, etc., must be ironed out. It calls for a degree of cooperation between various powerful private interests as well as government officials.

The auto industry must play an increasingly important part. The period is over when the manufacturer loses interest when his car, truck or bus leaves the assembly line and the salesroom. Gasoline, oil, tire and other related businesses should put their shoulders to the wheel. Safety organizations and insurance companies, the press, screen, radio, television and the theater should help.

There must be a freer exchange of information, more discussion of difficulties, more inspections of successful installations, and above all better leadership. By such means we can have, before long, general agreement on an adequate program and schedule with enough flexibility to insure the cooperation of the national, sectional and diverse other interests which control our motorized civilization.

If half the ingenuity, thought, and effort which go into the styling and sale of cars were applied to roads and their regulation we would gradually make our motor civilization really work. Our greatest domestic menace and liability would soon become an asset of incalculable value. All that is needed is a genuine working partnership of the best brains in private enterprise with public administrators consistently supported by the press and the people. The alternative is a motorized chaos in which no one can in any sense make a decent living.

19

Family Doctors
and Consultants

FROM TIME TO TIME, OVER THE YEARS, I HAVE been asked to serve as a consultant on out-of-town problems similar to those with which I have had experience in New York. These excursions have been arranged on my vacation time, or I have taken short leaves of absence from my regular jobs. Actually, the hard work is usually done by staffs made up of the best men available for the special kind of studies required. My part is merely to direct the surveys and review the findings and recommendations.

Whatever value these reports may have for others, the experiences have been most interesting and helpful to me. We learn a lot about the problems of diverse communities and get a better perspective on our own. Answers to such problems are not to be found in abstract formulas and generalized conclusions, and the best solutions, for one reason or another, are not always adopted.

We had such an experience in Baltimore some years ago. It convinced me that no group of outsiders, no matter how well motivated and equipped, can do anything substantial for a city that the local people do not really badly want themselves. I took down to Baltimore the best equipped, the most experienced, and the most practical men in every field that had the remotest relation to the arterial and housing program we were to study. I had great difficulty in getting some of the men to go down because the compensation they received meant little to them. My task in writing a director's report was a comparatively easy one. There were no differences of opinion or even mental reservations among the experts. I stress this fact because our recommendations were not those of a staff under orders from one person, but the consensus of consultants who have a legitimate pride of opinion and the courage of their convictions.

Among other things, we reached the unanimous conclusion that the arterial highway problem of Baltimore could in a large measure be solved by building an expressway through the heart of the city. We recommended a genuine municipal improvement of wide scope, with depressed express lanes, attractively designed bridges, landscaped slopes, wide service roads and incidental walks and promenades, with park and recreational facilities such as we have in New York and other places.

What Happened to the Plan

I am sure that if we were called upon again, we would make the same recommendations all over. However, if in the course of cutting a swath through a big city like Baltimore—an old city with many people who do not like to be stepped on, inconvenienced, discommoded—if in that process, for example, we propose to wipe out a slum which the community does not want to do anything about, of course, the thing bogs down. This is what happened in Baltimore. In city after city, where they have attemptd to imitate what has been done in New York, and some other cities, the plans fall down because the local people are not there to carry them out.

Consultants Are Not Family Doctors

Consultants are diagnosticians, engaged to indicate what seems wrong and what remedies adopted elsewhere would be likely to prove effective in specific cases. They do not take the place of a family doctor who is continuously at hand, or of a local surgeon if there is an operation to be performed. A diagnosis is only as good as those who make it, and the patients are under no obligation to take our advice if they do not like it.

For equally obvious reasons, consultants on public work have no responsibility for persuasion or propaganda. They cannot claim special knowledge of localities. Their value comes from their familiarity with somewhat similar conditions elsewhere; their freedom from local bias and connections which might consciously or unconsciously influence their conclusions. But it is important to employ technicians with experience and records of accomplishment in comparable work. Apprentices should not be engaged to learn their trade at the expense of communities seeking advice regarding public improvements.

I have mentioned New Orleans as an illustration of unusual conditions favorable to the creation of a modern arterial system. As director of a consultants' survey and report on an arterial plan for New Orleans, I was able to recommend a comprehensive program which was well regarded locally and has since been progressing. Unlike Baltimore, New Orleans, because of her original street pattern and canal system, can solve her basic arterial problems with a minimum of dislocation of residence, business and industry.

The trouble with most city plans is that they are too grandiose. They flatter the community temporarily, but in the end are not taken seriously by conservative officials who have to foot the bills. New Orleans is by its location and history accustomed to fairly large expenditures, Federal, state and municipal, for public purposes. The great levees and revetments which hold back the Mississippi, the pumps which keep the city dry, the docks which invite commerce and the rails and roads which in turn feed the waterfront, not to speak of the Sugar Bowl and Huey P. Long Bridge, are all public and quasi-public works which no private enterprise could supply, and which prepared the average citizen for a postwar works program of reasonable and logical expansion.

There was, however, a decided limit to the kind of program New Orleans could carry out, beyond which lies the domain of sterile, academic planning which produces nothing tangible within our means and in our time. We therefore proposed a plan and schedule which seemed to us to be within the powers, resources and grasp of New Orleans with, of course, substantial help from Baton Rouge and Washington because of the genuine regional character of the improvements and their relation to state and national planning.

To expedite the advance planning of certain special and limited improvements, we recommended the employment of able and experienced consulting firms on a contract basis for both design and supervision. We urged this not because civil service was unable to furnish competent men, but because the hiring of such men, who had never worked together as a team, on a competitive basis for distinctly temporary service would be wasteful, slow and unsatisfactory. It was hardly necessary to add that no selfish or personal motive was back of this advice since none of our consultants was seeking employment in connection with this work.

WHEN AUTHORITIES DISAGREE

The extensive replanning and rebuilding of Pittsburgh, Pennsylvania, especially in the famous Golden Triangle, received its impetus before the last war. I was engaged to advise on arterial problems in 1939, but we did not limit our report to such improvements. Our plan centered on the Golden Triangle, with its complex of bridges and thoroughfares, and took in the entire area. We proposed the reclamation of the waterfront and the creation of a genuine park in which the historic Blockhouse would be given a place of honor in the area so like the topography of Lower Manhattan.

Instead of restoring the buried ruins of Fort Pitt, I suggested a gigantic shaft of Pennsylvania block granite, steel, glass and aluminum, which would represent a tribute by the modern Steel City to old Fort Pitt, and symbolize the meeting of the Allegheny and Monongahela rivers in the Ohio. My proposal was rejected. Perhaps some of the new Pittsburgh millionaires thought it might reflect on their reputations as collectors of Siennese primitives. Great strides have since been made in the Pittsburgh arterial and rebuilding program.

Occasionally we have been called upon for advice in cases where other agencies are not in agreement over arterial and other plans. Some years ago a group of substantial interests in Hartford, Connecticut, employed consultants to make a general report on an arterial program that had been proposed. I was asked to review their report and recommendations. There had been recommendations by the

Flood Commission, the State Highway Department and the Department of Engineering of the city, as to various routes for important arteries. One of the proposals involved cutting through Bushnell Park. This seemed to rest on the assumption of some right-of-way engineers that parks exist primarily to afford cheap, convenient and easy locations for heavy traffic. I dismissed this proposal with the assertion that it merely proved that the curricula of our engineering schools need broadening.

Because of differences of opinion over a route for an expressway through New Britain, Connecticut, the Mayor of the city and chairman of a special expressway committee asked me to give them the impartial view of an outsider on this and related matters. I could give little time to the subject, except during the vacation period, but recommended a group of consultants and agreed to review their findings. In this instance it was our conclusion that the New Britain expressway, as laid out by the State Highway Department, could not be financed within the required period from available funds, and an alternative route—one of several previously studied by state officials—was proposed. In our studies we had the wholehearted cooperation of the State Highway Department, and in my report I expressed the hope that the matter could be resolved without controversy. I came in for severe criticism from a local newspaper editor, who insisted that our study was a waste of money. The Mayor should have engaged the editor to make the study.

SOME WAR-TIME PROBLEMS

During the last war a number of special problems developed and I was asked by Rear Admiral Ben Moreell, Chief of the Bureau of Yards and Docks, with the approval of Lieutenant General Brehon Somervell, Commanding General of the Services of Supply, to act as coordinator of a survey of five of the most important congested war production areas, to ascertain existing conditions and determine what measures were desirable or necessary to improve conditions and attain maximum efficiency.

The most troublesome areas of congestion were at San Diego, San Francisco Bay, Portland, Maine, Newport, Rhode Island, and

Hampton Roads at Norfolk, Virginia. Concise but comprehensive reports were made of each of these areas and I wrote the covering report. The conditions we found were appalling in some respects and called for drastic measures. The consultants merely presented facts which any one could verify. My job was to take these facts, get at their real meaning, find out the causes, name those responsible and propose remedies.

Conditions in all these areas were similar, but those at Hampton Roads were the most serious. Here naval and military installations and private plants engaged in war work had brought a vast new population into an area which included five cities, two towns and parts of four counties. All public and private facilities were wholly inadequate. The attempt to improvise such facilities after we entered the war was an almost impossible task. In the absence of any real organizing and directing force there was something like chaos.

It seemed obvious that the only way to improve the situation and coordinate the various activities and public facilities was to centralize authority in one man, give him the help and material he needed, and hold him responsible for results. After all we were at war and the government had created the congestion. But this meant disregarding personalities, stepping on the toes of high-ranking naval and other officials and over-riding civilian agencies in Washington. We ran into some prize examples of stuffed shirts under imposing uniforms. One admiral said he was too busy to go over the problems in his port. I had to say in my report that he lacked the combination of qualities which would enable him to bring order out of the existing confusion. I guess it was my bluntness that caused the report to be marked "confidential." At any rate it was never published.

EXPERIENCES IN POST-WAR PLANNING

During the war I was also called upon for consultation regarding an expressway from Detroit past the Ford plant at River Rouge to the bomber factories at Willow Run, together with a proposed cross-town extension of this expressway through the heart of Detroit. The expressway to the two big war plants was promptly constructed and was one of the busiest defense highways in the country while the war was on. In design it closely follows our expressways in New York.

Presumably because of my experience with toll facilities, I was asked to study and comment on a report of the Illinois State Super-highway Commission on a system of state toll roads in Illinois, to be built after the war. This was a unique project. While there had been authorities that financed, built and operated traffic facilities on a local or regional basis, the proposal to set up such an authority on a statewide basis was something new. While I claim no intimate knowledge of all parts of Illinois, and had to assume that the traffic and cost figures were accurate, the several projects proposed seemed to be well selected and worth while. The main points of my comment had to do with financing and scheduling.

Of the various projects proposed for the state, there were two, both in Chicago, which I felt might attract responsible underwriters. Only one of these, the proposed Northwest Expressway, promised to be wholly self-liquidating. I recommended that this project be got under way promptly. Experience has demonstrated that once a successful project of this kind has been launched, further projects are less difficult to finance, especially if grants, subventions or contributions can be obtained from the Federal government. One successful project will gain confidence and support for others.

Again following precedents in New York, I strongly recommended that part of the right-of-way, including a section in the heart of the city, be developed and turned over to the Chicago Park District for play spaces to include facilities for small children and for older boys and girls, and sitting parks for older people; the cost of establishing such playgrounds to be a part of the expressway project, but conveyed to the city for park purposes.

PORTLAND, OREGON, IMPROVEMENT

While World War II was still going on, many of us became concerned over what would happen when it ended. There was no lack of confidence in our victory, but with the depression of the thirties in mind, we did fear unemployment on a large scale during the period of transition from war to peace. This fear was intensified by the views of practically all our leading economists. What was feared did not happen, fortunately, but the effort and money put into post-war planning was well worth while. One of the cities which it was felt would face a serious problem growing out of a large increase in population owing to rapidly expanded war industries was Portland, Oregon.

In 1943 I was asked to supervise the activities of a group of engineers and attorneys in preparing a general report and recommendations for a postwar program for the City of Portland and Multnomah County. The scope of the report was limited to certain definite recommendations, all looking toward the expediting of needed and desirable public works to afford employment, stimulate business and help bridge the gap between the end of the war and the full assumption of private activity.

Portland had stood the strain of her stepped up war work very well, and many of the community leaders were confident that the future of the entire region was assured. Further rapid development of water power from the Columbia River was expected to attract new industry and provide work. The Kaiser associates had revived shipbuilding, at the instance of the Federal government, and some felt that the Kaiser interests and the government had a moral responsibility to see that the new population was provided with work.

All these speculations, prophecies and hopes were interesting, but if we had pursued them far we would never have reached the limited conclusions as to which our opinion had been asked. It seems originally to have been the thought of those who invited us to make the report that we could justify a works program of $100 million to employ 30,000 people in the Portland area in the eighteen months after the war. We found that a $60 million construction program, employing a varying number up to 20,000 for two years, represented all that the area could afford and all that was necessary and justifiable.

I said at the time that to theoretical planners, who will accept nothing short of a revolution in urban life, our report was bound to be disappointing because in accordance with our instructions we only recommended limited public improvements in the urgent class which Portland, with help from the state and Federal governments, could afford to compress and expedite in order to help meet a postwar emergency.

It was also pointed out that critics would raise the question of cost, not only of construction but also of upkeep. The program proposed did not represent mere enthusiasm for public construction and was not a substitute for private enterprise. It seemed to us merely the minimum of insurance which a self-reliant community could take if it hoped to escape, or at least to minimize, relief expedients which had followed the depression in the thirties. To get away from any suggestion of a return to "work relief" I proposed that we call the program "Portland Improvement."

NATIONAL ECONOMIC PLANNING

While we did not have widespread unemployment following the last war, I still think our postwar planning was wise. Furthermore, I think such advanced planning is the best insurance we can have against recessions during cold wars and other periods of economic readjustments. Unfortunately interest in national economic planning follows instead of preceding slumps.

In 1953 and early 1954, there was a drop in employment and a corresponding flurry of interest in Washington. I was invited to a meeting of an advisory group on state and local planning of the Council of Economic Advisers held in the executive office of the President on December 16, 1953. It was not very fruitful. I was disappointed that none of the three members of the President's Council of Economic Advisers could find time to attend the meeting to which a number of well informed people had been invited. The Council was represented by Mr. Robinson Newcomb, who later sent me a copy of the minutes of the meeting. No stenographer was present and in a letter to Mr. Newcomb I later took exception to the account, especially to the report of my part in the discussion.

I went to Washington to urge the Federal government to prepare a public works program which could become operative when unemployment increased to a point where it threatened economic stability. An unemployment total of 5 million was tentatively proposed. It was suggested that if and when this happened the President put the program into effect simply by declaring an emergency.

There was considerable discussion as to how state and local governments through proposed new legislation could be aided in raising funds. While a Uniform Bond Law, such as had been proposed, is desirable it is my feeling that states and municipalities should not overburden themselves with indebtedness. They should not be expected to throw themselves head over heels in debt during a period of economic recession in order to minimize the financial burdens which should be undertaken by the Federal government.

If public works are advantageous as a means of combating economic recession, the Federal government should do its part, and indeed, should accept part of the burden of public works benefiting various states and municipalities. Certain Federal aid programs, such as highways and public housing, would be among those steps which could be undertaken readily by the United States. Additional means of participation by the Federal government in works programs could be in the field of aid for local revenue-producing projects.

President Eisenhower had said that his administration was determined to take whatever steps were available and necessary to prevent distress. However, my conclusion was that if the minutes of this meeting were supposed to reflect the actual thinking of the Council of Economic Advisers, we have learned little from the past and are not likely to face the future in the event of a recession without breadlines and boondoggling. As I said at the meeting, the human note seemed completely lacking, the plight of the man out of a job was not even referred to in the agenda, and statistics do not furnish bread for the hungry.

Some Long-Distance Telephone Calls

Modern communications seem to have extended the consulting field considerably. While I have declined to take on assignments in New York State involving fees, as President of the Long Island State Park Commission I was glad to be of service in advising County Executive J. Russel Sprague of Nassau County on the Atlantic Beach Bridge, an important metropolitan arterial link. We also made a study and recommendations regarding the proposed enlargement of Michie Stadium and facilities for handling the increased traffic involved at West Point. Later we made a report on a proposed new City Hall in Flint, Michigan, a survey and plan for Canton, Ohio, and other places.

More unusual have been some long-distance telephone calls. Two short visits, casual reading and more or less desultory talks with local officials and visitors did not entitle me to authoritative opinions, but I was happy to be invited by Governor Morris F. DeCastro to a meeting of the Virgin Islands Planning Commission and later to summarize my impressions of some of the problems of this insular possession of the United States.

I suggested that the functions of the Island's Planning Commission should be defined—otherwise it would deal only with vague abstractions, slogans or petty details and the word would get around that it was not serious business and the members themselves would lose interest. The commission should be a center or clearing house of all plans involving the future growth of the islands, so that these may be coordinated and reconciled. It should meet regularly, have at least a full-time executive secretary and a stenographer and whatever additional help it required to carry out any program decided upon.

The Islands' Basic Problem

In this instance planning is not merely mapping public improvements, zoning and checking projects for conformity. A much more basic problem exists, and one which planning agencies in established urban communities with pretty well defined objectives do not face. The commission after deliberation with the Governor and other authorities must decide what fundamentally they want the Virgin Islands to be, and for whom. If the future is to be primarily rural and agricultural and for the present population and its descendants, that is one thing. If, on the other hand, the aim is primarily to attract winter or year-round residents and tourists from the mainland, and if substantial worker immigration from Puerto Rico and perhaps other Caribbean Islands is anticipated to serve them and build up the islands' economy, that is quite another story. Planning may conceivably aim at both objectives at the same time, but one must certainly be regarded as more important than the other.

There is no sense in an attempt to industrialize the Virgin Islands —at least so far as heavy industry is concerned. There is no cheap power, as in Puerto Rico, and there is a lack of dependable skilled labor. Some light industries might be attracted if tax exemptions are continued and extended. Enterprises of this type, however desirable, certainly can only be an incident in the economic future of the islands.

I know nothing about agriculture, and did not presume to suggest anything except that Puerto Rican and probably European immigration appeared inevitable if the islands expected to grow things successfully for the domestic use of an increasing population and for more or less sophisticated visitors who look for some local foods as distinguished from feeding out of cans and off frozen imports. As to truck farming it seems strange to a visitor that vegetables and fruit can be grown in the British West Indies and sold advantageously in the Virgin Islands. There is little difference in soil conditions. There must be other explanations which call for frank analysis and discussion.

The serious implications of attracting outside labor to settle permanently in the islands must of course be considered. I should think the effects in the long run, if the process is regulated and gradual, would be good, socially, economically and politically. The Puerto Ricans cannot be kept out in any event, whether the present land owners and natives want them or not, and especially if there is a promise of greater prosperity and a better life than in overcrowded Puerto Rico. As to an immediate and necessarily limited program of improvements, I suggested the following as a conservative start:

Map the shorefront areas and high, scenic vantage points, both publicly and privately owned, most attractive for harbor, hotel, club and private residential development, as well as public recreation, indicating roughly, where it has not already been done, logical subdivisions and approaches. Obviously the kind of people to be attracted should be studied, and I assume that those who demand excitement, gambling, artificial amusements and noisy, catchpenny devices would not be aimed at.

Make rough cost estimates covering dredging, access roads, adequate and dependable water supply, sewage and garbage disposal, and other public utilities, landscaping and planning. The harbors and beaches and the land just back of them are the islands' greatest asset, which should be fully capitalized. Present harbors need dredging. The sand which is dredged up can be used to build up beaches and roads. Small docks are required at a number of places. St. John's especially needs docks and roads. Buck Island, for example, could be reached easily by boat from the nearest point on St. Croix if there were adequate docks and roads on both sides. Seaplanes or amphibians would be desirable at several points.

Publicly owned land, particularly shorefront land, should be sold for private development after installation of the basic public facilities, leaving, however, enough accessible beaches for public recreation. A considerable part if not all of the cost of such public facilities could be recovered by prudent subdivision and more or less leisurely sale of public lands, not to speak of the taxes which would be collected later.

Funds for such improvements might be advanced through the Virgin Islands Corporation, with additional subventions from Washington on a basis which would make them in time in substantial part self-liquidating. A new Virgin Islands Planning Authority, perhaps an outgrowth of the present Planning Commission, might be created as an alternative, with public waterfront lands placed in its charge. I doubt whether asking for more Federal funds in the annual island budget or the return of a larger share of excise money would have the same appeal at Washington as a program in considerable part revenue-producing and in the hands of experienced persons not closely identified with local politics.

Next I suggested that a practical official report be made by a successful commercial fishery corporation on the mainland and by a cold-storage company looking to the establishment of several small public fish markets in centers such as Charlotte Amalie, Christiansted and Fredericksted. Fish might be combined with other market wares. This responsibility should be financed and administered like others involving public improvements, and the aim should be to make it as nearly as possible self supporting.

I also urged that remaining slum areas be cleared by obtaining additional low-rental public housing funds and also by attracting private capital under the provisions of Title I of the National Housing Act and FHA guarantees if the resulting rentals would not be too high. The proper use of areas thus cleared should be decided in advance. Those not held for future public housing might be available for street widening, public squares, small parks, etc. Finally, I urged restoration, protection and exhibition of the islands' antiquities and their historical places and associations, their architecture, and of course careful conservation of their natural beauties. In part this may be done by establishment of additional national monuments and appropriations to repair and maintain them. In part zoning restrictions should be the instrument. In part special laws and regulations should be invoked such as those which have been effective in the Vieux Carré in New Orleans.

ROLLING DOWN TOWARD RIO

In 1947, I was invited by Nelson Rockefeller, as head of the International Basic Economy Corporation and IBEC Technical Services Corporation, to make surveys and recommendations for public improvements for Caracas, the capital of Venezuela. Caracas has a population of some half a million, about 100,000 of the inhabitants being people who have been drawn to the capital from the country and have become squatters in shacks on the surrounding hills.

The most pressing problem, next to housing, was providing main highways. The city itself had narrow streets and is twenty-five miles from La Guaira, on the coast. The coastal town and the capital were connected by a narrow, winding highway which rose three thousand feet and took an hour and a half to make the dangerous trip. Our most important recommendation was for a modern expressway from La Guaira to Caracas. We also proposed other arterial highways, a civic center for the capital, parks, playgrounds and additional improvements. In general these proposals have been acted upon. The expressway is now open, the civic center is taking form and Caracas is rapidly becoming a modern city.

OUR EXPERIENCE IN BRAZIL

We had an even more extensive and intensive consulting experience in São Paulo, Brazil, again following an invitation from Nelson Rockefeller and the Mayor and Council of São Paulo, to organize a group of technical consultants to make a report and survey of the city. It was an interesting and challenging assignment.

São Paulo, with a population of over two million, has many of the aspects of New York, Chicago, Miami and the new cities in Texas. It is the most rapidly growing city in the Americas and has been quicker than most of our metropolitan areas to recognize that the extraordinary expansion requires programs of construction and regulation to insure orderly progress in future, before the difficulties become insuperable, as is the case in so many of our urban areas.

The framework of the São Paulo government, is, from our point of view, extremely unorthodox. There is only partial and limited home rule. The municipality is the creature of the state. The Mayor was an appointee of the Governor; many functions which our cities perform are discharged directly by the state. I believe some changes must be made in the direction of greater local autonomy and responsibility, but it would have been presumptuous for us to suggest such changes.

The state collects revenues and exercises control, yet in the case of main highways the state stops at the city limits. Drainage is a city matter, sewage a state matter; the state assumes responsibility for police and fire protection, and even city traffic regulation. In such matters as unregulated land speculation and subdivision, São Paulo, with its enormous acreage, is better off than most of our more progressive cities, our boom towns and our planless, expanding suburbs.

The most conspicuous and basic neglect in São Paulo is that of an official city map. Such a map, based upon up-to-date air and ground surveys, does not exist. There are only fragments and odds and ends of a zoning resolution, and the building code or codes do not cover the whole city. Yet intelligent and farsighted urban plans have been made by widely recognized experts, and solid, substantial, enduring improvements had actually been carried out or were well under way when we first went to São Paulo.

The main outlines and features of its city plan had already been determined. There was nothing revolutionary about it. The average Paulista, however proud of his city, eager for its advancement and jealous of its reputation, is a middle-of-the-road citizen, at heart no revolutionary in his philosophy of municipal administration.

The program we proposed for São Paulo was modest, but definite as to objectives, timing and finance. There were no luxuries, no extravagances, no iridescent dreams and will-o'-the-wisps—only first things. The recommendations covered mapping and zoning, a comprehensive arterial system, mass transportation, parks and playgrounds, water supply, sewage treatment, land reclamation and suggestions for financing specific projects. My visits to Brazil, and the progress made there in developing public improvements, have been most gratifying, and I prize highly the medal of the Order of the Southern Cross, presented to me on behalf of the late President Getulio Vargas.

Flight, Followed by Silence

In 1947, General Lucius Clay, then Military Governor of the American Occupation Zone, invited me to visit Germany and make suggestions as to what might be done to improve conditions in the war-wrecked areas. I flew over and spent three weeks, looking over the wreckage, talking with officials and others and gathering as much material as I could. My knowledge of Germany and the language were extremely helpful, and on my return to New York I made a report to General Clay in which I summarized my impressions of the situation and made some suggestions which I hoped might lead to improvement.

My report was sent by the General to Robert P. Patterson, Secretary of War, with an urgent recommendation that it be made public immediately. However, it was felt that it might embarrass negotiations then going on between this government and our allies. It was suggested by General Clay that the report might be modified to remove any of my remarks which our allies might not like. The report was not modified, and it remains unpublished, but later the *St. Louis Post-Dispatch* asked me to write a series of articles on my trip.[26]

In these articles I described what I had seen in Germany and repeated some of the suggestions made in my memorandum to General Clay. Conditions at that time were truly appalling. A quarter of all German housing had been destroyed. In many cities 70 per cent of all former housing units were beyond repair. This necessitated a doubling up and sardine living on an inhuman scale in small rooms, cellars and partially restored houses.

Many of the people were too young or too old to comprehend what had happened. This was obvious from the sad eyes of little children peering out of slits in concrete bomb shelters converted into housing, and the faces of dazed, defeated old men and women at cellar windows, resigned, sour, arrogant, expressionless, preoccupied, bitter, grim, anything but alert or gay.

In my chamber of horrors, the most dramatic wreckage in Germany was not to be found at the Reichschancellery in Berlin, nor at the entrance to Hitler's bunker—scene of the Nordic goetterdaemmerung, where they soaked the bodies of the Fuehrer and Eva Braun with kerosene and burned them—nor at the fantastic mountain hideouts of the top Nazis at Obersalsberg high in the Bavarian Alps above Berchtesgaden, nor yet in gutted public buildings and within the yawning residences of the big and small people, but in the heart of Essen.

No word picture, photograph or movie can give an adequate impression of the wreckage of German cities. It had to be seen. Over the vast acreage of tortured, twisted steel and broken stone which once was the great Krupp mine, steel and munition works of Essen, where the grim Vulcan of German might had his favorite smithy, brooded the haunting stillness of death, interrupted only by the puny activities of human ants carrying off crumbs of debris. Until there was more coal, a lifting of the levels of industry for postwar Germany fixed by the Big Four, and a more realistic attitude toward so-called war potentials, it seemed obvious that this giant would remain prostrate.

THE PROBLEM OF RECOVERY

In the reshuffling, grabbing and dividing that followed the close of the war, we got the dirty end of the stick, Russia the best. The British and French did not do so badly with the Ruhr and the Saar. Nevertheless, a real amalgamation of the United States and British zones with the Saar annexed to France looked like a good bet. The population was swollen, but industrial recovery would provide the means to feed it.

Of the four nations in Germany, the United States was the most idealistic, confused and inexperienced. We had the advantage of such imponderables as distance, detachment and unselfishness, but we did not have much time left to make good in Western Germany. If communism was not halted, the entire European economy seemed sure to be Russian, leaving us isolated in a vast Soviet zone feebly defending a dying capitalism in Europe.

Up to that time the allied record in the Ruhr had been one of failure. It was a British failure, but we shared responsibility for it. I suggested that we could turn this failure into success by the same methods which have made our great public authorities successful, that is by establishing a Ruhr Coal Authority, which would enjoy all the advantages of decentralized government control and private or semi-public financing and management. I argued that such a public authority, organized on business lines, borrowing from the International Bank, under allied supervision and with the old cartels and private interests eliminated, could successfuly run the Ruhr mines, supply food, houses, consumer goods, and help revive Germany's industry without creating any German war hazard or potential.

Three years after I made this proposal, on May 11, 1950, the then French Foreign Minister Schuman officially announced the enlarged plan for a High Authority, backed by the Western nations, to take over and operate the German coal and steel industries. This plan, worked out by Jean Monnet, was the most constructive contribution made in stimulating European recovery and the creation of a more stable economy during this critical period.

The Public Works "Task Force"

My most important and interesting assignment as a consultant came in 1948, when former President Herbert Hoover asked me to head the Public Works Task Force of the Commission on the Organization of the Executive Branch of the Federal Government. This was indeed a high commission, and its objectives were of special interest to me. Nearly thirty years had passed since I participated in the successful efforts of Governor Alfred E. Smith in reorganizing the New York State government.

During the intervening years I had been particularly active in matters having to do with all phases of public work and had gained some knowledge of the problems not only of construction of physical improvements but of the laws and agencies involved. I was especially happy to work under Mr. Hoover, one of the great engineers of our time. As chief consultant of a task force, I assembled a staff of experts in all the related fields who undertook the study with enthusiasm, eager to render a public service.

I have more faith in men than in forms of government administration, but the Hoover study of the Organization of the Executive Branch of the Federal Government was long overdue. No man had a better understanding of this need than the former President, whose training and experience made him the logical person to direct a study of needed reforms. He was to go into all phases of administrative activities, and to bring forth a plan which, if adopted, would raise the standards of efficiency in national administration to new levels.

Our special task was to study the functions of the innumerable, scattered agencies under the President which have to do with public works. This covers a large area of government, involves much of our peacetime expenditures and imposes a good part of the crushing responsibility that rests on the President.

The main purpose of the Hoover Commission was to provide a responsible, economical government, with the President as the real instead of the nominal head, and with a rearrangement of departments and personnel in such a way as to leave the President free to deal with major problems, unburdened by too much administrative detail. To do this, agencies outside of the Cabinet circle, conflicting with established departments and only theoretically reporting to the President, should be brought into proper relation with the major departments headed by the President's Cabinet advisers.

A PUBLIC WORKS DEPARTMENT

To accomplish this objective, we recommended a Federal Department of Public Works, headed by a Secretary of Cabinet rank. This new agency would assimilate all Federal engineering and related functions, including a Special Board of Impartial Analysis to investigate every major proposal affecting water development and control, and promotion and conservation of natural resources. It was also proposed that the Secretary of Public Works, as well as the Secretary of Defense, be given representation on the Atomic Energy Commission. In half a dozen main divisions we proposed to concentrate the functions of some twenty-three existing agencies. In addition, the new department would provide engineering services to a score of other agencies which now have independent engineering divisions.

The conclusions in our report were reached almost unanimously, and were duly presented to Mr. Hoover in 1949. His recommendations were later presented to the President and to Congress. Some of his proposals have been acted upon, but not those relating to public works. The national government is still following its old methods. This cannot go on if we are to meet the increasing needs of the new day, and the competition of our realistic and aggressive adversaries.

20

Preparation
for Public Service

NO IDEOLOGY, HOWEVER DEMOCRATIC IN ITS ORIGIN
and purpose, can furnish the services, initiative, competition and rewards which are indispensable to a healthy society. Having spent most
of my life in government work, I cannot see how any country in which
everyone is a government employee and all business is bureaucratic
can be other than a cruel and inefficient autocracy in which suffrage
is limited and power tends more and more to be concentrated and
perpetuated in the hands of trimmers, incompetents and fanatics.

Russia must educate not only leaders but the entire rank and file
of 200 million people for a type of civilization to which they are as
yet unaccustomed. It is one thing to announce five- or ten-year
plans, and another to carry them out by fist and fiat. Education,
formal or informal, takes time, and cannot be fed in capsule form.
The task in a gigantic bureaucracy from which private enterprise is
excluded is, judging from our own none too happy experience in the
rapid expansion of government, staggering.

Democracy's problems, while formidable, are different. Compact,
responsive and responsible organization is important, but the men
picked to execute are much more important than the machine they
operate. A first-class man can make shift to run a second-rate machine. He will somehow find expedients to make it work. A second- or
third-string fellow will ruin the most delicate plant or instrument.
That is why Russia will take years to make a mechanized industrial

civilization, modeled after our own, run smoothly in the way in which our ingenious, mechanically minded and democratically educated and motivated people make it work. That is also why the U.S.S.R. may become so absorbed in perfecting its domestic administration that it will be less provocative, realizing its deficiencies in plant, skill, incentives, production and prosperity, the folly of territorial and ideological overexpansion, and the utter futility of another global war.

THE INDIVIDUAL POTENTIAL

No community can realize its potentialities without leadership. The same need is felt by states, nations and even international organizations. Without vision—which means men of light and learning—the people perish. In this content biography continues to be the greatest educator. Lots of our best minds in public and private affairs were untrammeled by prolonged higher academic education, and it is a question whether they would have been half as salty, original and productive under other conditions. Think, for example, of Abraham Lincoln, of his great biographer Carl Sandburg, of Thomas A. Edison and Henry Ford, of David Sarnoff. Think also of masters of simple, forceful English prose, unaffected by academic pretensions, such as Frank Cobb, of the old *World*, and Henry L. Mencken. Mencken got his education by a combination of reading and observation of life, and his seminars were the stables, the Krausmeyers' alleys and the McFaddens' flats of Aurignacian Baltimore. That is how he became the greatest authority on the American language—not by lucubrations among professors of semantics leading to a treatise on "The Split Infinitive Among the Ozark Mountaineers."

Leadership in a democracy takes many forms and often operates over broad and diverse fields. The late John Huston Finley was a farm boy from the Western Reserve who was in his time literally "Mr. New York," the indefatigable man about town, peripatetic stroller, coverer of the waterfront, chronicler of our past, and wise and kindly guide to youth, who make the future. He knew the whole town as few knew it. All peoples and all creeds looked up to him, and whether he was the great educator at Albany, and at City College, editor of

The New York Times or the orator proclaiming, like Walt Whitman, that New York was no mean city, his vitality, enthusiasm, loyalty and leadership were an unfailing stimulus.

One of the foremost graduates of City College is Bernard M. Baruch, who has earned the luxury of speaking his mind fearlessly on public questions. During the depression, Mr. Baruch resurrected the homely, almost forgotten adage that what you don't have to work for isn't worth having. He said that what the country needed was to go back to work, stop striking, and quit demanding high pay and double time for ever shorter hours, and deliberately reduced production. There is nothing academic about Mr. Baruch's pronouncements.

Laziness, lack of incentives and stimulus, and that overworked and misunderstood word "security" are responsible for the monotony, dullness and mediocrity of much of our government service. There are as good and often better men and women in public than in private business, but only a fool would claim that the average is what it should be.

THE VALUE OF EDUCATION

The improvement of our environment, like every other human enterprise, depends upon leadership, which is partly a matter of education and partly a God-given quality which has little relation to anything we can analyze or control. Life is a game or race in which there are many adventitious and theoretically unfair advantages and handicaps. The advantages are not absolute, and can easily be lost. The handicaps are there to be overcome, and strong men become stronger in the process. A college education gives a head start. It should enable a good man to compete successfully against a naturally better man who has to teach himself and learn without lectures, ivy and leisure.

A good elementary and high school education is a right which should be enjoyed by the average youth, and the effect of such education on the average student is the test of a successful school system. College and university training, however, is a privilege to be enjoyed only by exceptional people with above average aptitudes and promise, and the measure of the success of higher education is the leaders it produces. This is a distinction often lost sight of, or played down because in some quarters it is not considered democratic. For obvious reasons, we need men and women who have had special training to do the kind of work government must perform.

These specialists in many fields need broad general education, followed by training in the branch of science or technology for which they wish to fit themselves. For those who have no specialty, but desire to enter public service, public administrations offer many opportunities. Washington and many state and local governments are eager to recruit college graduates with good general knowledge of government, for posts as administrative assistants.

A young person interested in this type of work would be wise to major in political science and public administration at college. Many universities give good courses in this field. As a matter of fact, any student who is contemplating a public service career, irrespective of his specialty, should study history, political science and public administration and take all the English theme and rhetoric courses open to him and, if possible, write for the college papers and practice debating.

THE CRY FOR VISION

It should not be necessary to attract college men to public work by beating the tomtoms of evangelism. We should not have to ask them to wait for a "call," as they say in the ministry, to go into government, as if they were deciding whether or not to be missionaries in Africa. We need not split hairs as to whether it is at one level of administration or another. The grass roots of towns and counties, the pavements of cities, the state capitols as well as the ant hills of a crawling Federal bureaucracy cry equally for young men whose vision encompasses something more challenging than radical exhibitionism, revolutionary vaporing, mere money-making, or short hours, security and the easy life.

A certain amount of radicalism is a healthy characteristic of generous early youth. Usually it does not last long. A friend once found himself sitting next to a girl on a train headed for Poughkeepsie. She was studying college books, and he asked if she was at Vassar. She said "Yes." Then he inquired: "Are you a Communist?" "No," she replied, "I'm a Senior."

This is a competitive society in which deeds rather than words should be our objective. If one has no stomach for a fight, if one's aim is to retire to some pleasant Walden, there to observe nature and meditate, I concede that this too, like matrimony, is an honorable estate and one not to be entered into lightly. However, the ambition and lot of most of us, at least in our earlier years, is in the main current and not in the mountain lakes and backwaters.

All the vaunted achievements we celebrate are not necessarily progress. As our physicians prolong life and as we escape further and further from fear and want, and have more and more security, we are likely to develop an increasing number of clock watchers, marking time and waiting eagerly for the days when they can retire to the deep South to play shuffleboard, do square dances, or just sit. But most of us aim to compete with others, not necessarily for ignoble ends, but to expand our interests, to keep fully alive, to help others, to justify our brief existence and to vindicate our theory that it is the individual who really counts. Whatever the risks and penalties, life is indeed a battle. We can set up high standards. The fact that we are not always strong enough to keep the faith does not make that faith invalid or contemptible. If we fall occasionally, we can pick ourselves up and go on.

BIG AND LITTLE COLLEGES

The older one grows in years, experience and, it is to be hoped, wisdom, the more foolish seem the claims that one college or another consistently produces most of the best men in this or that calling or profession. No doubt some institutions have longer and more impressive records than others, faculties which maintain higher standards, rare individual teachers with a profounder influence on their pupils, talk, debate and extracurricular activities of greater vitality and surroundings of charm and more lasting claim on graduate loyalty. But the notion that to be a success we must matriculate here or there, if needed anywhere, cannot stand the simplest laboratory test, or survive an hour's debate in a rough-and-tumble forum.

I like small colleges. I also like endowed private colleges which live on the gifts, the endowments, and the current contributions, as well as the traditions, the memories and the loyalty and piety of their alumni. I devoutly hope that all higher education will not become public, because it is to the independence of our private institutions that we must look for freedom from politics, from the winds of doctrine, from passing fancies, from slogans, from polls of public opinion, from mob rule and from the current worship of the lowest common denominator.

It is one of the glories of this country that there is room in it for a variety of educational institutions and that in this field we are as yet not forced into one common mold. I was happy during a recent season of commencements to have been honored by a Catholic College of the Christian Brothers in New York, a revitalized urban university in Brooklyn and a former Baptist stronghold, now nonsectarian, in Oneida. Each has its individuality and its place in our scheme of things. Nothing will be gained if they slavishly ape each other to such a point that their peculiar virtues disappear. The only thing which could be worse would be to have them all absorbed by the state or, because they are tax exempt, to have the state dictate their policies beyond fixing minimum curricular standards.

The small, modest country colleges, not ambitious to be educational department stores, which do not boast of waves of students wafted in over the seven seas from the four corners of the earth, not ambitious for vast laboratories and magnificent new quadrangles, not competing for paid gladiators, happy in the presence of Gamaliels who teach rather than lecture, these academies which have turned out so many of our great leaders and thoughtful citizens in the past, I devoutly hope will continue to be magnets that attract the solid talent of the future.

Numbers are at once the reason and the curse of colleges in crowded urban areas, where busy boys and girls who cannot get away study in shifts and burn the midnight watts for a chance at early advancement. They are perforce more concerned with vocational training and making a living than with the liberal arts, which is unfortunate. But colleges in such locations have their solid advantages. Here is the clinic as well as the classroom. Here the student of law has the inns of court just across the street. Here the budding political scientist can see politics at work; the engineer and architect can make contact with the city planner and builder; and the tyro in commerce can study business and industry at first hand.

New York City has many such institutions where academic grove and forum are side by side. Long Island University, in the Brooklyn Civic Center area, is the newest and is rapidly expanding. I hope that in the new buildings that are to rise on the enlarged campus, the architects and builders will spare the plateglass and chromium. I hope they will remember that the function of a cathedral of learning is to lift the human spirit, and that the iconoclastic ultra-modern architect has not yet produced anything of durable, lasting appeal remotely comparable to the works of the great rapt, pious, dedicated and anonymous builders of the past.

Colleges must have bricks and mortar, grass, shrubs and ivy as well as teachers. Teachers gifted and decently paid are still the biggest factor, and it remains true that Mark Hopkins at the end of a log and a student at the other, without any elaborate trimmings, is a university—but a Hopkins on his end and a thousand students on the other is a seesaw that will not work.

CLARITY IN WRITING AND SPEAKING

The small college, not overrun as are our larger universities by Christmas shoppers hunting in crowded basements for educational bargains, has at least a chance of producing graduates with a vocabulary of over a hundred words and a passing acquaintance with such dated literature as the Bible, Shakespeare and the pungent English prose writers of the golden eighteenth century. It has always seemed to me reasonable that all graduates, bachelors and masters of the sciences as well as the arts should be able to read English fluently, write it intelligibly and speak simply and to the point in plain, ordinary Anglo-Saxon.

I particularly urge upon technical colleges training in speaking and writing the English language. Engineering, to be sure, deals with facts, but even the language of fact must be understandable and may be eloquent. I am sick and tired of "engineering English" which has to be edited, cut down and given brevity, sequence and punch. I still find myself giving hours to this chore, as though I were a college daily themes instructor or a rewrite man on a newspaper.

Those of us who supervise the prosaic everyday work of correspondence and reports do not ask of engineers the gifts of expression, style, foreign idiom, rhetoric and humor or even the racy lingo of the sports writer. We are, however, entitled to compactness, logic, progression of thought, simplicity without adornment, grammar, syntax and reasonably good spelling. A good secretary can supply some but not all of these requisites. I would not give any engineer a degree who cannot write simple English. All I ask is the ruthless logic of Euclid and the stark simplicity of Caesar's *Commentaries.* Or, if you prefer a homelier metaphor, I want ham and eggs without trimmings. By the same token, the most respected faculty, instead of the most neglected, in an engineering institution should be the department of English.

But Heaven forbid that I should advocate making every engineer an author. Some years ago my friend, Colonel Frederick Stuart Greene, then Superintendent of Public Works of New York State, and a distinguished pioneer in modern road building, having sold an article called "Highways and Highwaymen," telling how he reorganized the state road administration, got the itch for writing, known to the old Latins as *furor scribendi.* He enrolled in a university extension course on the short story and emerged with a thriller called "The Cat and the Cane Brake," which made *The Saturday Evening Post* and a collection of the Best Stories of the Year.

Admiring friends told him he was wasting his life on dirt moving. Others, probably engineers, snorted that he should get back to cuts and fills and leave the fine arts alone. Thereafter, Colonel Greene was a thwarted man who could never make up his mind whether he was Baron Georges Eugène Haussmann or Henri René Albert Guy de Maupassant. This is an error engineers generally should avoid. The engineer is by nature and training an honest and a modest man. The engineer does not share the curious superstition that everyone in these United States is a mine of hidden artistic talents awaiting only the rig and shaft, the drill and plunger for the uncovering and gushing of vast natural resources.

Someone will no doubt admonish that there have been great writers of fiction with remarkable insight into the human soul whose basic training was in engineering. I admit that an errant mathematician—not exactly an engineer—invented *Alice in Wonderland*. Da Cunha, the author of that truly great Brazilian classic, *Os Sertões*, or *Rebellion in the Backlands*, was indeed a practicing engineer, who dealt in romantic history rather than historical romance. Here was an engineer with imagination. He wrote about fanatical mixed-blood frontiersmen and refugees fighting from every shadow and vantage for the parched soil of their blasted countryside against a uniformed and conventionally equipped expeditionary force—a bloody parade through a continuous, terrifying ambush.

Unfortunately, the besetting vice of Da Cunha, a typical engineering failing, was floundering in technical detail. He was unfortunately at home and happiest in minute particulars and loved them for their own sake. Colonel Brian Fawcett, another surveyor, engineer and explorer, who disappeared mysteriously in Brazil some thirty years ago, author of one of the great adventure diaries of all time, suffered from the same fault—diffuseness which hid the crawling jungle in a tangled mass of detail.

The ability to write and speak good English is the most valuable qualification for public service in all important grades. The more literate the man, the better his training, the better the job he will get and the faster he will rise. The government official who can speak and write official reports in clear, terse language, for ordinary folks, not for technicians and the intelligentsia, will quickly attract attention and accumulate public respect for their work.

ARCHITECTURE AND ENGINEERING

In these days the professions have a way of overlapping or running together—engineering and chemistry, chemistry and physics, physics and mathematics, mathematics and philosophy. This is nature's way of curing overspecialization. Architects, to give another example, have been under severe strain because of modern building and material inventions which primarily involve structural engineering principles. To make matters worse for them, they have sought to destroy the integrity of their profession and the reason for their existence by violent efforts to wipe out magnificent traditions and established standards of beauty which alone have distinguished them from engineers. This tendency has been aggravated by the widespread use of words such as "functional" and "organic" which merely serve to confuse architects with hawkers of digestive pills, doctors of internal medicine, rubbers in Turkish baths and practitioners in beauty salons.

We must keep abreast of the times, without flouting tradition and making a joke of established standards in matters of design, architecture, and art. The conservative holds fast to what is good until something is proven better. Public structures of long life must wear well, not only physically but also in style and taste. A French Gothic bridge of the thirteenth century still delights the eye and also carries heavy motor traffic. In so-called long-range planning, we must avoid unproven, radical assumptions that all present aggregations of people are unhealthy, uncivilized and obsolete, and that folks must be plucked up willy-nilly and rearranged on new principles of dispersion, decentralization, "satellite" villages, roadside towns, atom-proof troglodyte, underground plants, etc. We cannot rely for inspiration or accomplishment on the brassy revolutionary doctrines and slogans of academic planners. There is some truth in George Bernard Shaw's impish observation that "Those who can, do. Those who can't, teach."

The academic groves are packed with revolutionary planners. Frank Lloyd Wright once told a group at Princeton that they should quit wasting time at school and go back to the land. Gropius, of the German Bauhaus School, and Eliel Saarinen, the great Finnish architect, had barely landed here before they concluded that everything in this country was wrong and that we sadly lack European culture. Dean Hudnut of Harvard characterized the entire West Side Improvement in New York City, which reclaimed our waterfront for recreation, as an escape corridor to the country. Lewis Mumford told the boys at Dartmouth and the sophisticated clientele of *The New Yorker* that they should be for abandoning all our big cities, and Le Corbusier (Corbu, as they called him in the United Nations headquarters planning board), when some of us questioned his complete indifference to cost, snorted: "Bah! Money!" and stalked out of the conference.

No better illustration of the gap between plan and reality can be found than the selection of the world capital. The original Headquarters Committee of the United Nations published to all and sundry that this capital required forty square miles of virgin countryside as a setting for its efforts—something completely extraterritorial, remote, self-contained and uncontaminated by the fleshpots of a great city. To the horror of the eagle-eyed, global planners, the majority of the United Nations concluded that the charms of solitude were exaggerated, accepted Mr. Rockefeller's generous gift and ended up happily with twenty-two acres in midtown Manhattan.

ENGINEERING: OLD AND NEW

Artifacts dug up by archeologists show that there was crude, practical engineering before the dawn of history. The modern science of engineering is, however, a product of the nineteenth and twentieth centuries. The civilization of the Western world is founded on engineering and cannot live without it. With the advent of fission we have fashioned an engineering Frankenstein monster which must be controlled and put to constructive and benevolent work if it is to serve and not to destroy us. If we fail, the responsibility for this cosmic joke is clear; for as Shakespeare, who seems to have anticipated just about everything, said in *Hamlet*, a very modern play:

> For 'tis the sport to have the enginer
> Hoist with his own petar.

At the moment our engineering genius seems to have outstripped our character, our better instincts, our ability to get along with each other, our capacity to live harmoniously with superficially different people on a shrinking globe. There are today no fixed laws of phase and change. Faith is probably the only certainty. We are in a terrible predicament, for as our technical knowledge increases, certainty becomes shakier, mystery as to the future deepens, the imponderables become weightier, hitherto unchallenged principles are attacked, authority is undermined and the area of surmise widens.

These are problems for the parent, the teacher, the doctor, the statesman, the philosopher, the priest and the prophet rather than for the engineer. It is the task of the engineer to supply material rather than spiritual wants. This is his contribution. If our civilization is not what it should be, do not blame the engineer. Today we are handing over to millions of unprepared, untrained and often irresponsible people for operation the keenest tools conceived of by the mightiest minds and fashioned by the most ingenious machines.

Relatively few first-rate engineers practice engineering after they are forty. They become managers, executives, etc., and their slide rules, trigonometry and calculus are forgotten. The engineer who likes management becomes a business executive. The engineer who likes risks becomes a contractor. The engineer who is rigid, tough, unyielding, inflexible, and no back-slapper or hail-fellow-well-met will never be a successful politician. Perhaps that is why there are so few engineers in politics, and maybe it is just as well; but they have a great responsibility.

ENGINEERS SHOULD BE LEADERS

I would respectfully ask whether the engineering profession in its many forms, guises and manifestations has concentrated sufficiently and applied enough of its resources in recent years to the solution of such practical problems as fixing instead of guessing at the durability of concrete roads; the life of all sorts of buildings, especially commercial ones; the extraction of salt from sea water to make it drinkable; the harnessing of the sun's rays, the tides and other natural forces to create usable energy; the conversion of plankton and similar ocean life and vegetation to food; refrigeration in warm climates; mechanical aids to medicine? I do not even remotely charge that these subjects have been neglected. I merely suggest that they have not advanced from basic to applied research with anything like the speed which has accompanied the many recent inventions in the fields, let us say, of transmission of sound and sight.

I am not bright enough to figure out how much faster progress in these promising fields can be made by university endowments, foundation projects, corporate research and large prizes than by waiting patiently for discoveries and inventions by lone geniuses operating with crude instruments in obscure, homemade laboratories. I suppose we need them all, as the doctors do in their attack on cancer or arthritis.

It is hard for me to understand why engineering know-how has not produced durable prefabricated, assembly-line, poured, bolted, or other mass production houses, single and multi-family, at reasonable prices. Moreover, whatever you call Frank Lloyd Wright's creations—extraordinary, fantastic, distinguished, fascinating, freakish, stimulating, livable, crazy—you cannot say they are cheap or that they meet the five-and-ten demand.

WOMEN AND PUBLIC AFFAIRS

There are almost endless unrealized opportunities for women in public and semipublic affairs. Why there are not more girls in the so-called planning field has been a mystery to me for years. Here brains, originality, imagination and persistence are badly needed— not the kind that run to pretty pictures, but the type that represents the conversion into beauty and utility of the needs, ideas, aspirations and mechanical advances of our American genius.[27]

That great master of rhetoric Anatole France paid to woman the greatest and most subtle tribute I can recall in the whole library of secular literature. In *Le Livre de Mon Ami* there is a paragraph in which he is philosophizing over a human skull. He etches with light, quick, brilliant strokes the rise of man from beast to numskull, from numskull to artisan, and finally reaches the great divide which separates the clod from the spirit. He pauses, and then remarks, as though inscribing a milestone in history beyond doubt and controversy:

"*Le sourire naquit sur les lèvres de la femme*"—the smile was born on woman's lips.

There, according to that great Frenchman, was the beginning of civilization. Women who have been conditioned to suspect masculine flattery may smile at this profound observation as a bit of mere gallantry. But—if they do—they are laughing off not only a major biological cause of the well-known human race but also, next to religion, the most significant mainspring of its uncertain inspiration and slow advancement.

I do not claim that everything can be accomplished by allure, but there is nothing wrong with the proper use by women in public affairs of the superior intuition, the curious and inexplicable feminine logic, the hunches, the subtlety, the understanding of motives and character which men lack and which constitute tremendous assets in all human relations. Not to speak of more obvious attractions.

One great difficulty in the path of women in public affairs lies, of course, in the fact that most of them still regard a business or public career as a stopgap, a temporary distraction, or a bridge between college and home. Our aggravated servant problem has not helped in this dilemma. There was a time not far back when the career woman could hire a reliable nurse or maid to come by the day for four dollars or sleep in for a hunded a month, and make enough more herself to justify her absence from home. Today she may find a domestic-science graduate or something right out of the bog or canebrake who takes French leave when the baby gets the grippe or the last Wedgewood cup is broken. At this point the career yields, and men again usurp the field. God help us males if women are ever permitted to compete on equal terms with us!

The inherent difficulties of recruiting and advancing competent government personnel have been increased in many jurisdictions by absolute veteran preference. I repeat that a veteran should certainly have some special credit, but absolute preference in promotion as well as initial appointment is government cutting its own throat. The older men and the new ones are grossly discriminated against. Certainly a percentage advantage ought to be enough reward for veterans, many of whom saw no dangerous service or came out of the war without injury.

When the time comes to promote someone to a position in which the imponderables of leadership, judgment, force, courage, ingenuity, personality and reliability, rather than technical skill, are decisive, the list of eligibles shrinks quickly. The place where a man was educated is rarely mentioned, and extraneous social considerations, though still prevalent, become relatively less influential in a competitive economy. That is why any system of formal examination, Chinese or American, for the highest offices is dubious. In our efforts to eliminate favoritism, we are likely also to strain out the only qualities which are truly important. In civil and particularly public work, as in war, you cannot tell what a man can do until he is in a tight spot.

SOME PITFALLS TO AVOID

Despite the many handicaps, I feel that public service is decidedly worth while. It is important, of course, to know what one is driving at, and to be unafraid of novelty or size. It is a mistake to assume that government is an inverted triangle with steep sides and a huge base with room for everybody at the top. One cannot become a big shot until they have been successful as a small one. The Montessori blocks and abc's have to be learned.

The public administrator soon learns that in launching important public improvements, timing is everything. Things can be accomplished today which could not have been done yesterday and may be impossible tomorrow. It often needs what the rhetoricians call a concatenation of circumstances to set the stage, not to speak of the actors to take the cues.

In planning and administration it is essential to study every inch of the community and to be honestly absorbed in its problems and future. One must weigh and gauge the resources—human, financial and material—at hand and in sight. It is essential, also, to study the personalities, equipment, outlook, ties, resources of superiors; to learn to recognize the limitations under which they work.

Public works, if necessary, and well and honestly executed, are a great asset to elected officials, even if they are expensive. People can see, touch and use them. They cannot be laughed off like claims of superior administrative efficiency in other phases of public service.

It is important, therefore, to give the lion's share of credit to others if there is anything to celebrate. Let elected officials have the spotlight and applause at groundbreakings, cornerstone layings, dedications, tape cuttings, flag-raisings and public drives. If anything goes wrong the elected officials get the worst punishment.

Under our intricate constitutions, charters and codes, there are rarely less than a dozen agencies involved in any big public enterprise. Teamwork is not easy in the face of pride of opinion, demand for star parts, and plain, old-fashioned, high-minded envy. It is not necessary to be a sycophant, and one need not be afraid of being in a minority, but it does not pay to get too far ahead of the procession. People are sure to shy away from public servants, no matter how well-meaning, who get a reputation for being unrealistic, unreasonable, wild or eccentric.

There is sure to be plenty of criticism, and it is a mistake to ask much in the way of rewards or gratitude. The public servant must run the gantlet between those against all change and those who favor change for its own sake. It takes nerve to make decisions and genius to make both sides happy. Unfortunately, those who have guts are rarely gifted with diplomacy.

This dangerous trade of public service is full of anomalies and apparent contradictions, which can, however, be reconciled if we do not attempt over-simplification. I believe in both far horizons and limited objectives. Where there is no vision the people perish, and where there are only visionaries there is no progress and no accomplishment. Young men who only see visions are soon old men who have nothing to look back on but dreams. The interval should have been filled with constructive action, necessarily limited because even exceptional men have little time and strength for more.

There are many generations in a millennium, and we have today a new face in our midst—at least new to most of us. It is the face of the pejorist. A pejorist, those who studied Latin will remember, is a comparative fellow. He does not say the world is bad. He isn't an out-and-out pessimist. He merely thinks the world is getting worse, not only abroad but here at home. The age of opportunity, he says, is over. The future is dim and threatening. The country is filling up.

The individual is lost in the crowd. All frontiers have been conquered.

Why complain about the disappearance of geographical frontiers? They are relatively unimportant. The frontiers of science are boundless. Those of the human spirit are infinite, and unless we begin to explore them, expanded science will be of little avail and there will be no survival for humans. This is indeed the showdown, the crucial third act of a vast global drama, the hour of final verdict in the struggle between good and evil which began in the Gardens of Eden and Gethsemane and will end at some terrible Armageddon. How can anyone with an instinct for a clean fight in a great cause regret being born in this age of decision? How can those who are armed with a great faith fear the outcome?

When have we ever before had so marvellous an opportunity to apply the lessons of the past, to justify our existence, to vindicate our essential humanity? Man was not created, as Pope said, only to draw nourishment, propagate and rot. He was meant to fight against the hosts of darkness who are massing today for the final assault. I know of no field in which there is greater need for such effort than in public service.

I am no cynic and have not lost the true faith. I am for limited objectives and for reaching them. I repeat, like Cardinal Newman I do not ask to see the distant scene; one step enough for me. But it must be a long step forward and not too far ahead of the procession. We cannot afford to waste the short span allotted us on lost causes. We cannot hope to please everybody. We must labor in the public vineyard with the tools, the resources, the men and the support we can muster in our time. We are finally measured by our results, not by our pretensions.

I have no feeling against idealistic, visionary or theoretical people, so long as they are not obstructionists. Vision and idealism we must have, but we need creative realism to give them meaning. There is no reason to abandon a principle because fallible human beings find difficulty in living up to it. By the same token, there is no sense in clinging to a dogma because it has seemed valid in the past, if it is meaningless today and may become a handicap tomorrow. We are going through a period of political and economic readjustment in this country in the course of which we shall at least bridge, and perhaps fill, the gap between theory and practice. The thinker and the doer each has his contribution to make in this task of human engineering.

Competition with an alien philosophy has in a sense been stimulating and certainly has done us no harm. We have been compelled to re-examine our vaunted democracy and private enterprise to be sure that, both as intellectual concepts and as working systems, they offer more to the average man and can, therefore, compete successfully with communism.

We have discovered that there is more to this soul searching than quoting Thomas Jefferson and Horatio Alger against Karl Marx and Stalin. We find that our principles are valid, but some of our practices are considerably short of our preachments and we have set about the task of squaring them.

We have rediscovered the wellsprings of our democratic strength. The real meaning of liberty is not to be found in slogans. The test to be applied to any shift from private enterprise to government should be simply this: will it work better? Nor need the choice be absolute and irrevocable, the possibilities of cooperation among business, universities and government are in the earliest stages. Atomic research is an exciting illustration. In the cold war, time runs in our favor, not because we have a lead in atomic weapons, but because human nature is much the same the world over, and will not indefinitely tolerate a terroristic vacuum in one area of society. Meantime, by dealing realistically with the problems of democratic government, we can face the future with full confidence in our cause and strength, and the good humor and serenity of a clear conscience.

Publisher's Note:

Summary of Important Dates
and Duties of Robert Moses

1888   Born December 18 at New Haven, Connecticut; son of Emanuel and Bella M. Moses.

1913   Began as municipal investigator, New York City.

1915   Married Mary Louise Sims; children: Barbara (Mrs. Richard J. Olds), Jane (Mrs. Frederic A. Collins).

1919   Chief of Staff, New York State Reconstruction Commission.

1921   Secretary, New York State Association; Secretary, New York City Municipal Campaign.

1924   Assumed presidency of Long Island State Park Commission, chairmanship of New York State Council of Parks, which positions he still holds.

1924–27   Member of the State Fine Arts Commission.

1926–30   Chairman, Metropolitan Conference on Parks.

1927–28   Secretary of State; Chairman, Committee on Public Improvements of New York.

1929   Moreland Commissioner to investigate the State Banking Department.

1933   Chairman, Emergency Public Works Commission; Chairman, Jones Beach State Parkway Authority and Bethpage Park Authority; declined Fusion nomination for Mayor of New York City.

1934   Republican candidate for governor of New York; appointed by Mayor Fiorello La Guardia as City Park Commissioner to consolidate and administer city park and parkway system and coordinate with state and suburban systems; reappointed by Mayors O'Dwyer, Impellitteri, and Wagner; appointed member of Triborough Bridge Authority, and sole member Henry Hudson and Marine Parkway Bridge authorities.

1936   Chairman, Triborough Bridge Authority; Executive Officer, New York City World's Fair Commission; delegate to Republican National Convention.

1938   Became sole member of New York City Parkway Authority, which absorbed the Henry Hudson and Marine Parkway authorities, and built the Cross Bay Parkway Bridge and shorefront improvements in the Rockaways; delegate to State Constitutional Convention; Chairman, Committee on Highways, Parkways, and Grade Crossings.

1939   Consultant, Pittsburgh Regional Planning Association on arterial plan; Centennial lecturer, Duke University; Godkin lecturer, Harvard University.

1940   Stafford Little lecturer, Princeton University.

1942   Appointed to New York City Planning Commission by Mayor La Guardia, since reappointed by Mayors O'Dwyer and Wagner; Chairman, State Committee on Post War Employment; reviewed highway and parkway plans for the Detroit area for State of Michigan and Huron-Clinton Metropolitan Authority; member, New York State Postwar Public Works Commission.

1943   Coordinator of Congested War Production Areas for the Army and Navy Munitions Board; Director, Postwar Plan for Portland, Oregon.

1944   Director, Arterial Plan for Baltimore, Maryland; Consultant, Illinois Superhighway Commission.

1945   Secretary and Chief Executive Officer, New York City Tunnel Authority.

1946   Chairman, consolidated Triborough Bridge and New York City Tunnel Authorities; Chairman, Mayor's Emergency Committee on Housing; Director, Arterial Plan for New Orleans; Chairman, Mayor's Committee for permanent world capital; New York City Construction Coordinator; lecturer, Miami University.

1947   Reported to War Department on German occupation problems.

1948   Consultant on arterial system for Caracas, Venezuela; Chief Consultant on Public Works to Commission on Organization of the Executive Branch of the United States Government; Chairman, Mayor's Slum Clearance Committee.

1949   Member, New York City Traffic Commission; Consultant, Arterial System for Hartford, Connecticut; Adviser, Nassau County Transit Commission.

1950   Consultant, International Basic Economy Corporation; Director of Report on City of São Paulo, Brazil; member, Long Island Rail Road Commission.

1951   Reported on Expressway program for New Britain, Connecticut.

1952   Director of Report on Canton, Ohio.

1953   Winner, General Motors Better Highways Award; Report on New City Hall, Flint, Michigan.

1954   Appointed Chairman of New York State Power Authority by Governor Dewey; lectured at Syracuse University, Swarthmore, Cornell University, and Harvard University.

B.A., Yale University, 1909; B.A., Oxford University, with honors in jurisprudence, 1911; Ph.D. in political science, Columbia University, 1914. Honorary degrees: A.M., Yale University, 1936; LL.D., New York State College of Forestry, Syracuse University, 1936; Union, 1945; Princeton University, 1947; Hofstra College, 1948; D.E., New York University, 1950; LL.D., Columbia University, 1952; LL.D., Yale University, 1952; LL.D., Harvard University, 1953; D.E., University of Michigan, 1953; D.E., Manhattan College, 1954; LL.D., Long Island University, 1954; L.H.D., Colgate University, 1954.

In addition to his many academic honors, Robert Moses has been the recipient of innumerable medals, citations, and testimonials from civic, educational and other groups in the city, state, and nation. He is an honorary citizen of São Paulo and the Order of Cruziero do Sol was conferred on him by the government of Brazil in 1952. He makes frequent contributions to magazines and newspapers, and is prolific in the art of letter writing. He has an apartment in Manhattan overlooking Gracie Square and the Mayor's Mansion, and a summer place at Babylon, Long Island. His various offices are at 270 Broadway; The Arsenal, Central Park; Randall's Island, New York City; Belmont Lake State Park, Babylon, Long Island.

Notes

Material for various chapters in this book has been drawn from speeches, reports, interviews, letters, and articles that have appeared in magazines and newspapers. Articles from which excerpts have been taken in large part, or adapted, and the publications in which they appeared, are as follows:

1. Interview for New York Life Insurance Company, published in The Ladies Home Journal, November, 1953.

2. "The Challenge of Party Politics," Woman's Day, September, 1954.

3. Review of "Beau James," by Gene Fowler, New York Times Book Review, April 10, 1944.

4. "What's The Matter With New York": New York Times Magazine, August 1, 1942.

5. "From an Independent Independent Republican," Life Magazine, October 20, 1952.

6. "Government Can't Be 'Just Like Business,'" New York Times Magazine, November 25, 1951.

7. "Current Planning Literature," New York World-Telegram, December 2, 1953.

8. "The Changing City," Architectural Forum, March, 1940.

9. "Is Urban Life Doomed?" St. Louis Post-Dispatch, October 5, 1947.

10. "Plan For Your City," Elks' Magazine, January, 1945.

11. "What's The Matter With New York": New York Times Magazine, August 1, 1942.

12. "The Challenge of the City," Christian Advocate, February 18, 1954.

13. Ibid.

14. "Is Urban Life Doomed?" St. Louis Post-Dispatch, October 5, 1947.

15. Ibid.

16. "The Challenge of the City," Christian Advocate, February 18, 1954.

17. Ibid.

18. This chapter is largely adapted from a series of articles appearing in The New York Daily News, November 13-17, 1953.

19. "What's The Matter With New York?" New York Times Magazine, August 1, 1942.

20. United Nations' World, November, 1940.

21. "The Changing City," Architectural Forum, March, 1940.

22. "Highways and Means," Town and Country Magazine, April, 1953.

23. "To Turn Back the Killer, Speed," New York Times Magazine, January 4, 1953.

24. "Highways and Means," Town and Country Magazine, April, 1953.

25. General Motors Prize Essay. Some of the material from this Essay also appears in chapters 16 and 17.

26. St. Louis Post-Dispatch, August 17-20, 1947.

27. "The Challenge of Party Politics," Woman's Day, September, 1954.

Index

Adams, John, 32
Adirondack, Forest Preserve, 155; region, 186
Adonis, Joe, 145
Agassiz, Alexander, 170
Alabama, 166
Alba, 50
Albany, 80, 100, 102, 103, 117, 249
Alger, Horatio, 24, 265
Alice in Wonderland, 256
Allegheny: region, 151; River, 231
Alley Pond Park, 77
Aluminum Company of America, 182
Amalgamated Clothing Workers of America, 112
Amalgamated Houses, 111-112
Amateur Athletic Union, 143
American Association of Highway Officials, 215
American Museum of Natural History, 107, 150
American Society of Civil Engineers, 65
Amsterdam, 86
Aquarium, Coney Island, 123, 139; Battery, 139
Architectural Forum, x
Argentina, 43

Aristotle, 38, 54
Ark of the Covenant, 138
Armageddon, 264
Arsenal, Central Park, 269
Art Commission, city, 141
Arverne Houses, 160
Astoria, 77
Athens, 50, 51, 85
Atomic Energy Commission, 247
Auburn, 86
Augustan Age, 102
Aurora, Illinois, 52
Automotive Safety Foundation, 215

Babylon, 86; L. I., 269
Baldwin, David M., 197
Baltimore, 228, 229, 249, 268
Barge Canal Terminal, 106
Barnhart Island, 188, 190
Baruch, Bernard M., 34, 63, 75, 250; Houses, 112
Basin Street, 87
Bassett, Edward M., 29
Baton Rouge, 230
Battery, 138; Park, 139, 161; Tunnel, 161
Bauhaus, 257; influence, 65
Bavarian Alps, 244
Bay Ridge, 210

Set in Linotype Electra
Format by Marguerite Swanton
Manufactured by The Haddon Craftsmen, Inc.
Published by HARPER & BROTHERS, *New York*